Systematic Approaches to Comparative Politics

By RICHARD L. MERRITT
University of Illinois

Rand McNally & Company · **Chicago**

RAND McNALLY POLITICAL SCIENCE SERIES

Harry Eckstein, *Advisory Editor in International Relations and Comparative Politics*

*For Ruth
and Karl*

PREFACE

This book is about the uses of quantitative data in cross-national political research. Its purpose is to present to students of comparative politics an approach—a frame of reference with which to view political institutions, processes, and perspectives. It is a framework with a quantitative bias, one that asks How many? or How frequently? or With what covariance? when facing a problem for political research. It is a framework that seeks to use principles of scientific inquiry to formulate and test hypotheses within a theoretical structure. It is a framework that is alert to the possibility for quantitative analysis and that searches out and uses quantitative data for cross-national research.

More specifically, this book focuses on the uses, limitations, and outcomes of alternative research strategies stemming from this quantitative orientation. These strategies include the use of aggregated data such as census and event statistics, content analysis, systematic means to analyze characteristics of elites and their behavior, survey research, and other approaches stemming from the behavioral sciences. With respect to these strategies, I shall discuss, first of all, some of the purposes of political research to which they may be put. Second, I want to surface some relevant problems facing the analyst who would use such techniques, and give an indication of how past researchers have dealt with them. Finally, where feasible, I shall outline some of the findings of major studies utilizing each of these systematic approaches to comparative politics.

There are several things that this book is not. It is not a discussion of comparative politics per se. Nowhere will it describe the structures and functions of the British government, or compare and contrast the constitutional safeguards of civil liberties in modern France and West Germany, or consider the different roles of the Wehrbeauftragter in West Germany and the Ombudsman in Sweden. The book does not present a new theory of comparative politics. Indeed, I have stolen shamelessly the ideas and research of other scholars, with the aim of placing them in the perspective of systematic approaches and quantitative data as a means to show the interplay between theory and data. The book is not a series of "how to" chapters—how to perform content analysis, or how to draw a stratified random sample of a population. The reader will nonetheless find ample references to methodological "cookbooks" and technical expositions of methods. Finally, the book is not a discussion of statistical techniques of analysis. It does not define a measure of the extent to which curves are skewed, nor does it explain the difference between the Student's t and the Kolmogorov-Smirnov tests for relationships among data.

If my presentation is sufficiently clear, then I would hope that the student of comparative politics will gain from the book an appreciation of and feel for systematic cross-national research. Even better would be that students use some of the methods and findings of such research in their term papers and other academic work. But the best outcome would be if the reader were to adopt this style of thinking, either in whole or in part, as his own, and initiate substantial research projects designed to improve our scientific methodology and contribute to the small but growing body of verified knowledge about political institutions, processes, and perspectives.

In stressing systematic approaches and quantitative data, I do not mean to suggest that these are the only means appropriate for political scientists. To the contrary, every competent political scientist will doubtless have a rich store of historical information, familiarity with the reasoning of the classical political philosophers, skill in logical analysis, and, above all, a perspicacity about the political and social world that surrounds him. The point is rather that hard data can temper and fill out his judgments and, when such data are available or obtainable, he would be foolish to ignore them.

Some portions of this volume I wrote at earlier dates and have previously appeared elsewhere: "The Emergence of American Nationalism: A Quantitative Approach," *American Quarterly,* 17:2, pt. 2 (Summer 1965), 319–335, copyright 1965, Trustees of the University of Pennsylvania; "The Organization and Promotion of Political Research in the United States," in *Comparing Nations: The Use of Quantitative Data in Cross-National Research,* eds. Richard L. Merritt and Stein Rokkan (New Haven and London: Yale University Press, 1966), pp. 383–409; "The Representational Model in Cross-National Content Analysis," in *Mathematical Applications in Political Science, II,* ed. Joseph L. Bernd (Dallas, Texas: Southern Methodist University Press, 1966), pp. 44–71; "Political Science and Computer Research," in *Computers in Humanistic*

Research: Readings and Perspectives, ed. Edmund A. Bowles (Engle-wood Cliffs, N.J.: Prentice-Hall, Inc., © 1967, reprinted by publisher's permission), pp. 90–107; and "The USIA Surveys: Tools for Policy and Analysis," in *Western European Perspectives on International Affairs: Public Opinion Studies and Evaluations,* eds. Richard L. Merritt and Donald J. Puchala (New York: Frederick A. Praeger, 1968), pp. 3–30. The manuscript was completed in the late summer of 1968 and revised slightly a year later. In the meantime a companion volume to facilitate research has appeared: Richard L. Merritt and Gloria J. Pyszka, *The Student Political Scientist's Handbook* (Cambridge, Mass.: Schenkman Publishing Company, 1969). It contains considerable information of a practical nature, including bibliographies and sources of data for cross-national research.

Finally, it gives me great pleasure to be able to acknowledge my intellectual debts to several teachers, colleagues, and friends: most notably to Karl W. Deutsch of Harvard University; also to Samuel Flagg Bemis, Robert E. Lane, and Harold D. Lasswell of Yale University, Hayward R. Alker, Jr., of the Massachusetts Institute of Technology, J. Zvi Namenwirth of the University of Connecticut, Stein Rokkan of The Chr. Michelsen Institute in Bergen, Norway, and Erwin K. Scheuch of the University of Cologne. From each of these men I have learned a great deal; I can only hope that some of what I have learned from them made its way relatively unscathed into this volume.

Most important of all, I am indebted to Anna—just for being Anna!

R.L.M.

Urbana, Illinois
4 September 1969

CONTENTS

Systematic Approaches to Comparative Politics

1

THE STUDY OF
COMPARATIVE POLITICS

Comparative politics as a field of inquiry is the comparative analysis of political structures and processes both within and across nations. Its primary concern is *politics,* which, in the classic words of Harold D. Lasswell (1936), is the study of "who gets what, when, how." It thus deals with the distribution of valued resources such as power, wealth, and skill in a political community. And, in a larger sense, it is concerned with the control of human behavior in the process of distributing and redistributing these valued resources.

Our emphasis, however, is on the *comparative*—laying bare the crucial aspects of political systems, noting uniformities as well as differences from one system to the next, searching for laws about the relationship of variables, and attempting to account for such similarities, differences, and relationships by means of systematic and integrated theory. The comparative method is the closest political scientists can get to controlled experimentation. Unlike the social psychologist who can study experimental groups under controlled conditions, only rarely can the political scientist impose such controls on the groups and processes —legislative committees, cabinets, the enactment of civil rights legislation—that interest him. If he can analyze a larger number of legislative committees or the passage of several items of legislation, then it is sometimes possible for him to go from case to case observing what outcomes appear to be related to what sets of conditions. Such an approach is in important respects like the replication of a laboratory experiment. At the same time there are basic differences. The researcher cannot be sure he has completely controlled his experimentation; moreover, the probability that someone could replicate his study and produce similar results may be lower than the level of probability that would satisfy laboratory scientists. But, if the political scientist recognizes his imprecision, then he may work toward its reduction.

Since the world is made up of myriad political systems, it makes good sense to broaden our experimentation to cross-national comparisons. To do this gives us, first of all, a much larger sample of such cases as legislatures and cabinets to work with. More important, it forces us to expand our perspectives. The nominating convention is highly significant in the American political scene, for instance, but not of much importance or even nonexistent in other Western democracies. The Ombudsman in Sweden and the Wehrbeauftragter in the Federal Republic of Germany play roles that are not clearly defined in the American national political system (although the office is a part of some municipal systems). And relationships between socioeconomic variables and voting patterns differ from one country to the next. Cross-national comparisons enable us to sort out the unique from the universal, to work toward a general rather than a parochial theory of politics.

Toward the Comparative Study of Politics

Traditional Approaches. As Roy C. Macridis (1955) has pointed out, the traditional study of comparative politics has failed us in important respects. It was less analytical than descriptive. If there was any theoretical framework to the descriptions it was usually an implicit theory of progress, which viewed all political institutions as moving less or more perfectly but nonetheless inexorably in the direction of a democratic ideal. Totalitarian regimes and dictatorships were seen as aberrations from this democratic ideal rather than as types of political systems in themselves. The traditional approach was rarely comparative. It most often gave in parallel form descriptions of the governmental institutions of various countries, or described how a particular institution, such as a legislature or cabinet, worked in several countries. The traditional approach emphasized legal forms and norms, focusing upon constitutional provisions, upon how institutions should work rather than how they do in fact work. It was anecdotal. Examples, more or less aptly chosen, were used to illustrate principles, with seldom any indication given of how frequently the events described in the examples occurred and what the frequency of counterexamples was. The traditional approach was parochial in its attention to Western European political systems, to the exclusion of any consideration of non-Western areas. It was static—even when it described political change—for it was unable to account for the dynamic changes of growth and decay in the infrastructure of politics.

Not until the publication of Carl J. Friedrich's *Constitutional Government and Politics* (1937) did the study of comparative politics become

4

truly comparative and begin to employ a theoretical framework. But even Friedrich, in his analysis of legislative functions or of political executives, for example, often did little more than juxtapose the practices of several states and draw conclusions about the juxtaposition. His was nonetheless a seminal work—one which, in its revised form (1968) is still widely read today and which has spawned numerous theoretical approaches to the study of comparative politics. For close to two decades it stood as a beacon light in the fog of a tradition-bound field of inquiry.

Recent Approaches. In the years since World War II, and particularly since the mid-1950s, the study of comparative politics has moved in two separate but related directions. The first is toward a concern with micropolitics. This approach concentrates upon the political behavior of individuals and small groups, such as the family, acting as single units. Why do people get involved in politics? What leads a person to adopt a given set of political perspectives? How important is parental influence in the formation of his attitudes, as opposed to that exerted by his classmates at school or co-workers in an office? What are the political consequences when a person has an implicit faith in people that stems from his earliest childhood? Micropolitics seeks to learn as much as possible about specific aspects of people's perspectives and their behavior. In the absence of a theory or a conceptual framework to integrate the particular facts that are discovered into a meaningful whole, however, it runs the risk of producing collections of curiosities not unlike Ripley's "Believe It or Not!"

The second development is toward a concern with *macro*politics. It deals with the interrelationships of structures and processes in the political system as a whole, and is especially interested in the effects of structural relationships within the system upon the behavior of the elements (individuals, groups, institutions) comprising the system. What influence do patterns of communication have upon the social mobilization of groups at the periphery of the system? What role does the economic structure of a society—whether it be organized more along laissez-faire or planned lines—play in economic growth? What patterns of recruitment of new men into positions of power are most conducive to political modernization and stability in emerging nations? In the absence of concrete facts to support theoretical statements about relationships within political systems, it must be added, the statements themselves may be reduced to the level of glittering generalities.

The position of macropolitics is actually a middle one. It is as far from the narrowly focused microtheoretical concern with individual human behavior as it is from broad theory of a speculative nature that postulates the existence of universal principles of behavior underlying and causing all human action and interaction, such as Marx's concept of class or Toynbee's notions of challenge and response. Macropolitics comprises what Robert K. Merton (1957, pp. 5–6) has called theories of the middle range: "theories intermediate to the minor working hypotheses evolved in abundance during the day-by-day routines of research, and the all-inclusive speculations comprising a master conceptual scheme from which it is hoped to derive a very large number of empirically observed uniformities of social behavior." As such it seems to hold out the brightest prospects for advancement of the field of comparative politics, particularly to the extent that it can incorporate and even account for the findings produced empirically at the microtheoretical level (see Holt & Richardson, 1968; LaPalombara, 1968; Macridis, 1968; and Teune & Przeworski, 1969).

With the new theoretical concerns has come a revolution in style of political research. The traditional mode of research, which, of course, varied from one researcher to another, tended toward the more descriptive, literary, and anecdotal patterns for organizing and analyzing data; above all, it was highly personalized, resting to a large extent upon the insight of the person performing the research. The newer mode is behavioral. It stresses data that are impersonal, subject to verification by an independent scholar, and, where possible, quantified. In the words of Robert A. Dahl (1961, p. 767):

> . . . The behavioral approach is an attempt to improve our understanding of politics by seeking to explain the empirical aspects of political life by means of methods, theories, and criteria of proof that are acceptable according to the canons, conventions, and assumptions of modern empirical science.

The behavioral mood implies the acceptance of a style of thinking— a style that focuses on frequencies, distributions, and covariance. It implies the acceptance of the viewpoint of probability, which treats individual events or outcomes as members of a family or ensemble of possible events or outcomes that might have occurred with a greater, or lesser, or equal probability in a roughly similar situation. A crucial element in this style of thinking is the use of analytical tools that are statistical in nature. These techniques enable us to *describe* events and processes in terms of central tendencies, variances, and other attributes; to *generalize* about the characteristics of an entire population or class of items through sampling procedures; and to *show relationships* between variables through correlative tests.

It is the behavioral approach that underlines this volume. Without denying the scholar's need for a wealth of historical information, for broad-gauged speculation, and for value orientations toward both his research and the real world surrounding him, the book spotlights means to organize quantitative and qualitative information into data useful for testing politically significant propositions simply, directly, and clearly.

Systematic Approaches to the Study of Politics

Both micropolitics and macropolitics rely upon principles of scientific inquiry in their search for verified theory. What these principles are, alas, is often quite misunderstood. We frequently talk about the scientific method as though it were a rigidly formulated approach to analysis, one requiring the researcher to follow a preordained series of steps sharply outlined in a scientific cookbook. Such cookbooks exist, to be sure, but they often fail to convey what is of the essence in the scientific method —an inquiring mind, careful to detail, alert to the implications of expected or unexpected findings, and, withal, conscious of the nature and limitations of the conceptual framework within which the researcher is working.

Data in Political Research. At the heart of scientific research is the analysis of observed fact. A person casting a ballot is a fact, as is an angry mob casting stones at the police; and so is an Englishman's shipment of a gift to his cousin in Ohio. "Strictly speaking, a fact is the sum of an observed set of properties," wrote Eugene J. Meehan (1967, p. 11); and, generally, "facts are stipulated in terms of space, time, and distance." Hence they can be produced through and, in principle at least, are verifiable by, observation.

Data are organized bits of information, facts put through a sieve. Some are quantitative in nature: the number of students in a classroom; the per capita gross national product of a group of countries; the size of a nation's armed forces; the percentage of votes cast for a candidate in an election. Such data generally lend themselves readily to statistical treatment. But what about nonquantitative data (sometimes called qualitative data)? They may be thought of in several different lights. First of all, they may be grouped into several exhaustive but mutually exclusive *nominal* categories. Thus we may distinguish among democratic, oligarchic, totalitarian, and other forms of government. If we have specified what we mean by such terms, then the proposition "Country *X* has a democratic form of government" poses a simple research task: Either the country does or does not have a government with attributes corresponding to those we have labeled democratic. From

Civic Culture (handwritten annotation in left margin)

there it is a short step to the use of *ordinal* scales, which rank countries according to the extent to which they possess certain characteristics (such as a democratic form of government). In this sense the proposition "Country X has a more democratic form of government than does country Y" is a reasonable basis for research. The question to be asked then is "How much more?" It may be possible that our operational definition of a democratic form of government provides for gradations along some form of *interval* scale that enables us to say, "The form of government of country X is twice (or some other fraction) as democratic as that of country Y." By now, of course, our qualitative distinctions (of kind) are changing into quantitative distinctions (of amount). Even more important is the fact that, when we categorize qualitative data along nominal, ordinal, or interval scales, we are in effect assigning numbers to them—numbers that are then subject to mathematical and statistical modes of analysis (Singer, 1965).

Propositions: Verbal and Mathematical. A major task of political research is to generate data, within a general theoretical framework, to test propositions about political systems, events, and behavior (see Buchanan, 1969). Behavior, in this sense, may include causal and noncausal relationships as well as random, habitual, and other nonrational elements. Propositions about such behavior may be descriptive, explanatory, or evaluative (Meehan, 1967). Thus "Jones is a United States senator" is a fair *descriptive* proposition. The criteria for membership in the Senate are quite clearcut: Either Jones meets these criteria (and the proposition is confirmed) or he does not (and the proposition may be rejected). "Jones was elected senator because he is a member of clique z" purports to be an *explanatory* proposition. If it can be ascertained that the probability is quite high that any member of clique z will be elected to the post he is seeking, and if we can establish that Jones is in fact a member in good standing of the clique, then we would have some evidence for accepting the proposition (although we must recognize the possibility of intervening variables that would "explain" both the success of the clique and Jones's success in the senatorial race). So is the assertion "Jones is a good senator" a fair *evaluative* proposition *if* we are sufficiently sharp in specifying (operationalizing) what we mean by the term good—for example, his voting record on a given array of issues—that an impartial investigator can directly observe the difference between good and not good. But the assertion that "Senator Jones is in a state of grace" will in all likelihood not be a satisfactory descriptive, explanatory, or evaluative proposition. Since being in a state of grace generally rests upon nonobservable characteristics, it would be impossible—in this life at least—to determine whether the assertion is true or false. Of key importance, then, is the extent to which the terms of a proposition can be operationalized for the test of data.

Although propositions can be phrased in verbal symbols, highly abstract propositions often take the form of mathematical assertions. The usefulness of the mathematical assertion lies in the fact that completely abstract symbols are less ambiguous, and hence easier to understand, than verbal symbols, which often bear a variety of connotations. (Paul F. Lazarsfeld [1955a, p. 4] goes so far as to say that, in the social sciences, "there is no idea or proposition . . . which cannot be put into mathematical language, although the utility of doing so can very well be doubted.") Whether expressed in terms of mathematical or verbal symbols, however, the essence of the assertion is the set of logical relationships among the symbols (which, in the former case, it expresses in the form of equations). The assertion itself may or may not be deduced properly according to the canons of logical analysis; it may not be, but hopefully is, parsimonious; it may even be elegant—but, whatever its particular properties, it is free of specific content.

Of what value are such mathematical assertions in political research? Perhaps the best answer to this question came from Herbert A. Simon (1957, p. 99), who, in his restatement of Homans' theory of group dynamics, demonstrated "how mathematization of a body of theory can help in the clarification of concepts, in the examination of the independence or nonindependence of postulates, and in the derivation of new propositions that suggest additional ways of subjecting the theory to empirical testing." It seems fair to conclude that most political scientists do not build mathematical models solely because of the aesthetic pleasure involved in the task. Of more importance is the fact that they may be of value in the empirical study of political events and processes. Even so, the emphasis in the mathematical model is on the abstract logical relationship, not the empirical utility. As Hayward R. Alker, Jr., has written (1965, pp. 9–10):

> Whatever empirical meaning mathematical statements have is due entirely to the interpretations which are given to these formulas and to the assumptions from which the formulas are derived. In this sense, the correctly deduced but uninterpreted mathematical statements are neither true nor false; their applications to particular realms of experience, however, are legitimate subjects of debate.

The applications, of course, take the form of empirical propositions that may be proved true or false.

Although their numbers are increasing, relatively few political scientists use purely mathematical models. Most of those engaged in systematic research are interested in propositions with empirical content, in explanatory models that account for a specific occurrence or class of occurrences. When the mathematical formulas have been operationalized to apply to data in an imaginary or real world, whether in the distant past, the present, or the future, then we have entered the realm of what we may call the statistical model. The primary concern of the political scientist at this level may be collecting appropriate data to confirm or reject specific propositions within the framework of such statistical models (see Golembiewski, Welsh & Crotty, 1969).

The Confrontation of Theory and Data. Ideally, the scientific method calls for the formulation of precise hypotheses (propositions) and their confirmation or rejection through empirical tests. Sometimes this is exactly what happens. At other times, however, the process of scientific research is neither so neat nor so orderly. The scholar gathers a considerable amount of data about observable experience and then examines them to see what regular patterns of interaction exist. Such a process is what we call a fishing expedition. Although not as efficient as other approaches, it sometimes produces interesting hypotheses and challenging findings. Another scholar may be examining a body of data and happen quite by chance upon something of interest that he did not expect and was not looking for. As testified by the classic instances of scientific serendipity—the discovery of X-rays by Wilhelm Conrad Roentgen in 1895, perhaps, or the later discovery of penicillin by Alexander Fleming —it takes a remarkable observer to recognize, not that his experiment has gone awry, but that he has discovered something new and exciting.

The typical procedure is more probably a high level of interplay between the data-gathering and the hypothesis-forming stages of scientific inquiry. The scholar works a great deal with his data and sorts out his various hunches to see which seem most worthwhile to pursue. (Note, by the way, the underlying normative basis of such decisions.) After settling upon one or two working hypotheses, he will begin in a systematic way to determine which types of evidence can be brought to bear upon them in the most efficient manner possible. At some point he will revise his hunches and rough hypotheses into the form of propositions —assertions (and their converse formulations) that can be proved true or false by the test of data derived from observable experience. Then begins the often lengthy process of collecting the data. When the data have been applied to the propositions, the researcher evaluates his findings, using them in turn as a foundation for the development of new hypotheses. Thus the principle of scientific inquiry entails a continuing confrontation of theory and data.

The Uses of Political Data

The term data has been defined as information organized so that it can test propositions. But what does this really mean in the context of political science? Surely, there are some assertions that merely require simple quantitative answers: "Candidate X secured a majority of votes in a particular election"; "The propensity of the military to intervene in the politics of African states is increasing rather than decreasing"; "The mutual flow of trade transactions among the countries of the European Economic Community reached a peak in the late 1950s and has leveled off since then." Other aspects of politics, however, are more difficult to measure. Is there a single instrument or set of data that can "measure" the growth of nationalism among groups of people? Or hostility in the international environment? Or love or fear or hate in an individual personality?

Measurement and Indicators. Measurement in the social sciences is in principle similar to measurement in the natural or physical sciences: Both deal with large systems and a few cases, and both result at best in probability statements about the large systems based on analyses of the few cases. The reliability of such probability statements depends upon such factors as the appropriateness of the cases as a representative sample of the larger universe, the extent to which the conditions created in the experiment or analysis simulate those existing in the larger universe, and the care with which the analysis was conducted. The ability to design experimental research and to conduct repeatable experiments under controlled conditions is, as I noted earlier, more limited in the social sciences than in the natural and physical sciences, but this fact scarcely diminishes the usefulness of quantitative research and measurement in such fields as political science, history, and sociology.

When an event or class of events does not lend itself to quantitative measurement, however, or when it is an indivisible event or object (such as the human body) from which it is impossible or difficult to draw representative samples for close analysis, it is sometimes useful to consider those aspects of the event that are measurable. Such indices or indicators, in the context of other indicators and of concepts tying them together into a coherent pattern, may be used to infer the nature and content of the entire class of events. The modern doctor, for example, with his background in anatomy, physiology, and organic chemistry, uses such indicators as temperature readings, pulse-counts, urinalyses, and blood tests in considering the condition of a patient after an operation. Although each indicator by itself may tell the doctor little about his patient, used together and in conjunction with a cogent concept about the behavior and functioning of the human body, they can perform a great diagnostic service.

It has been only in recent years that social scientists have begun to use indicators to analyze events previously the subjects of numerous and often conflicting judgments. In spite of the newness of some of the indicators, however, the time is past when economists, investment brokers, and politicians can afford to rely solely upon their own intuition in viewing the state of the national economy, the future growth of an industry, or the political climate. The intuition of a learned and discerning social scientist is, of course, a valuable research aid: It is indispensable in seeing and formulating research problems, finding relationships between events or concepts, and drawing warranted and fruitful conclusions. But where it is used in analyzing such an event as a national economy or a political community, it must be tested against all available evidence. Modern economic analysis rests not upon theory alone but upon such indicators as employment patterns, gross national product, per capita income and consumption, capital equipment, and investment figures.

There is still another way of viewing indicators, more deductive in character than the approach outlined above. "Any given theory," Eugene J. Webb and his associates have pointed out (1966, p. 28), "has innumerable implications and makes innumerable predictions which are unaccessible to available measures at any given time." Borrowing a concept from the science of geology, they went on to note: "The testing of the theory can only be done at available outcroppings, those points where theoretical predictions and available instrumentation meet." Theories of personality, for instance, argue that people misstate—and presumably misremember—their own behavior to make it more congruent with their images of social norms (see Deutsch & Merritt, 1965). If we accept these theories, then we might predict that, in a country that considers voting a civic duty, more people would report having voted in an election than the number who in fact did so. Data from a major study of the American presidential elections of 1952 and 1956 bear out this prediction: About 12 per cent more persons claimed to have voted in these elections, and 3 per cent more claimed to have voted for the victorious candidate than had done so in fact (Campbell, Converse, Miller & Stokes, 1960, p. 94).

Similarly, Herbert Hyman (1944–1945) presented data showing that as many as 42 per cent of the respondents in a survey during World War II distorted their actual record about such matters as war-bond purchases, the display of government posters, and absenteeism. In both

SYSTEMATIC APPROACHES TO COMPARATIVE POLITICS

instances survey research techniques were used to determine whether
and the extent to which people misstated or misremembered their behavior in situations about which the research team had prior (general
or specific) knowledge of their actual behavior.

What are the characteristics of a useful indicator? First, it must be
subject to quantitative measurement. Thus the thermometer measures
bodily heat in terms of degrees Fahrenheit, the barometer measures air
pressure in inches, and public opinion polls measure the climate of
opinion in terms of the number of responses to particular questions.
Second, the indicator must be systematic, that is, it must represent an
appropriate sample of the universe of observable facts from which it was
drawn (or, in some cases, it may comprise the universe itself). Each
item in the sample must be analyzed or measured with equal care. Third,
the indicator as well as the sampling procedure must be explicit, orderly,
and repeatable—or, in a word, objective. If this requirement of reliability
is met, an independent analyst, by repeating the processes of measurement, should get results similar to those produced by the original analyst.
And, finally, if there are several possible indicators available to him, the
researcher should choose those that will give him the greatest amount of
useful information most efficiently.

Some Pitfalls in the Use of Quantitative Data and Indicators. If indicators are valuable research tools, there are at the same time certain
dangers in their use. The analyst must be certain that the indicator
actually indicates what it is supposed to indicate. This is the issue of
validity. A temperature reading will not indicate a patient's blood pressure, nor will unemployment statistics reveal the state of manager-
employee relations. The obverse of this is the temptation to draw too
extensive or comprehensive a conclusion from the information given by
the indicator. The thermometer measures only the bodily heat of the
patient, not the state of his health. Both of the above points, it may be
added, are merely other ways of saying that there must be a clear theoretical relationship between the event or process being studied and those
aspects of it that the indicators are measuring. Another danger is that
the investigator may rely too heavily upon any single indicator. Whenever possible he should use a multi-indicator approach to the events or
processes that interest him.

To these must be added still another danger, particularly relevant for
cross-national research: the problem of *functional equivalence.* In brief,
it poses the question "Do the indicators used in a comparative study tap
the same underlying dimensions of perspectives or behavior in each of
the countries included?" A simple example might be an investigator's

Almond!

effort to ascertain latent levels of patriotism by asking respondents in several countries about their favorite colors. A response of "red, white, and blue" might be considered patriotic for respondents in the United States or France, but a functionally equivalent answer in postwar Germany might be "black, red, and gold," and, in Italy, "green, white, and red." Similarly, a content analysis of newspapers in various Western European countries would have to consider the extent to which the press in these countries is truly comparable in terms of readership, credibility among various categories of readers, independence from political parties, and, more generally, their role in the political process. The issue of functional equivalence, so important for any comparative research, is one that runs like a red thread through the chapters that follow (most particularly, Chapter 5).

This is not the place to discuss in any detail problems of causal inference from statistical relationships among sets of data (see Simon, 1957; Lazarsfeld, 1958; Lazarsfeld, 1961; Blalock, 1965; Alker, 1965). But some *inferential fallacies* facing the unwary researcher should be noted. Alker (1965, pp. 101–105) has discussed seven such fallacies. The best known of these is the *ecological* fallacy (Robinson, 1950; Scheuch, 1966; Alker, 1966). Very simply, it states that correlatives of aggregated data for a group may not hold for individual members of that group. One of William S. Robinson's examples pointed to a highly negative statistical correlation between levels of literacy and percentage of black inhabitants both according to states ($\emptyset = .77$) and to the larger census regions ($\emptyset = .95$). The hasty conclusion that Blacks tend to be illiterates would be wrong, for it turns out that correlating the same data on an individual rather than an aggregated basis washes out the relationship almost entirely ($\emptyset = .20$). In short, the statistical correlation on literacy in areas with different racial mixes says precious little about the literacy of individual Blacks in the United States.

The opposite of this is the *individualistic* fallacy, which would attribute to a group the characteristics of an individual. "To assume that competition among individuals will universally produce industrious citizens does not mean, *necessarily*, that the nation with the most competitors will be the most industrious," Alker noted (1965, p. 103); "Laissez faire arguments need to be independently validated at all levels of cooperation and competition."

A third major type is the *universal* fallacy. If the ecological fallacy occurs when the analyst draws inferences from a larger group to its individual members, the universal fallacy occurs when he fails to notice that the absence of a statistically significant relationship between a pair of variables for a universe covers up a significant relationship for the variables within subgroups. Thus, for all countries for which data are available, the relationship between per capita income and McClelland's index of achievement motivation is insignificant ($r^2 = .02$); it is positively significant ($r^2 = .43$), however, for the Latin American countries (Alker, 1964).

Other types of fallacies include the _selective_ fallacy, in which the analyst selects for analysis only those data that fit the point he wants to make and then infers from the evidence that his point has indeed been substantiated. In the _contextual_ fallacy, the analyst ignores the fact that the environment may influence the validity of a relationship among variables ("One man's meat is another man's poison," says the old proverb). The _historical_ fallacy incorrectly assumes that a process discoverable in history (for example, the political effects of economic development) will apply to a cross-section of countries at various stages of development at any given time; and the _cross-sectional_ fallacy incorrectly assumes the opposite, namely, that a relationship valid at a given time for a large number of units at various stages of development will apply to the historical path of development for any single unit as well.

Empirical research in political science is relatively new. The instruments that researchers have developed as measures or indicators are, generally speaking, crude. They lack the sophistication of some of those created by physical and natural scientists, and, as will be seen in the following chapters, the most well-developed of the quantitative techniques and indicators in political science borrow heavily from the other social sciences, most notably social psychology. Time and again the reader of empirical political studies will find that the indicator used by the researcher is inadequate, invalid, or downright irrelevant. Time and again he will lament the fact that the investigator ignored important bodies of data or treated them improperly. Time and again he will leave such studies with a feeling of dissatisfaction—a feeling that the researcher has tried to do something akin to analyzing measles by counting the red spots on the body, a feeling that the researcher has missed politically relevant points because of his concern solely with mindless quantification and statistical analysis within a narrowly conceived conceptual framework. Much of this disappointment is justified. And, as will become increasingly evident in the chapters that follow, I share some of this disappointment.

Yet this is not sufficient cause to give up hope on empirical political research. For one thing, the field has made great strides in recent years. As this volume will also demonstrate, the techniques used today are far more sophisticated than those of a decade ago, and the growing intellectual commitment of younger scholars together with the growing financial commitment by foundations to empirical research makes it quite likely that the field will develop even more rapidly during the coming decade.

Furthermore, however poor the indicator, it can always be of some value to the insightful political researcher. At the very least, its inadequacy can tell us how something should not be done, and it may possibly suggest to a well-trained analyst a better way of approaching the same topic. Sometimes, too, findings are valid even though based on a faulty indicator; in such cases it is the task of the researcher to dig more deeply into the putative relationship, to find out why the relationship holds, and to seek better ways to demonstrate it empirically. Or such findings may generate new propositions about politics that can be pursued in other ways. That Newton's gravitational theory ultimately turned out to be less than completely adequate did not prevent it from making a significant contribution to science and industry. By the same token, a healthy degree of skepticism in viewing the results of behavioral research does not mean that we must disregard its findings. They can be used as a springboard for more sophisticated research.

In sum, empirical political research is just beginning to attain its potential. And in no respect, perhaps, has it advanced so far as in techniques for generating data from the universe of observable facts.

The Data Basis for Political Research

Techniques for observing this universe of politically relevant facts vary with the researcher. Some are content merely to record their impressions, to describe more or less analytically their external environment as well as aspects of their own personal behavior. More and more frequently, however, social scientists are seeking to measure dimensions of such ongoing processes and cultural artifacts. It is this mensurative focus that concerns us here.

Unobtrusive Measures. One approach to systematic observation entails the use of what Eugene J. Webb and his associates (1966) have termed unobtrusive measures. It concentrates upon the observation of behavior in situations in which the actors do not know that they are being observed and hence are unable to correct their behavior to take into account the fact of observation. To take a simple example, we all know of people with charming smiles who, when they see a friend approaching with a camera, immediately and almost unconsciously freeze their face into an artificial and often unattractive grin. Webb and his associates have discussed a number of ingenious unobtrusive measures that researchers have used to examine aspects of social processes (p. 2):

> . . . One investigator wanted to learn the level of whisky consumption in a town which was officially "dry." He did so by counting empty bottles in ashcans.
>
> Library withdrawals were used to demonstrate the effect of the introduction of television into a community. Fiction titles dropped, nonfiction titles were unaffected.
>
> Sir Francis Galton employed surveying hardware to estimate the bodily dimensions of African women whose language he did not speak.
>
> Racial attitudes in two colleges were compared by noting the degree of clustering of Negroes and whites in lecture halls.

Carried to an extreme, unobtrusive measures of ongoing processes might include the use of "bugging" devices to eavesdrop on conversations, concealed cameras or tape recorders to observe people's covert behavior, and similar electronic devices. (This suggestion, of course, points to the moral dilemma that exists in the use of unobtrusive measures: To what extent is the researcher engaged in legitimate research and to what extent is he merely invading the privacy of individuals? What "ought" to be the allowable limits as far as the use of unobtrusive measures by social scientists is concerned? To what extent can the social scientist prevent the use of the methods he has created by unscrupulous outsiders seeking personal gain?)

The situation of political scientists interested in cross-national research is considerably different from that of the social psychologist when it comes to the use of unobtrusive measures. To the extent that both are concerned with the actions and perspectives of human beings, their problems are similar: Recognition that he is being studied may alter the behavior of an individual, thereby biasing the findings of the study. The political scientist is also likely to pay attention to the behavior of large institutions, such as the nation-state. When he compares on a cross-national basis the government revenues of states, the sizes of their military forces, or their patterns of political leadership, the likelihood is small that the fact of observation by itself will have any impact upon the countries under study. In the long run, of course, the product of such a scientific inquiry (on economic or political development, for example) may feed into the decision-making process of one or more countries; but in this case the effect is due not to the fact that the observations were made but to the fact that they were reported and interpreted.

One type of unobtrusive measure used by political scientists interested in cross-national research rests upon the analysis of *aggregate data* about nations and their component elements. The way was led by econometricians who, as early as the late nineteenth century, perceived that some aspects of economic events and processes lent themselves to measurement. They devised the concept of a national demand curve made up of the aggregate of individual demand curves, the concept of gross national product, comprising the sum of goods and services produced in a country, and other indicators of the aggregated behavior of individuals. More recently sociologists and political scientists have examined census data to establish and compare social mobility rates among various countries, military participation rations (the proportion of men in the military age category who are in the armed forces of the country), and rates of urbanization. They have studied the importance of religion as a political variable by comparing votes for religious parties expressed as a percentage of a country's total vote in an election. They have sought to determine levels of domestic violence by looking at crime rates, workdays lost due to strikes, and the incidence of anti-government demonstrations. The use made in cross-national comparisons of such aggregate data—census data, electoral data, and "event" statistics—will be explored in Chapter 2 of this volume.

The products of any culture are many and rich in variation. They include the beliefs, attitudes, and values that govern human relationships; styles of dress and home furnishing; temples, palaces, and tombs; practical tools and ornamental objects; drawings; modes of thinking and communicating; patterns of family life and childrearing; instruments of government. And, it goes virtually without saying, one important way to understand any given culture, whether it exists in the present or disintegrated before the time of recorded history, is to examine its products.

What is true in principle, however, is often exceedingly difficult in practice. Little by way of artifacts has come down to us from cultures that flourished in preliterate times—a few potsherds, perhaps, or a necklace or two, some primitive tools, a few drawings made on the walls of caves. How can the scholar, taking into account only these remnants that have survived the ravages of time, reconstruct the patterns of culture that characterized these ancient peoples? Nor is the problem much different for students of more recent societies. To be sure, the artifacts of eigtheenth-century America are vastly greater in number and variety than those remaining from most preliterate societies. And, what is more important, a storehouse of written communications—diaries, letters, pamphlets, newspapers, narrative descriptions—produced by early Americans has passed into the hands of modern scholars. Even so, the basic task of the researcher is to utilize all these forms of information to reconstruct aspects of more general cultural structures and processes.

The method of research most commonly used to examine cultural artifacts is known as *content analysis.* At first blush, the term seems to imply nothing new. Is that not what we do daily when we "analyze" the "content" of a book, speech, painting, or other communication? Is that not what the historian does when he examines a body of documents to infer their "true" meaning? In a sense, the answer to both these questions is yes. The modern social sciences, however, have sought means to turn this general approach into a systematic methodology useful for the scientific analysis of cultures and cultural phenomena. Quantitative content analysis, in the words of Alexander L. George (1959, p. 8), "substitutes controlled observation and systematic counting for impressionistic ways of observing frequencies of occurrence" of content variables. Examples of such content variables include words (or symbols), concepts, images, words in context, sentence lengths or structures, designs on vases, and even stylistic elements of drawings made by children. It is in this sense—the systematic tabulation of the frequency and covariance with which certain predetermined symbols or other variables appear in a given body of information covering a specific period of time—that content analysis is discussed in Chapter 3 of this volume. To the extent that it is useful in politically relevant cross-cultural studies, particularly of preliterate societies, content analysis also finds a place in Chapter 6.

A third type of unobtrusive measure focuses upon the political leadership of countries and especially upon the distribution of *social background characteristics of elites.* One interesting hypothesis in this regard is that the origin of a leader explains to some extent the beliefs, attitudes, and values that govern his day-to-day behavior and policy decisions. An alternative hypothesis, equally testable in principle, holds that the office shapes the man rather than vice versa: Leaders with similar positions will come to share a common set of perspectives regardless of their differential social background; what is important is their role in the political process rather than their origins. Chapter 4, which discusses the cross-national analysis of elites, will look into the usefulness of data about the social background of elites to test such hypotheses, as well as to investigate other ways to study the characteristics of elites.

Intrusive Measures. In contrast to such unobtrusive measures are what may be called intrusive measures of continuing processes. For the social psychologist these may include experimentation with small groups, observation of individuals and groups performing task assignments such as decision-making, and other situations in which participants are aware of the researcher's presence. Another variety of intrusive measure is the method of field research used by cultural anthropologists and others who sit on the sidelines or who even participate in a real-world situation (as discussed in part in Chapter 6).

Except for survey research, political scientists interested in cross-national research have done little to date of a systematic character using these approaches. Indeed, not until the publication in 1961 of Sidney Verba's *Small Groups and Political Behavior* was the concern of experiments based on behavior within face-to-face groups explicitly political. Recent studies of budgetary committees by Aaron Wildavsky (1964) and town finance committees by James D. Barber (1966) suggest that this approach will bear heavy fruit for the study of political life, even if it may be some years before comparable cross-national studies will appear. Not quite so bright are the prospects for research using experimental techniques on nonexperimental populations in the real world. It is clearly out of the question, for instance, that responsible social scientists would initiate crises in human communities to observe the reactions of their fellow beings. In some circumstances something similar has been possible. The American and other occupation authorities experimented with democracy in postwar Japan and Germany, although, to be sure, not in any scientific way using control groups or formal propositions for testing. Another conscious effort to initiate change was the Vicos Project. The director of this project, Allan R. Holmberg, described its aims as follows (1965, p. 3):

> . . . Cornell University, in 1952—in collaboration with the Peruvian Indianist Institute—embarked on an experimental program of induced technical and social change which was focused on the problem of transforming one of Peru's most unproductive, highly dependent manor systems into a productive, independent, self-governing community adapted to the reality of the modern Peruvian state.

The approach toward the Indians of *Hacienda Vicos* followed by the project was one of active manipulation (Lasswell, 1965, p. 31). It brought "the scientific observer explicitly into the context of interaction," turning him into a benevolent *patron* who, through the manipulation of rewards and punishments, could guide the *peons* toward modernity. Like the efforts to democratize postwar Japan and Germany, however, the Vicos Project was not one that seriously undertook controlled experimentation.

Because of the virtual absence of experimental studies at once cross-national in scope, systematic in orientation, and using intrusive measures, this volume will not pay much attention to them. Only in Chapter 7, which deals with computer applications, among other things, will one such approach be considered at length: gaming and simulation using experimental small groups.

A more common intrusive measure is direct inquiry. Increasing numbers of political scientists are fairly comfortable using quantitative data stemming from *survey research*. The techniques, uses, limitations, and implications of public opinion polling both for scholarly research and for the world of day-to-day politics have become part of our intellectual life. So, too, has that variety of elite analysis that administers questionnaires to political leaders, businessmen, and top-level civil servants. Such methods are considered in three separate chapters of this book: Chapter 4, which focuses on the comparative study of elites, discusses the tasks entailed in interviews of leadership groups; Chapter 5 deals with the general problems of cross-national surveying, taking into account some of the concerns that face the researcher who wants to initiate such a survey as well as issues of secondary analysis of survey research; and Chapter 6 looks at some direct inquiries made of schoolchildren and other samples not intended to be representative of national populations.

The use of quantitative and organized qualitative data as indicators to test politically interesting propositions has opened whole new areas of research in comparative politics. Some of the areas that can be explored, and some of the methods of procedure that can be used in exploring them are outlined in the following chapters on aggregate data analysis, content analysis, the comparative study of elites, survey research, and contributions from other areas of the behavioral sciences. Organizational issues and the prospects for analyzing such data using highspeed electronic computers—routines for enlarging the data basis, for statistical analysis, and for gaming and simulation—are discussed in Chapter 7. It is the combination of the new style of thinking about political events and processes, discussed above, and computerized techniques for the generation and analysis of data that is revolutionizing the study of comparative politics.

REFERENCES

Alker, Hayward R., Jr. *Mathematics and Politics.* New York: The Macmillan Company, 1965.

Alker, Hayward R., Jr. "Regionalism Versus Universalism in Comparing Nations." In Russett, Alker, Deutsch & Lasswell (1964), pp. 322–340.

Alker, Hayward R., Jr. "A Typology of Ecological Fallacies." In Dogan and Rokkan (1969), pp. 68–86.

Barber, James D. *Power in Committees: An Experiment in the Governmental Process.* Chicago: Rand McNally & Company, 1966.

Blalock, Hubert M., Jr. *Causal Inferences in Nonexperimental Research.* Chapel Hill: University of North Carolina Press, 1964.

Buchanan, William. *Understanding Political Variables.* New York: Charles Scribner's Sons, 1969.

Campbell, Angus, Philip E. Converse, Warren E. Miller, and Donald E. Stokes. *The American Voter.* New York: John Wiley & Sons, Inc., 1960.

Dahl, Robert A. "The Behavioral Approach in Political Science: Epitaph for a Monument to a Successful Protest," *The American Political Science Review.* 55:4 (December 1961), 763–772.

Deutsch, Karl W., and Richard L. Merritt. "Effects of Events on National and International Images." In Kelman (1965), pp. 132–187.

Dogan, Mattei, and Stein Rokkan, editors. *Quantitative Ecological Analysis in the Social Sciences.* Cambridge, Mass., and London: M.I.T. Press, 1969.

Friedrich, Carl J. *Constitutional Government and Democracy.* 4th ed.; Boston: Blaisdell Publishing Company, 1968.

Friedrich, Carl J. *Constitutional Government and Politics: Nature and Development.* New York and London: Harper & Brothers, 1937.

George, Alexander L. "Quantitative and Qualitative Approaches to Content Analysis." In Pool (1959), pp. 7–32.

Golembiewski, Robert T., and William A. Welsh and William J. Crotty. *A Methodoligical Primer for Political Scientists.* Chicago: Rand McNally & Company, 1969.

Holmberg, Allan R. "The Changing Values and Institutions of Vicos in the Context of National Development," *The American Behavioral Scientist.* 8:7 (March 1965), 3–8.

Holt, Robert T., and John M. Richardson, Jr. *The State of Theory in Comparative Politics.* Minneapolis: University of Minnesota, Office of International Programs, Center for Comparative Studies in Technological Development and Social Change, 1968 (mimeographed).

Hyman, Herbert H. "Do They Tell the Truth?" *The Public Opinion Quarterly.* 8:4 (Winter 1944–1945), 557–559.

Kelman, Herbert C., editor. *International Behavior: A Social-Psychological Approach.* New York: Holt, Rinehart and Winston, 1965.

LaPalombara, Joseph. "Macrotheories and Microapplications in Comparative Politics: A Widening Chasm," *Comparative Politics.* 1:1 (October 1968), 52–78.

Lasswell, Harold D. "The Emerging Policy Sciences of Development: The Vicos Case," *The American Behavioral Scientist.* 8:7 (March 1965), 28–33.

Lasswell, Harold D. *Politics: Who Gets What, When, How.* New York: McGraw-Hill Book Company, Inc., 1936.

Lazarsfeld, Paul F. "The Algebra of Dichotomous Systems." In Solomon (1961), pp. 111–157.

Lazarsfeld, Paul F. "Evidence and Inference in Social Research," *Daedalus*. 87:4 (Fall 1958), 99–130.

Lazarsfeld, Paul F. "Introduction: Mathematical Thinking in the Social Sciences" [1955a]. In Lazarsfeld (1955b), pp. 3–16.

Lazarsfeld, Paul F., editor. *Mathematical Thinking in the Social Sciences*. 2d ed.; Glencoe, Ill.: The Free Press, 1955b.

Macridis, Roy C. "Comparative Politics and the Study of Government: The Search for Focus," *Comparative Politics*. 1:1 (October 1968), 79–90.

Macridis, Roy C. *The Study of Comparative Government*. New York: Random House, 1955.

Meehan, Eugene J. *Contemporary Political Thought: A Critical Study*. Homewood, Ill.: The Dorsey Press, 1967.

Merritt, Richard L., and Stein Rokkan, editors. *Comparing Nations: The Use of Quantitative Data in Cross-National Research*. New Haven and London: Yale University Press, 1966.

Merton, Robert K. *Social Theory and Social Structure* (rev. and enlarged ed.). Glencoe, Ill.: The Free Press, 1957.

Pool, Ithiel de Sola, editor. *Trends in Content Analysis*. Urbana: University of Illinois Press, 1959.

Robinson, W. S. "Ecological Correlations and the Behavior of Individuals," *American Sociological Review*. 15:3 (June 1950), 351–357.

Russett, Bruce M., and Hayward R. Alker, Jr., Karl W. Deutsch, and Harold D. Lasswell. *World Handbook of Political and Social Indicators*. New Haven and London: Yale University Press, 1964. 2ⁿᵈ ed: Hudson & Taylor

Scheuch, Erwin K. "Cross-National Comparisons Using Aggregate Data: Some Substantive and Methodological Problems." In Merritt & Rokkan (1966), pp. 131–167.

Simon, Herbert A. *Models of Man: Social and Rational*. New York: John Wiley & Sons, Inc., 1957.

Singer, J. David. "Data-Making in International Relations." *Behavioral Science*. 10:1 (March 1965), 68–80.

Solomon, Herbert, editor. *Studies in Item Analysis and Prediction*. Stanford, Calif.: Stanford University Press, 1961.

Teune, Henry, and Adam Przeworski. *The Logic of Comparative Social Inquiry*. New York: John Wiley & Sons, Inc., 1969.

Verba, Sidney. *Small Groups and Political Behavior: A Study of Leadership*. Princeton, N.J.: Princeton University Press, 1961.

Webb, Eugene J., Donald T. Campbell, Richard D. Schwartz, and Lee Sechrest. *Unobtrusive Measures: Nonreactive Research in the Social Sciences*. Chicago: Rand McNally & Company, 1966.

Wildavsky, Aaron. *The Politics of the Budgetary Process*. Boston: Little, Brown, 1964.

2

AGGREGATE DATA IN
CROSS-NATIONAL RESEARCH

Aggregate data describe the characteristics of an entire population or aggregate of individuals—the size of the population, the ratio of men to women, their racial or ethnic composition, the extent to which they are literate, their living standard, their propensity to save or invest, and so forth (see Merritt & Rokkan, 1966; Taylor, 1968; and Dogan & Rokkan, 1969). Generally speaking, such data are of two varieties. Sometimes, aggregate data comprise the sum total of individual behavior. The number of babies born, of people who marry, or who die (expressed in a standard unit, such as per 100,000 persons in the population) constitute, respectively, that population's birth, marriage, and death rates. The total number of people murdered during the course of a year, similarly standardized, is the population's homicide rate. In other circumstances, however, the whole is not the sum of its parts, but rather more or less than this sum. "To count the percentage of authoritarian persons, or to ascertain the proportion of individuals who come close to a particular notion of a 'democratic, civic culture' in their opinions" does not necessarily say whether or not the society as a whole is democratic (Scheuch, 1966, p. 159).

C.C.

It is quite possible to imagine a society that is democratic in its orientation comprising large numbers of individuals whose personalities have a bent toward authoritarianism. And it is equally possible to imagine a basically democratic population that accepts or has accommodated itself to a dictatorial regime. This second type of aggregate data, then, comprises what Raymond B. Cattell and his associates (Cattell, Breul & Hartman, 1951, p. 408) have called syntality variables, that is, "characteristics of the group when acting as a group, e.g., its aggressiveness, its support of artistic production," and even the behavior of its official representatives when they cast their votes in a meeting of the United Nations General Assembly or send a diplomatic protest to another country. As it turns out, keeping separate these two concepts of aggregate data sometimes proves problematic in empirical political research.

Aggregate Data as Indicators

Cross-national research using aggregate data concentrates upon the collection and analysis of such summary data for a large number of individual polities. If we know the population size of 120 countries, for instance, we can order them into a ranking from the most to the least populous. Other *distributions* could rank the countries according to their consumption patterns, the number of doctors or hospitals, their literacy rates. Such cross-national distributions of data are of more than intrinsic interest. Some of them may serve as *indicators* of underlying processes, as discussed in the previous chapter. We are interested in the height of the mercury in a thermometer, for example, not because the liquid itself or its shifting position in a glass tube is particularly fascinating but because we have a theory about the even expansion of mercury (and other liquids) in response to changes in temperature that enables us to use the thermometer as an instrument to indicate the temperature. Similarly, we may be interested in the number of inhabitants per doctor or hospital bed as indicators of health standards in a set of countries. Combining single indicators of temperature and humidity gives us an *index* (a discomfort index) that summarizes for us a more general picture of the weather (Lazarsfeld & Rosenberg, 1955, pp. 15–16). A similar collection of individual indicators of economic activity may be combined into an overall index of gross national product.

Indicators serve a variety of purposes. They enable us to understand complex events, processes, or concepts. If we find, for instance, that one indicator of a concept varies directly with changes in another indicator, then we have added to our comprehension of the concept itself. If the relationship is a causal one, then we may use one indicator as a predictor of the other. Second, and this is a point that will not be considered in any detail in this chapter, indicators aid in the formulation and evaluation of policy. They provide yardsticks of past performance regarding the national economy or a drive to increase literacy. These standards enable us to evaluate current performance, to see whether we are doing better, worse, or about the same as before. Third, and implicit in both of the earlier points, indicators can assist us in making projections into the future.

The procedure for using indicators in research is simply described but sometimes exceedingly difficult to apply (see Lazarsfeld, 1959). The starting point is a concept of interest to the researcher: political development, civil violence, values in political life, the state of the national economy, and still others. The next step is to construct a model of the concept, that is, to present it in a carefully designed analytical formulation. The researcher must then search out those aspects of his model that lend themselves to direct or indirect measurement. In effect he is "operationalizing" his propositions by matching them with measurable variables. Fnding ways to make these measurements, submitting a body of information to the measuring instruments, and compiling the data comprise the next procedure. Finally, the researcher must recombine his statistical indicators (perhaps with other data) into an index of the concept modeled. Two examples may make this procedure clearer.

Karl W. Deutsch (1961) was interested in the concept of social mobilization, which he defines as "the process in which major clusters of old social, economic and psychological commitments are eroded or broken and people become available for new patterns of socialization and behavior" (p. 494). He broke the concept down into its constituent parts, which he represented by the symbols $m_1, m_2, \ldots, m_n$ (p. 495):

> Thus we may call m_1 the exposure to aspects of modern life through demonstrations of machinery, buildings, installations, consumer goods, show windows, rumor, governmental, medical or military practices, as well as through mass media of communication. The m_2 may stand for a narrower concept, exposure to these mass media alone. And m_3 may stand for change of residence; m_4 for urbanization; m_5 for change from agricultural occupations; m_6 for literacy; m_7 for per capita income; and so on.

(In the rest of his article, it must be added, Deutsch concentrates only upon m_1 through m_7.) He then proceeded to a double task: to find quantitative indicators of his subconcepts and to find critical thresholds for these indicators in terms of modernization. Let us look more closely at his indicator for m_6, literacy (p. 496):

> Each of the seven processes chosen could itself be measured by several different indicators, but in each case these subindicators are apt to be very closely correlated and almost completely interchangeable. Literacy, for instance, can be measured as a percentage of the population above fifteen or above ten, or above seven years of age; it could be defined as the ability to recognize a few words, or to read consecutively, or to write. Each of these particular definitions would yield a different numerical answer, but so long as the same definition was used for each country, or for each period within the same country, each of these yardsticks would reveal much the same state of affairs. If applied to Morocco between 1920 and 1950, e.g., each of these tests would have shown how the number of literate Moroccans began to outgrow the number of literate Frenchmen in that country, with obvious implications for its political future.

In his search for the critical level of literacy in terms of processes of political modernization, Deutsch writes (p. 497):

> It has often been remarked that even a considerable advance in literacy, say from 10 per cent to 60 per cent of the population above fifteen years

of age, does not seem to be correlated with any significant change in the birthrate, if one compares literacy and birthrate levels of a large number of countries in the 1950s. At the level of 80 per cent literacy, however, there appears a conspicuous change: for the same collection of countries, not one with a literacy rate above 80 per cent has a birthrate above 3 per cent per year. As a provisional hypothesis for further testing, one might conjecture that a literacy rate of more than 80 per cent might indicate such an advanced and thoroughgoing stage of social mobilization and modernization as to influence even those intimate patterns of family life that find their expression in the birthrate of a country. Obviously such a hypothesis would require other evidence for confirmation, but even in its quite tentative stage it may illustrate our point. If it were true, then the 80 per cent level would be a threshould of criticality on the particular scale of literacy as an indicator of social mobilization.

Deutsch then recombined his individual indicators in a quantitative model of the social mobilization process (p. 502–506).

An analysis of civil violence by Ted Gurr with Charles Ruttenberg (1967; see also Gurr, 1968) provides another example. For them, civil violence comprises "all collective, nongovernmental attacks on persons or property, resulting in intentional damage to them, that occur within the boundaries of an autonomous or colonial political unit" (p. 28). To get an index of the magnitude of civil violence, they first of all delineate five basic measures or indicators: number of participants, social area affected, number of casualties, property damage, and duration. These indicators are combined into three intermediate indices of pervasiveness, intensity, and amplitude, which in turn build a final weighted combination or index of the magnitude of civil violence. This final weighted combination, along with other data (for example, type of civil violence —turmoil, conspiracy, or internal war), contribute to their theoretical model consisting of "an interrelated set of propositions about variables that determine the likelihood and magnitude of civil violence" (p. 106).

It should be clear that the concepts and indicators are very closely interrelated. Indeed, Oskar Morgenstern (1963, p. 244) goes so far as to say that "nothing can be measured for which there exist no good concepts, and concepts, no matter how precise, are of little practical value if the corresponding measurements cannot be performed."

Types of Aggregated Data

Several types of aggregated data (summation or syntality variables) are appropriate for quantitative indicators of underlying concepts. One general type consists of standard enumerations: census data, governmental or quasi-official statistics, and sample surveys seeking either behavioral or perceptual data. Another general type comprises content analytic data: systematic content analyses of various forms of communication, "event" statistics, and judgmental data. The six subtypes suggested are ranked in terms of their "hardness," that is, the probability that they are both reliable (highly replicable) and the extent of agreement on what individual indicators are likely to mean (a problem in validity). Each type of data is subject to errors both general and specific, and each raises problems about validity. Discussions of error and validity will follow descriptions of the types of data the researcher most typically uses.

Census Data. The government of the United States conducts a full-scale census every tenth year. Other countries with developed statistical offices conduct censuses more or less frequently, and some countries have even introduced annual microcensuses, using sampling techniques, for the purpose of keeping abreast of developments in the periods between decennial censuses. In brief, the census technique entails the distribution of questionnaires to the entire population (or, in the cases of microcensuses, a carefully selected sample of that population). Individual questions ask about the number of people in the household, their age, sex, marital status, educational level; the number of rooms in the dwelling, how long the family has lived there; and so forth. Heads of households or interviewers fill out the questionnaires and return them to government offices, where the responses are tabulated. Ultimately these data appear in census reports, statistical abstracts, yearbooks, and other government publications. In the period since World War II, the United Nations Statistical Office has undertaken to publish annual *Demographic Yearbooks,* containing what data of this sort are available from all countries.

The availability of census data—particularly, in the case of the more modernized countries for which long time-series are available—has made them virtually the first type to which researchers have turned when interested in using aggregate data to investigate political concepts. Each of the major collections of politically relevant aggregate data includes such variables as population, annual increase in population, percentage of population in cities over 20,000, wage and salary earners, and age and sex breakdowns for populations.

Governmental or Quasi-Official Statistics. In each country the central statistical office and branches of individual agencies, no less than offices in such private and quasi-official concerns as banks, hospitals, and national associations, produce statistics about their operations. On the one hand, they record the occurrence of certain events: births, deaths, illnesses of various types, marriages, homicides, suicides, attendance at movie theaters, military personnel, consumption of electricity, and a host of other events. Indeed, in such numbers-conscious societies as the United States, it sometimes seems that statistics are kept about everything imaginable, from the production of miniskirts to records on flagpole sitting. On the other hand, some countries have agencies that utilize statistics stemming either from enumerations or from reports by governmental, quasi-official, or private agencies to construct complicated indices designed to tell us something about the state of the economy. Such econometric data include cost of living, gross national product, balance of payments, and, more generally, national accounting statistics. To these should be added a third type of process-produced data: the results of elections (see MacRae & Meldrum, 1969) and even roll-call votes in national legislatures.

Sample Surveys. Although public opinion surveys will be discussed in greater detail in Chapter 5, their use as aggregate data in building indicators and indices should be noted (Linz, 1969). The popularity of such surveys to get information about people's behavior and perspectives is on the rise. Many of the more developed countries of the world have several agencies polling the population about its buying habits, church attendance, images of other countries, attitudes toward foreigners or minority groups, and basic societal values. Such data are still not available in quantity for most of the countries of the world. In some of these other countries, academicians and foreign governments are encouraging the development of such techniques. The United States Information Agency, for instance, commissions polls in about 33 countries (Merritt, 1968). In principle it is nonetheless possible to piece together relevant survey data for a number of countries and to use them as indicators for aggregate data analysis. This is particularly the case when we turn from topics that are directly political to media analyses, such as the reading and radio-listening habits of populations across the globe. Still, the value of such multinational surveys as those commissioned by the United Nations (Buchanan & Cantril, 1953), the United States Information Agency (Merritt & Puchala, 1968), the worldwide affiliates of the Gallup Polls, or occasional endeavors sponsored by research foundations (Almond & Verba, 1963; Osgood, 1967) should not be discounted.

Content Analysis. The more general uses of content analysis for cross-national research must await Chapter 3 for detailed discussion, but it

Taylor & Hudson

1972

is worth noting here that some types of findings could be useful as indicators in aggregate data analysis. The Yale Political Data Program →(Russett, Alker, Deutsch & Lasswell, 1964) used as one of its 75 political and social indicators David C. McClelland's content analysis of children's readers (1961), which produced an index of achievement motivation for 41 countries. Similarly, in principle at least, an extension of the RADIR (Hoover Institute's study of Revolution and the Development of International Relations) world attention surveys, initiated by Harold D. Lasswell, Daniel Lerner, and Ithiel de Sola Pool (1952), could provide a useful indicator of cross-national attention patterns. The possibilities for using such data for cross-national indicators will expand with the development of computer technologies facilitating content analysis.

Event Statistics. Some events of particular interest to political researchers occur too infrequently to be recorded in statistical yearbooks or are suppressed by some governments because they cast their country in a bad light. These include assassinations, resignations from high political office, strikes, mass demonstrations, riots, and even civil war. If the entire world is viewed as an entity, however, the occurrence of such events is sufficiently frequent that some method of recording them is desirable. In the last decade a number of scholars have begun to search out such "event" statistics for cross-national research. The technique is straightforward enough. After delineating which variables are important for his research and operationalizing them (by no means, of course, simple tasks), the scholar conducts a systematic search of a variety of yearbooks and other sources to determine when and where these events took place.

The Dimensionality of Nations project, initiated by Harold Guetzkow and carried out by Rudolph J. Rummel and subsequently by Raymond Tanter, was the first major project to focus upon such typically political events. The variables that Rummel (1964a) first analyzed included nine measures of domestic and thirteen measures of foreign conflict. The domestic conflict measures were, in addition to the presence or absence of guerrilla warfare, the number of assassinations, general strikes, major government crises, purges, riots, revolutions, anti-government demonstrations, and people killed in all forms of domestic violence. His foreign conflict variables were, besides the presence or absence of military action, the number of anti-foreign demonstrations, negative sanctions, protests, countries with which diplomatic relations were severed, ambassadors expelled or recalled, threats, wars, troop movements, mobilizations, accusations, and people killed in all forms of foreign conflict

30

behavior (p. 5). The initial period covered by Rummel was 1955–1957. Later studies by Rummel and Tanter (Tanter, 1965; Rummel, 1966; Tanter, 1966) extended the period to cover the first decade and a half after World War II, from 1945 to 1960. The sources of data, it might be noted, were five: the *New York Times Index,* the *New International Yearbook, Keesing's Contemporary Archives, Facts on File,* and the *Britannica Book of the Year.* The number of countries ranged up to 113. Since the analytic technique used by both Rummel and Tanter was factor analysis, as will be discussed later in this chapter, neither of them attempted to construct indices out of their individual indicators (except in the sense that factors are indices).

Ivo K. and Rosalind L. Feierabend (1966a; in expanded form in Feierabend, Feierabend & Nesvold, 1969; see also Nesvold, 1969) delineated similar variables for 84 countries. For the seven years 1955–1961, they counted each occurrence in each country of each of 28 types of events, ordered along a scale from 0 (extreme stability) to 6 (extreme instability). Typical of positions on the scale are the following events (p. 252):

0. General election [1]
1. Resignation of cabinet official [8]
2. Peaceful demonstrations [6]
3. Assassination of a significant political figure [15]
4. Mass arrests [35]
5. Coup d'état [14]
6. Civil war [5]

They then categorized the countries according to the most serious event (that is, the highest on the scale) befalling each of them during the period as a whole. (The numbers in brackets above designate the number of countries in each category.) Finally, to get a rank ordering of the countries in each category, they calculated the "sum total of each country's stability ratings," that is, all such events occurring in each country. More recently the Feierabends (1966b) have developed a six-point scale of "coerciveness versus permissiveness." In assigning individual countries to the different categories, they asked three questions: "I. To what degree are civil rights present and protected? II. To what extent is political opposition tolerated and effective? III. How democratic is the polity?" (p. 9). Thus the "most permissive" type of polity (1 on the scale) might have the following profile (p. 9):

civil rights present and protected; right of political opposition protected, i.e.,
   in press, parliament, party formation, etc.;
government elected at regularized intervals in fair, free elections;
public opinion effective in policy formation;
significant heads of government limited in power and duration of office;

legislative bodies effective participants in decision process;

judicial bodies independent and have regularized procedures;

tradition of structures mediating between individual and central government, e.g., strong local government, states' rights, etc.;

constitution representative of sectors and interests within population, respected yet not impossible to amend.

And the "most coercive" polity (6 on the scale) would have these characteristics (p. 11):

civil rights nonexistent, i.e., entirely dependent on whim of government;

political opposition impossible, e.g., no parties or autonomous associational groups exist, government penetrates all institutions of society;

government perpetual, elections serve only showcase function;

public opinion disregarded in policy formation;

significant head of government has dictatorial and absolute powers;

legislative bodies serve only to reiterate executive decisions, have no powers of their own;

judicial bodies completely dependent;

no intermediary structures or institutions exist between the individual and central government;

constitution completely disregarded in practice, impossible to amend.

In the former case, the Feierabends derived their data from standard sources such as *Deadline Data on World Affairs* and the *Britannica Book of the Year;* in the latter they consulted about five sources of information for each country. And in both cases their indicators were used for correlative purposes with other indicators.

Work by Gurr and Ruttenberg, mentioned above, focuses upon civil violence. Regarding sources, they write: "they are listed in the order of their contribution in the final data set: the *New York Times* (via its Index), *Newsyear* (the annual volumes of *Facts on File), The Annual Register of World Events* (based on *The Times* of London), and, providing as a group the least amount of useful data, *Asian Recorder: Weekly Digest of Asian Events, Africa Diary: Weekly Record of Events in Africa, Africa Digest, Africa Report, East Europe: A Monthly Review of Eastern European Affairs,* and *Eastern Europe"* (pp. 36–37).

The basic measures Gurr and Ruttenberg are seeking for 119 countries for the 1961–1963 period, as noted earlier, are (pp. 31–32):

BM1: *Number of Participants* (per 100,000 population). Participants are all those reported to have been members of the group(s) engaging in violence, excluding the punitive forces opposing them. . . . [4]

BM2: *Social Area.* The extent of the polity affected by the most widespread strife event of the year. [4]

BM3: *Number of Casualties* (per 1,000 participants). This is the total number of deaths and injuries reported as direct consequences of civil violence. . . . [4]

BM4: *Property Damage.* This measure, having no direct relationship to
monetary value, is intended to reflect the amount of damage relative
to the scope of action indicated by the preceding Basic Measures. [3]

FIGURE 2.1
The Gurr-Ruttenberg Measures of Civil Violence

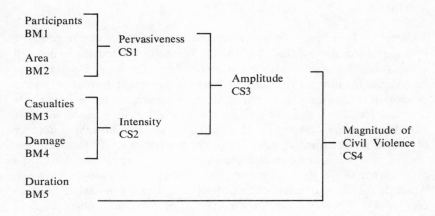

Source: Adapted from Gurr & Ruttenberg (1967), p. 36.

BM5: *Duration.* The total amount of time encompassed by all occurrences
of civil violence during any one calendar year. [4]
(The figures in brackets are the number of scaling points for each measure.)

Gurr and Ruttenberg then combine the grouped data for each basic
measure (for example, "Duration" is coded into four groups: t_1 = one
week or less, t_2 = one week to one month, t_3 = one month to six months,
and t_4 = six months to one year) into a set of four weighted scales or
indices (p. 33):

CS1: *Pervasiveness.* This scale combines BM1, Number of Participants, and
BM2, Area, to obtain a measure of the extent to which civil violence
is diffused throughout the polity. . . . [16]
CS2: *Intensity.* This scale combines BM3, Number of Casualties, and BM4,
Property Damage, to index the relative degree of violence resulting
from civil strife. . . . [12]
CS3. *Amplitude.* This scale combines Pervasiveness and Intensity by equal
weighting. . . . [16]

CS4: *Magnitude of Civil Violence.* This scale is the final weighted combination of all five Basic Measures. Amplitude is combined with Duration according to a rule that gives greater weight to Amplitude. . . . [64]

The scheme for combining these various indicators and indices is shown in Figure 2.1. The resulting scores for the individual polities range from 192.0 for the Congo (Léopoldville)—which means that this polity was scored 64 on CS4, Magnitude of Civil Violence, for each of three years —down to a group of 33 polities scoring 0.0 on the final weighted combination.

Judgmental Data. In principle, of course, each of the five categories of data discussed above entails judgments. What are the criteria to be used in reporting literacy data, for instance, or when does an anti-government demonstration turn into a riot or a major governmental crisis or even a revolution? The term judgmental data, however, is more commonly reserved for those generated when the researcher uses the opinion of experts about the distribution of a particular variable in a large number of countries. Frequently, the data useful for constructing them are not readily available in the standard statistical abstracts or handbooks. "Type of government" is one such indicator. Over two thousand years ago Aristotle divided governments into three pure types (monarchy, aristocracy, and democracy) and three corrupt types (tyranny, oligarchy, and mobocracy), depending upon whether rule was by the One, the Few, or the Many. And since then, many political observers have used roughly the same or quite different classificatory schemes to the same end. Recently, Seymour Martin Lipset (1960, p. 48) classified Western European and Western Hemisphere countries into democracies, unstable dictatorships, and stable dictatorships:

> The main criteria used to define European democracies are the uninterrupted continuation of political democracy since World War I *and* the absence over the past twenty-five years of a major political movement opposed to the democratic "rules of the game." The somewhat less stringent criterion for Latin America is whether a given country has had a history of more or less free elections for most of the post-World War I period. Where in Europe we look for stable democracies, in South America we look for countries which have not had fairly constant dictatorial rule.

Other analysts have used various sets of rules to sort out types of party structures, bureaucracies, leadership forms, legislative behavior, and so forth.

The most comprehensive attempt to classify a large number of countries according to carefully operationalized criteria was undertaken by Arthur S. Banks and Robert B. Textor (1963). Drawing upon relevant theoretical work in the social sciences, most particularly that of Gabriel A. Almond (1960), they developed 57 "raw characteristics" or variables, and sought information on each of them for 115 polities. One of their variables is "Constitutional status of present regime" (p. 83). Polities were coded into three main categories (with the number of polities in each category in brackets):

A. Constitutional (government conducted with reference to recognized constitutional norms) [51]
B. Authoritarian (no effective constitutional limitation, or fairly regular recourse to extra-constitutional powers. Arbitrary exercise of power confined largely to the political sector) [23]
C. Totalitarian (no effective constitutional limitation. Broad exercise of power by the regime in both political and social spheres) [16]

(The remaining polities were coded as ambiguous [5], unascertained [11], or unascertainable [9].) Other variables include "Ideological orientation" (doctrinal, developmental, situational, conventional, or traditional, "System style" (mobilizational, limited mobilizational, or non-mobilizational), and various forms of interest articulation and interest aggregation. Instructive about the basis of the judgments is the author's comment (p. 22):

> Banks devoted ten months, full-time, to the coding work underlying the present study. The problems he encountered were comparable in nature and inherent difficulty to those frequently complained about by cross-cultural researchers. There was, first, the serious problem of lack of data on many subjects. Beyond this was the equally serious problem that many of the analytical concepts and categories currently in use by comparative government specialists are not globally relevant and hence do not lend themselves to global comparisons. In short, it was often necessary to resist the blandishments of an otherwise interesting typology because of insoluble reliability problems, while it was also necessary to reject the temptation to fall back on categories of easy reliability where little would result that was fresh, valid, or analytically powerful.

Their initial analytical procedure was a correlation of each dichotomized variable with every other one; subsequently, the data were factor analyzed.

Russell H. Fitzgibbon (Fitzgibbon & Johnson, 1961) has experimented with panels of judges. At five-year intervals he sent questionnaires about Latin American developments to groups of well-known experts. For the most part the judges were professors at American universities, although some of them, like former Assistant Secretary of State Spruille Braden, were or had been American government officials, and others were journalists. The number of judges varied, from 10 each in the 1945 and 1950 panels, to 20 and 40 in 1955 and 1960, respectively; seven men participated in all four panels. The task of these experts was to rate each of 20 countries on 15 separate dimensions, using a five-point scale from "excellent" to "insignificant (virtually no) democratic achievement." The dimensions included "An educational level sufficient to give the political processes some substance and vitality," "A fairly adequate standard of living," "Free and competitive elections—honestly counted votes," and "Civilian supremacy over the military." And, as suggested, the purpose of the project was to secure an index of the progress that the Latin American countries were making toward democratic institutions and practices.

Perhaps the most persuasive plea for the use of more judgmental data in cross-national research was made by an anonymous reviewer (1964, p. 31) of the Yale Political Data Program's *World Handbook of Political and Social Indicators* (Russett, Alker, Deutsch & Lasswell, 1964). The Yale Political Data Program, he said,

> should seek to develop a new methodology of indicators. . . . Both *expert opinion* and *sample surveys* are so much more rapid, cheaper and flexible than censuses that ultimately they must replace them for the greater number of useful profiles of international conditions. . . . The panel technique needs to be perfected for cross-national comparisons. We can imagine a conversion of expert opinions into a quantitative ordering of unemployment phenomena that would be incomparably richer in meaning and in its own way much more "accurate" than the present set of data. The science of appraising conditions is well organized in welfare, mortgage-banking, and other occupational areas. Perhaps the Yale group might ponder the need for training social and behavioral appraisors to provide an adequate supply of standardized judgments on a large number of specified policy conditions. . . .

The United States State Department conducts both types of research: the panel technique through its desk officers and intelligence officers in individual countries, and the surveying through the worldwide polls commissioned by the United States Information Agency. To adapt these procedures to serve academic research purposes would greatly enhance the development and analysis of cross-national indicators.

Reliability: Margins of Error

Sources of Error. In the six types of data discussed above, there are many potential sources of error. Each type, of course, has error specific to it, but in general these may be classified into three groups: human error, reporting error, and willful error. *Human error* is inadvertent but pervasive. The clerk who analyzes statistics all day will doubtless misread a few figures, or transpose data columns, or commit punching errors when transferring his data to IBM punchcards. Careful checks may reduce error of this type, but even the most elaborate precautions do not prevent some anomalies from slipping into the final reports of such reliable agencies as the United States Bureau of the Census (Coale & Stephan, 1962). Interviewer bias, however unintentional, affects the results of sample surveys. The coder systematically analyzing the content of a body of material will occasionally fail to note the appearance of some variable, or two coders will place the same item into different categories. A judge rating a set of countries on some scale will inadvertently put a check mark in the wrong column. Without meaning to be antihumanistic, I would add machine error to this category. Desk calculators and even electronic computers, it turns out, sometimes suffer their version of a "nervous breakdown" and manipulate data incorrectly.

A second general source of error stems from inadequate *reporting systems*. In their comprehensive surveys of problems of accuracy in economic and social indicators, Oskar Morgenstern (1963), Raymond A. Bauer (1966a), and Albert D. Biderman (1966) list several ways in which statistical offices themselves generate error.

1. One of these results from varying definitions of a variable. Different field agencies may interpret a given variable to mean quite different things, producing data that are not comparable in any meaningful sense. Or the definition of a particular variable may expand over time to include more cases. Bauer (1966a, pp. 27–28), noting that "virtually every trend series pertaining to social problems has a built-in inflationary bias that would make it look as though things were 'getting worse,' unless the trend for improvement were very strong," goes on to cite the example of statistics on mental illness:

> The inflation begins with the phenomenon itself, in that some disorders that previously would have been considered to be physical diseases are now regarded as mental illness. To this has been added the expansion of the category of illness itself. What once was regarded as "odd behavior," or "bad behavior," is now recognized as a manifestation of disease.

2. Another source of institutional error derives from inadequate training of personnel, particularly those in the field who fill out questionnaires or compile data. As Morgenstern (1963, p. 5) writes:

> If the data be aggregates, these are necessarily made up from such large masses that this assumes particular significance because, as is often the case, they are usually made by hundreds, thousands, and even tens of thousands of "observers." These, as a rule, have only a limited training in observing, taking counts, recording answers. Mass observations have their own prob-

lems, even when undertaken in the best known manner. There is, for example, a summation of errors by the successive processing of data (observers at various stages not being able or trained to correct the errors of the lower stages). These errors frequently are cumulative. There is no guarantee that they will cancel out. . . . They have . . . shown up in population statistics with the consequence that even in modern times and in advanced countries sometimes millions of people are omitted or counted double. . . .

3. The natural growth of reporting agencies may mean that, as time goes on, they are more comprehensive in their reporting. This in turn means that reported changes in the incidence of particular events, such as homicides or mental illness, may indicate little more than that the reporting agency's facilities have become more extensive.

4. Sometimes reported data are in error over time because the dates of their observation vary. To take an absurd (but, alas, not implausible) example, if for one year sales of Christmas trees are recorded in the third week of December and for the next year sales are recorded in the last week of December, we would expect the findings to differ significantly. But would this difference really indicate differential sales of Christmas trees from the first year to the next? Similarly, images and attitudes sometimes fluctuate in response to external events (Deutsch & Merritt, 1965). The results of a survey asking Frenchmen their opinions of the Soviet Union, taken immediately before, let us say, the Soviet repression of the Hungarian uprising in 1956 or its launching of Sputnik I in 1957, would in all likelihood not be directly comparable to the results of a survey of Englishmen taken after these events.

5. Social conditions also affect the reliability of data. Bauer (1966a, p. 28) suggests three types of social conditions affecting the reporting of mental illness:

> . . . Mental illness has become socially acceptable to the extent that doctors will now record cases that previously they would have disguised under more polite labels.
> . . . Hospital admissions for mental illness are a function of available hospital beds. . . .
> As the population has become urbanized, the availability of relatives or servants to take care of the "odd" person has decreased, the size of the housing unit decreased, and, therefore, it has become less tolerable to keep such people at home. Hence, they are more likely to become a statistic in the indices of mental illness.

Similarly, in analyzing "the proud and true claim of Mississippi's white supremacists that their state had the lowest crime rate in the nation," Biderman (1966, p. 124) has pointed out:

> The substantial immunity enjoyed by whites who offend against Negroes doubtless reduces substantially the registration by the index of crimes of

SYSTEMATIC APPROACHES TO COMPARATIVE POLITICS

violence in Mississippi. . . . More important is that where offender and victim are known, the bulk of offenses are not interracial. Offender and victim usually are members of the same race. The most apparent source of the low crime rate for Mississippi is that crimes of Negroes against Negroes have been of little official concern to the all-white police forces of that state. Furthermore, police practices have done little to develop the attitude among the Negro population of the state that it is wise or moral to report to the police the offenses they suffer or witness.

Prejudice, local pride, and changing ecological circumstances all con- \ tribute their part to inaccuracies in aggregate data.

Reporting error is particularly problematic for those using "event" statistics. (Since content analysis and survey research will be discussed in subsequent chapters, we shall omit here a specific discussion of the types of error to which they are subject.) How likely is it, for instance, that the *New York Times Index* (or some other standard source) will have complete and reliable information about the domestic and international conflict behavior of a wide variety of countries? For one thing, reporting and the inclusion of items in the pages of the *New York Times* tend to be uneven. Censorship may prevent news of such behavior from being disseminated. Or if such news is disseminated, it may not get into the sources used because the country in which the unrest occurred is of little interest to the world at large (for example, demonstrations in Nepal or Uruguay), or the news goes unreported because it was concurrent with an event considered important enough to be reported in great depth (Rummel, 1964a, p. 6). For another, as George Lichtheim has complained (cited by Gurr & Ruttenberg, 1967, p. 37), however comprehensive the *New York Times* may be, it is preoccupied "with international events to the extent of allowing seriously inadequate coverage of intranational news." Third, it is well known that in the middle of an event such as a riot the observer's estimate of the extent of participation will vary with his vantage point. Finally, estimates of casualties or even property damage may vary widely with the facts, since many participants may prefer not to be treated at government-controlled hospitals or many choose not to prefer charges for property damage, fearing that such steps would give proof of participation that could lead to their arrest. As a simple example, in the very statistics-minded city of West Berlin, a political riot in June 1967 led to the death of one student and the hospitalization of nearly fifty others; for weeks afterward, the press carried reports that could be neither verified nor proved false that in fact a second student had died while hospitalized. It is not difficult to transfer this situation to a developing country with inadequate hospitals and statistical offices. (Although their efforts will not be discussed here, it should be added that econometricians and statistically-minded political scientists are currently developing techniques that will permit more precision in estimating the value of missing data.)

In some instances, *willful distortions* of data emerge from offices charged with the production of statistics. Reporting error-filled data to be entirely reliable is a frequent practice. "All offices must try to impress the public with the quality of their work," Morgenstern (1963, p. 11) has noted. "Should too many doubts be raised, financial support from Congress or other sources may not be forthcoming." Then, too, pride may lead some offices in some countries to report findings from data they have never collected. Feeling that it would be a blow to their self-esteem to have to report that they did not have a particular set of data, they might be willing to estimate its parameters and report them as reliable. Misleading reports aside, statistical offices have also been known to falsify their data. This may be done for reasons of international prestige. The importance of literacy and other indicators of a country's state of modernization may lead the political leadership of some countries to fudge a little on the true circumstances when they discuss, or issue statistical reports about, their own progress toward modernity. Something of the same thing operates when belligerants overestimate the damage—number of planes shot down, number of casualties—they have inflicted upon their enemies. Falsification may also serve policy purposes. Officials interested in underlining the effectiveness of their police in quelling a riot may deliberately overestimate the number of participants; those claiming that the rioters did not represent a significant proportion of the population may underestimate their numbers. Or a nation may report that it has more bombers and nuclear weapons than it in fact possesses as a means to intimidate its would-be opponents.

The possible sources of error are merely magnified when we turn to cross-national research. The definition of a variable, the units being counted, the ways of counting them, and forms of reporting the findings may all differ from country to country. And, of course, when we move from the more developed countries, some of which have had censuses and statistical offices for close to two centuries, to the newer nations of the world, the possibility of errors of these sorts may increase exponentially. The researcher using such data must be aware of sources of noncomparability. It should be added that international cooperation, through the League of Nations and the International Labor Office, and subsequently through the United Nations and various academic institutes and conferences, has made substantial gains in standardizing techniques of data collection (Rokkan, 1966).

Types of Error. Whatever its source—whether it stem from human fallibility, imperfections in the measuring instruments, or conscious design—error may be classified as either random or systematic. If it is truly due to *random* fluctuations occurring in the process of data collection, then we may anticipate that error in one direction will cancel out error in an opposite direction (bearing in mind the remarks by Morgenstern cited above). What this means is that, ceteris paribus, a distribution of data will probably be accurate though each of the individual bits comprising the distribution may be subject to random error. (The accuracy of a distribution as a whole, of course, should not lead us to assume that every item making up the distribution is equally accurate.) For correlative analyses of quantitative indicators, Russett (1965) has shown that the deliberate introduction of random error serves only to lower the coefficient of correlation slightly, without affecting the main findings significantly.

What is more problematic is *systematic* error, that is, when certain countries persistently over- or underestimate certain types of data. In his analyses, Rummel (1964b) found that systematic error was most likely to occur in demographic and economic-welfare data, and that levels of economic development and totalitarianism in the reporting countries accounted for the major part of the variation. Rummel also makes a useful distinction between univariate error, that is, present in only one of the indicators when two or more indicators are being compared, and multivariate error.

Quality Control. Few, if any, data are free from error. The question is how to deal with the error that is present. As a first step, the researcher must try to establish the *margin of error* characterizing his data. That this is not at all a simple task is suggested by standard treatments of cross-national data on population. Russett, Alker, Deutsch, and Lasswell (1964, p. 15) identify three sources of error in total population estimates: "the base, such as the census total, from which later annual estimates must be calculated; the method of adjusting for population increase; and the period of time from the base data for which an approximate adjustment must be made." Following procedures established by the Statistical Office of the United Nations, they then specify the approximate error ranges (in per cent of estimated population) for the base data alone:

A. Complete census of individuals
    1.0% in censuses taken at least decennially;
    2.0% in censuses taken sporadically;
    3.5% in censuses taken for the first time. . . .
B. Sample census or survey—5.0%

C. Partial census or registration; annual count (apparently this is the same as an "unconventional count"; e.g., a count of dwellings or a count from voting or tax registers)—10.0%

D. Conjecture—20.0% . . .

These estimates are then adjusted according to "the number of years since the base data were established" and "the range of annual per cent error imputed to the time adjustments" (pp. 15–16).

In the case of content analytic data and event statistics, the error margin is the reliability score, that is, the degree of agreement between two or more coders coding the same body of data. Feierabend and Feierabend (1966a, p. 252), for instance, found that intercoder reliability for their political stability index was very high (with the Pearsonian r ranging between .87 and .935). Tanter (1966, p. 44) reported intercoder agreement ranging from 85 to 100 per cent. And Gurr and Ruttenberg (1967, p. 37), discussing their basic measures of civil violence, wrote: "The level of agreement was .75—high, considering that one of the coders had had no prior experience with either the scales or the sources." In each case these scores represent roughly the probability that another researcher could, by applying the same measuring instruments to the original body of information, replicate the original findings.

Knowledge of error margins will affect the researcher's treatment of his data. That a set of data has a high margin of error—the reported value of the Soviet Union's gross national product, $122 billion in 1957, may vary in either direction by as much as 20 per cent, that is, its true value may be anywhere between $98 and $146 billion (Russett, Alker, Deutsch & Lasswell, 1964, p. 152)—should surely lead the researcher to interpret his findings cautiously. Such variability has prompted some (for example, Scheuch, 1966, p. 140) to propose *grouping* the data into intervals instead of treating the estimates as "true" values. "If there is any reason to suspect error," writes Scheuch, "one should sacrifice some information and settle for a rough measure." Gurr's solution (1966) is to develop what he terms "optimal intervals" permitting *adjustments* of the "best estimates" by rounding or rescaling. His procedure eliminates some of the false precision of the estimates; but leaves the ungrouped and "error-compensated" data in rank-order distributions.

Work performed by Rummel (1964a; 1966) and Tanter (1965; 1966) in the Dimensionality of National Project suggests still another procedure: using *dimensions of error as variables* in the analyses. Finding that censorship and the lack of world interest in particular countries were chief sources of error, they developed three indicators: (1) a three-point censorship scale based on the findings of the Inter-American Press Survey and the Survey of the World's Press by the International Press Institute; (2) a world-interest indicator comprising the number of embassies or legations in each country; and (3) another indicator of world interest based on the number of index cards per country in the cardfiles of *Deadline Data on World Affairs*. As Tanter (1966, pp. 44–45) explains it:

> These three error measures are included in the correlation and factor analysis. If censorship has no correlation with the conflict behavior measures, then systematic bias as tapped by the censorship measure does not distort the conclusions. Negative correlation of censorship and the conflict behavior measures is not crucial because one can assume the direction of systematic bias to be under- instead of overstated. Aside from possible exaggeration by the press, one would not expect nations to overstate the number of riots and revolutions it has. So if censorship is negatively correlated with riots, it might be inferred that the correlations between riots and the other conflict behavior measures would undergo little change even if censorship were suppressing knowledge of such incidents. Positive correlations between the censorship and the conflict behavior measures indicate that censorship in a nation could be distorting the results; positive correlation, however, is a necessary but not sufficient condition for such systematic error to distort the results of this study.
>
> A high positive correlation between the world interest measures and the conflict behavior measures might mean that lack of world interest in some countries could be causing their conflict behavior to go unreported. Positive correlation, however, is a necessary but not sufficient condition for such systematic error to distort the conclusions. . . .

In his study of conflict behavior in 1958–1960, Tanter found his world-interest indicators (p. 61)

> to correlate highly with the protest variable and also to have high pattern values on the *diplomatic* dimension. It was concluded that the level of world interest in a nation is related to the tendency for a nation's protests and (to a lesser extent) its expulsion of ambassadors to be reported. Hence, propositions about these two conflict measures should be qualified to the extent that the data of nations in which little interest is expressed *may not* be included in the correlations from which the propositions are inferred.

Data from their studies of other periods suggest that error plays an even lesser role in explaining the incidence of conflict behavior.

In short, if we know something about the extent and nature of the error in our aggregate data, it is possible to take it into account through various means, none of which may be wholly satisfactory. To be sure, the researcher should strive to improve the quality of his data. Ultimately, however, he must recognize what economists call the opportunity cost of gathering or improving any additional piece of information. To reduce the margin of error to, let us say, the 5 per cent level for many of the indicators discussed in this chapter would require an exhorbitant input of research time and funds. Wilfried Malenbaum (cited by Gross, 1966, p. 166) argues that "lack of precision is not a sufficient explanation for the failure to use" available statistics as indicators. These indicators must be used, it should be clear, but hopefully with a lively concern for the effects of error and possibly even an effort to compensate for it.

Validity

More basic than the problem of reliability is that of validity. Do the indicators really indicate what they are supposed to indicate? Is a set of data sufficiently related to a concept that a measure of the former will give us an accurate picture of the latter? Two criteria usually govern the generation of indicators for political research. The first is the researcher's deductive analysis of the concept that interests him. Once he has decided upon the types of indicators most appropriate to the concept, his task is to locate or devise the data that will constitute the indicators. The second criterion is the availability of certain types of data, particularly from government sources. But, alas, the reasons such agencies collect statistics may be far removed from those motivating the researcher. "Statistics are gathered not out of a general sense of curiosity," writes Bauer (1966a, p. 26), "but rather because it is presumed that they will be guides to planning and action." This presumption limits the efforts of any agency (pp. 25–26):

> There is little doubt that the statistical series collected by the U.S. government reflect those areas of concern that have occupied the minds of the American people, though with some lag in time. But they reflect these interests unevenly, since the probability of a given statistical series being developed is also affected by
>
> The articulateness and power of the group whose interest is involved.
> The susceptibility of the phenomenon to being measured.
> The extent to which the phenomenon is socially visible.
> The preferences and skills of the agency personnel who gather the statistics.

The availability and authority of such statistics—Elbridge Sibley (cited by Biderman, 1966, p. 97) notes: "Statistics published in the chaste and solemn 8 pt. and 6 pt. of the Government Printing Office possess a persuasive quality to which even the most rigorous academic discipline does not produce complete immunity"—tempt the political analyst to rely unquestioningly upon them and to despair at the thought of gathering new types of data for indicators. Sometimes, it would seem, the inductive criterion of availability silently subverts that postulating a need to gather certain types of data.

There may be many indicators for every concept. Which of those that the researcher discovers or devises should he use? The best test is whether or not a particular indicator can be validated by "coincident indicators determined according to different methodologies and giving results distinguishable from other known conceptual variables" (Alker, 1966, p. 6). After surveying several indices of gross national product, Russett, Alker, Deutsch, and Lasswell (1964, pp. 149–151) decided to include in their data bank the index developed by Mikoto Usui and Everett E. Hagen (1959). When challenged on this decision, Hayward R. Alker, Jr. (1966), demonstrated not only that the Usui-Hagen index and two other proposed indices were highly intercorrelated but that the "three rather different indicators of national economic development give strikingly similar results when correlated with representative aggregate political variables." Alker concluded that "these results greatly increase our assurance, within modest error margins, of their validity as cross-national indicators of economic activity" (p. 8). Thus, for the statistical analyses conducted by the Yale Political Data Program, the three indices were completely interchangeable at the cost of only a small loss of information (see Lazarsfeld, 1959, pp. 113–117). Efficiency may dictate that we eliminate from our analyses the more redundant indicators.

The Analysis of Aggregate Data

Once we have data that are reasonably accurate (or for which we have fairly reliable margins of error) and that are indicative of the underlying concept in which we are interested, the next task is to analyze them. The remainder of this chapter will outline some of the ways in which political researchers have used their aggregate data and some of the conclusions they have reached.

Univariate Analysis. The simplest analytical technique focuses upon single variables. Russett, Alker, Deutsch, and Lasswell (1964), for instance, present their data for each variable in the form of a rank ordering, which lists the countries from that having the most of the value measured to the country with the least (Figure 2.2). They go on to describe the properties of each rank ordering by means of simple statistical summary measures: the *range* (that is, the difference between the highest and the lowest values in the distribution), the *mean* (or average value for the distribution as a whole), the *median* (or middle

FIGURE 2.2
Annual Growth of G.N.P. Per Capita

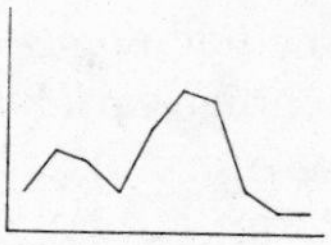

No. of Cases		68
Mean		2.99
Median		2.55
Modal Decile		VI
Range		9.8
Standard Deviation		2.22
Percentage of World Population		86

% of Table Population	Case Deciles	Rank	Country	G. N. P. per Cap. % Annual Change	Range Deciles	Years
	I	1	Japan	7.6	I	1953–60
		2.5	Austria	7.2		1948–60
		2.5	Yugoslavia[1]	7.2		1953–60
		4	Romania[1]	6.9[a]		1953–60
		5	Bulgaria[1]	6.5	II	1953–60
		6.5	Jamaica	6.3[a]		1954–59
		6.5	West Germany	6.3		1950–60
	II	8.5	Czechoslovakia[1]	6.0[a]		1952–60
		8.5	Trinidad & Tobago	6.0[a]		1952–60
		10.5	Israel	5.8[a]		1952–60
		10.5	Poland[1]	5.8		1953–60
18.0		12	U. S. S. R.	5.7[b]		1950–60
		13	China (Mainland)[1]	5.5[c]	III	1952–61
	III	14	Italy	5.4		1948–60
		15	Greece	5.3		1950–60
		16	Puerto Rico	5.0		1948–60
		17	Spain[2]	4.9		1950–59
		18	Hungary[1]	4.8[a]		1952–60
		19	Algeria	4.7		1950–58
		20	Venezuela[3]	4.4	IV	1950–60
	IV	21	Albania[1]	4.0[d]		1955–58
50.2		22	Burma[3]	3.9		1955–58
		23	Finland[4]	3.7		1948–60
		24	France	3.5	V	1950–60
		25	Switzerland[5]	3.4		1950–59
		27	Portugal	3.2		1948–60
		27	Netherlands	3.2		1948–60
	V	27	Taiwan	3.2		1953–60
		29.5	Brazil[6]	3.1		1948–60
		29.5	Denmark	3.1		1948–60
		31	Sweden	3.0		1948–60
		32.5	Congo (Leopoldville)[3]	2.8		1950–59
		32.5	Rhodesia & Nyasaland	2.8		1954–60
	VI	34	Norway	2.6	VI	1948–60
		35	Belgium	2.5		1948–60
		36.5	Philippines	2.4[a]		1952–60
		36.5	South Korea	2.4		1953–60
		38.5	Mexico	2.3		1948–59
		38.5	United Kingdom	2.3		1948–60
		40	Colombia	2.2		1950–59

% of Table Population	Case Deciles	Rank	Country	G. N. P. per Cap. % Annual Change	Range Deciles	Years
	VII	41	Tunisia	2.0[d]		1950–58
		44.5	Ecuador	1.8		1950–60
		44.5	El Salvador	1.8[e]		1953–59
		44.5	Ireland	1.8		1953–60
		44.5	Luxembourg	1.8		1953–59
		44.5	Turkey[4]	1.8[a]		1952–60
		44.5	United States	1.8		1948–60
	VIII	48	Thailand	1.7[a]	VII	1952–60
		50	Canada	1.6		1948–60
		50	Iceland	1.6		1954–60
74.5		50	Panama	1.6[e]		1950–58
		52.5	Indonesia[6]	1.5[e]		1951–59
		52.5	Peru	1.5		1950–58
		54	Cyprus	1.4		1950–60
		55	Chile	1.3		1950–60
	IX	57	Ceylon[3]	1.2		1950–60
		57	Guatemala	1.2		1948–60
		57	Nigeria	1.2		1953–57
		59.5	Cambodia[4]	1.0		1953–59
		59.5	India[6]	1.0		1948–59
		61	Malaya	0.6	VIII	1955–60
		62	Honduras	0.4[a]		1952–59
	X	63	Pakistan[2]	0.3		1953–60
		64	Bolivia	−0.2[d]		1950–55
		65	Argentina	−0.4	IX	1950–60
		66	Paraguay[6]	−1.0		1950–60
		67	Morocco	−1.9[a]	X	1952–60
		68	Syria[6]	−2.2[a]		1954–60

[1] Net material product.
[2] Net national product at factor cost.
[3] Gross domestic product at market prices.
[4] Gross domestic product at factor cost.
[5] Net national product at market prices.
[6] Net domestic product at factor cost.

Sources: Unless otherwise noted, U.N., *Statistical Yearbook, 1961* (New York, 1962).
[a] U.N., *Yearbook of National Accounts Statistics, 1962* (New York, 1963).
[b] Stanley H. Cohn, "The Gross National Product in the Soviet Union: Comparative Growth Rates," Joint Economic Committee, *Dimensions of Soviet Economic Power,* 87th Congress, 2d Session (Washington, D.C., 1962), p. 75. I am indebted to Professor Abram Bergson of Harvard University for the reference.
[c] U. N. E. C. A. F. E., *Economic Survey of Asia and the Far East, 1961* (Bangkok, 1962), p. 92.
[d] U.N., *Yearbook of National Accounts Statistics, 1960* (New York, 1961).
[e] U.N., *Compendium of Social Statistics, 1963* (New York, 1963).

Source: Russett, Alker, Deutsch & Lasswell (1964), pp. 160–161.

value, which has an equal number of countries located above it and below it in the distribution as a whole), and the *standard deviation* (which is a measure of the extent to which the individual countries vary from the mean). They also divide the entire array of data into deciles— first, according to the number of countries included in the array (number of countries divided by ten) and, second, according to the range as described above (range divided by ten). The range decile containing the greatest number of countries is the model decile. Finally, to give the reader a visual image of how many countries are in· each range decile, they graph the overall distribution.

A note of caution must be added about the use of rank-order profiles, particularly when the error margins of the data are substantial. The estimated population of Afghanistan in 1961 was 14,204,000, with an error margin of 20.0 per cent in either direction (Russett, Alker, Deutsch & Lasswell, 1964, p. 19). This means that the true value of Afghanistan's population could lie anywhere between 11.4 and 17.0 million. Its estimated population makes it the 35th most populous country (of 133 listed). If its true population were 17.0 million, however, it would be ranked in 29th place (assuming that the estimates for the other countries were correct); and if its true population were 11.4 million, it would drop to 39th place in the ranking. Similarly, Mali's ranking could conceivably be anywhere between 70th and 83rd place, and that of Somalia could range from 95th to 108th place. These facts have a double implication: First, and quite obviously, the researcher must take the error margins of his data into account when he interprets his findings; second, he must exercise extra care when he is using rank-order correlation procedures to relate his variables to one another.

Univariate analyses serve primarily descriptive purposes. First of all, listing countries' absolute scores on a particular variable or indicator demonstrates clearly the existence of differentiation in the world (Lasswell & Kaplan, 1950, p. 57). Second, putting them into a rank order permits the reader to locate any given country in its relationship to other countries. The most populous polity listed by Russett, Alker, Deutsch, and Lasswell (1964, pp. 18–20) is Communist China, which contains approximately 23 per cent of the world's total population; the least populous they include is Iceland, with less than 1/100 of 1 per cent. Similarly, the United States accounts for 38 per cent of the world's total gross national product, the Netherlands Antilles for less than 1/100 of 1 per cent (pp. 152–154). Closer examination reveals that a major portion of most resources are concentrated in but a handful of countries: The four most populous polities contain 50 per cent of the people on earth, and the four wealthiest account for 59 per cent of the world's

GNP. Not only are there inequalities in the world's distribution of resources, but these values also tend to cluster (Lasswell & Kaplan, 1950, p. 58). There are the "haves," who possess more of whatever there is to get, and the "have nots." Thus, regarding social services—infant mortality rates or the number of doctors and hospital beds (per 100,000 population) as indicators of a concern with health, or governmental expenditures on welfare measures—a few countries in nothern and western Europe regularly head the list. The United States, Great Britain, West Germany, and France are usually leaders on indicators of industrial development, such as GNP, capital investment, manufacturing output, and skilled labor. Finally, as suggested in the previous paragraph, summary measures can tell us something about the distribution and characteristics of a variable as a whole.

Bivariate Analysis. However useful univariate analysis may be for descriptive purposes, the political researcher is more frequently interested in the relationships among his variables. He may simply be interested in knowing whether there is any significant degree of association between two indicators or variables, a and b. Or he may have a model that predicts that shifts in the value of a will cause proportionate shifts in the value of b. In both cases (ignoring the differential assumptions and other tests that would have to be met), he would use standard statistical techniques producing indices of relation, called coefficients of correlation (or product-moment correlations). If two sets of ordered data for a group of countries are perfectly correlated ($r = +1.00$), then changes in one indicator are directly proportional to changes in the other. The higher on indicator a a country is, the higher it will be on indicator b. The reverse will be the case if the two sets of data are perfectly correlated in a negative direction ($r = -1.00$). And, if variations on one indicator are completely independent of variations on the other, then we may say that no relationship exists between the two indicators ($r = 0.00$). One type of correlation model is linear. If we plot the individual scores for a group of countries on a scattergram, with the vertical axis representing scores on indicator a and the horizontal axis representing scores on indicator b, then this model would enable us to determine the best-fitting straight (regression) line characterizing the array of data. (With standardized data, the slope of the regression line is equal to the correlation coefficient.)

Some of the major analyses of aggregate data have used linear regression coefficients as a first approach. Russett, Alker, Deutsch, and Lasswell (1964, pp. 261–292), using raw scores, correlated each of their 75 indicators with every other one. The result was a series of 75 matrices containing correlation coefficients. (To assist the reader, they omitted coefficients lower than ±.30, and underlined those greater than ±.50; using a table that is supplied, it is possible to figure out in a very rough sense the statistical significance of each correlation coefficient.) Individual variables correlate at the ±.50 level or greater with as many as 33 of the 74 other variables. And, out of a total of 2,755 possible bivariate relationships, 452 are at this level or greater. In effect, these 452 relationships comprise propositions of possible political relevance— propositions crying out either for further testing and/or for interpretation. Gross national product per capita, for instance, correlates quite highly with radios per 1,000 population (+.85) and television sets per 1,000 population (+.75), the percentage of working force in non-agricultural occupations (+.84), percentage literate (+.80), and life expectancy (+.86); and negatively with birth rate (−.76), infant mortality (−.76), and number of inhabitants per physician (−.81). Findings of this sort led the researchers to investigate more fully the characteristics of polities at various "stages" of economic and political development.

Feierabend and Feierabend (1966a) present another possibility: rank-order correlations. In this case, it is not a country's absolute value on a particular indicator—whether its GNP is $41.6 billion or $10.7 billion—that is important, but rather its position in the rank ordering of all countries on that indicator. The Feierabends' index of political stability, it will be recalled, first grouped 84 polities into 7 discrete categories and then ranked the polities within each category. A question that they asked was the extent to which the resulting rank-order scale compared to (rank-ordered) scales of political stability based upon absolute data. Using the Spearman rank-order correlation coefficient (a nonparametric statistical technique that does not require assumptions about the randomness of the data), they matched their index with Harry Eckstein's index (1963) "Deaths from domestic group violence per 1,000,000 population, 1950–1962" ($r_s = -.69$) and the Yale Political Data Program's index (Russett, Alker, Deutsch & Lasswell, 1964, pp. 101–104) "Executive stability: number of years independent/number of chief executives, 1945–1961" ($r_s = +.38$). Because of the ranking problems suggested in the previous section, it would seem that a product-moment correlation of absolute (or logged) scores is, where possible, more effective than a rank-order correlation. In this case, however, where the index was not scaled in absolute scores, the only way of getting a measure of association is through the use of rank-order correlations.

Sometimes, a linear regression merely distorts or obscures the true relationship between two variables. A glance at the scattergram showing the array of his data may suggest to the researcher that not a straight line but a curve (second- or even higher-order polynomial) would be the best fit. The Yale Political Data Program (Russett, Alker, Deutsch & Lasswell, 1964, pp. 304–310) found this to be the case in numerous instances. With "Annual percentage rate of increase in population, 1958–1961" and "Percentage literate of population aged 15 and over" as the two variables, for instance, the "use of the curvilinear regression raises the correlation coefficient fairly substantially, from $-.37$ to $-.49$," which leads to the hypothesis that "population increase is fastest at middle levels of literacy" (pp. 304–305). Another striking example— although not so significant in a statistical sense, since the curvilinear fit only raises the correlation from $-.43$ to $-.47$—is the relationship between "Deaths from domestic group violence per 1,000,000 population, 1950–1962" and "Annual growth of gross national product per capita," as shown in Figure 2.3. Finding that violence tends to be lower at both low and high levels of economic development, but somewhat higher at the middle level of development, the Yale researchers write (p. 307):

> This would suggest—to the extent that our cross-sectional model provides useful insights for change over time—that underdeveloped nations must expect a fairly high level of civil unrest for some time, and that very poor states should probably expect an increase, not a decrease, in domestic violence over the next few decades. The reasons, of course, are not hard to suggest. In a traditional society knowledge is limited, aspirations are limited, and expectations as to the proper activities of government are limited. All this changes with development.

Corroboration of this relationship is to be found in the analysis by Gurr and Ruttenberg (1967, p. 66). Their curvilinear correlation between their "Total magnitude of civil violence (logged)" index and logged per capita income for 1962 is presented in Figure 2.4. Again it must be added that a relationship based on cross-sectional data (data for many countries at a single point in time) may or may not be relevant for a longitudinal model (developments in a single country or set of countries over time).

Multivariate Analysis. Bivariate relationships are also subject to distortion because of the hidden effects of third (intervening) variables. To use a simple, nonstatistical example, we may see a happy married couple and hypothesize that their marriage (being togther) produces the happiness. A closer look at their home life however, indicates that they spend a good deal of their time together watching television. Subsequent tests might reveal that, with the television set operating, either of them

FIGURE 2.3
Economic Development Is Associated With
Political Violence, at Least in the Early Stages

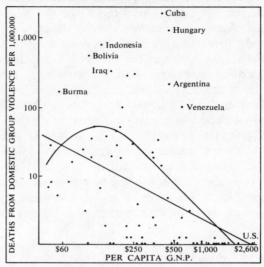

Source: Russett, Alker, Deutsch & Lasswell (1964), p. 307.

FIGURE 2.4
Levels of Strife and Per Capita Income, 1962

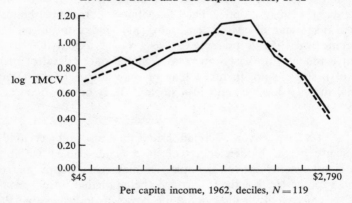

Source: Gurr & Ruttenberg (1967), p. 67.

would be happy alone or with each other and that, without it, they can be happy neither together nor alone. We would be justified in concluding that the television set goes farther in explaining their happiness than does the fact that they are married. The introduction of a "control variable" might also have the opposite effect of giving structure to apparently unstructured relationships. Thus Alker (1964b) shows how a slight negative relationship ($r = -.13$) between logged per capita income and scores on McClelland's index of need for achievement changes when the control factor of "geographic region" is introduced (Figures 2.5a–2.5e).

A related method is multiple regression, which permits the researcher "to identify the amount of variance in a variable 'explained' by two or more other variables" (Alker & Russett, 1964, p. 311). Phillips Cutright (1963) used this technique in studying the social correlates of national political development in 76 independent states outside Africa. First, he developed an index of political development, based upon the degree of party competition in national legislatures and procedures for electing chief executives. A bivariate (linear) correlation revealed that an indicator of communications development—based on standardized T scores of per capita newspaper readership, newsprint consumption, circulation of domestic mail, and telephones—was the best single predictor of levels of political development, accounting for 64 per cent of the variation in scores around the mean of the latter. "A multiple regression equation which added educational development, agricultural labor force, and degree of urbanization to the communication index as predictors of political development raised the level of explained variation to 72 per cent" (p. 582). Deane E. Neubauer (1967), however, pointing out that the above index really indicates "degree of democraticness" rather than political development, shows that a more refined index of democratic development negates Cutright's findings. Neubauer's multiple regression anlaysis based on 23 democracies suggests instead that (p. 1007)

> political development, to the extent that it represents democratic political development, is a threshold phenomenon. Certain levels of "basic" socio-economic development appear to be necessary to elevate countries to a level at which they can begin to support complex, nation-wide patterns of political interaction, one of which may be democracy. Once above this threshold, however, the degree to which a country will "maximize" certain forms of democratic practices is no longer a function of continued socioeconomic development.

Neubauer traces the development of democratic practices to the existence of ameliorative patterns of pluralism and to cleavages that are neither intense nor disruptive.

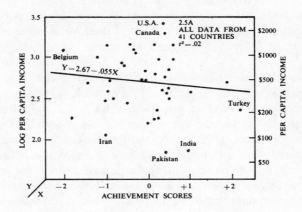

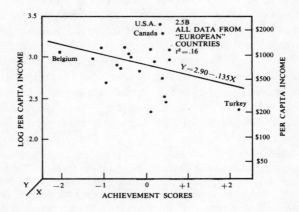

Source: Alker (1964b), p. 327.

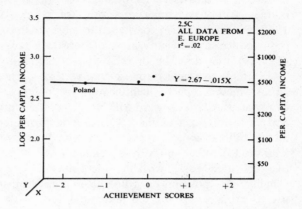

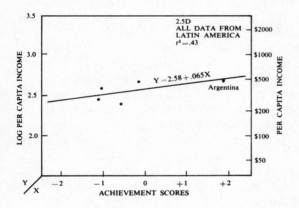

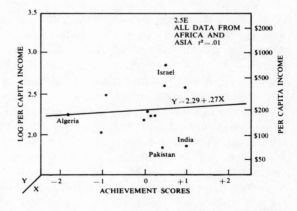

Several studies have factor analyzed the aggregate characteristics of polities. Although it may serve other purposes (Cattell, 1952; Harman, 1967; Rummel, 1967), perhaps the most common use of factor analysis is to reduce an unwieldy mass of data to a few underlying dimensions (factors) that describe or otherwise account for variation in the data. As a simple example, suppose that we know ten parameters of a population: income, party identification of parents, preferred presidential candidate, attitudes toward McCarthyism, the United Nations, Medicare, and so forth. Each of these variables is correlated to some extent with all the others; and, moreover, each may be viewed as a particular configuration of other, more basic (latent) variables. Our task is to isolate two or three basic variables—hypothetical constructs such as "personality" or "position on a liberalism-conservatism scale"—that we can use to explain why the ten individual variables were all intercorrelated in the first place. The hypothetical constructs (factors) are themselves statistically independent. Within each, however, the individual variables co-vary to a highly significant degree.

One of the more interesting uses of this technique is the factor analysis of roll-call voting in the United Nations General Assembly by Hayward R. Alker, Jr. (1964a; Alker & Russett, 1965; see also Vincent, 1968). In looking at the sessions of 1947, 1952, 1957, and 1961, he found two factors that together (averaged over the four seasons) accounted for 74 per cent of the variation (variance) in the members' voting patterns. The first of these (averaging 57 per cent) centered on Cold War and colonialism issues (or, as Alker terms them, issues of East vs. West), including UN membership for Communist China, disarmament, Soviet intervention in Hungary, UN military efforts in Korea, as well as several issues related to colonialism in Africa and elsewhere. The factor accounting for the next greatest amount of variance (averaging 17 per cent) was particularly concerned with the "have" and the "have not" nations (or issues of North vs. South): questions of multilateral economic aid channelled through the United Nations, the creation and financing of a UN emergency force in the Congo, nuclear testing, and the like. By plotting on two-dimensional charts each member's position with respect to the two sets of issues, Alker was able to delineate changing patterns of bloc-voting in the United Nations. Needless to say, such an analysis is not solely of interest to the scholarly world, for it also contains much of value for American foreign policy decision-makers, who sometimes confuse one kind of conflict with the other. It turns out, for instance, that many emerging nations support the United States on East-West issues, but not on North-South issues if the United States takes a "European" position. The danger for American policy-makers is that by taking too "Northern" a position on North-South issues (which are most salient for the developing countries) they may alienate those countries and lose their support on East-West issues.

Of the studies factor analyzing aggregate data constructed into indicators and indices, the first were by Raymond B. Cattell. He initially used 72 variables to delineate the nature of underlying culture patterns among 69 countries (Cattell, 1949; 1950). Later, after reducing the number of countries to 40 in an effort to eliminate imprecise data, he and his associates (1951) found 12 such dimensions, among them "enlightened affluence vs. narrow poverty," "vigorous order vs. unadapted rigidity," and "cultural pressure and complexity vs. direct ergic expression." The ultimate goal of Cattell's factor analyses was to produce hypotheses about the nature of cultural pressure, order, enlightenment, morale, and other cultural dimensions.

Brian J. L. Berry (1961) went beyond the discovery of basic patterns among variables to focus on regional variations. His first step was to rank order 95 countries on 43 economic and demographic variables such as railway density and intensity of railway use, foreign trade per capita, energy consumption, birth and death rates, and mail flow. His factor analysis revealed that four factors—technological development, economic-demographic development, contrasts in income and external relations, and size—sufficed to describe the patterns underlying the 43 variables. Berry was then able to use his findings to test some common-sense notions about regional levels of economic development, confirming some (such as the commonly accepted idea that "the more developed countries generally have commercialized and/or industrialized economies") and failing to confirm others. Of particular interest are some other of Berry's generalizations based on the factor analysis (p. 119):

> That there is some regional concentration of developmental levels on a subcontinental or continental level suggests possible regional typologies of economic development and the desirability of their development as a major channel for further research. That a tropical or equatorial location apparently has little to do with stage of economic development helps lay to rest one of the major intuitive assumptions of the developed West concerning the rest of the world. In turn, the fact that colonialism, or at least political colonialism, seems not to explain poverty but even in some instances to have countered it, is at variance with the assumptions of perhaps three-fourths the population of the world.

Clearly, however, it will be important to submit Berry's generalizations, which are based on data from the mid-1950s, to reexamination at some later date to determine the effect of time (and with it differential capital inputs, growth rates, and the like) upon his factors of economic development.

Rudolph J. Rummel (1964a), as indicated earlier, selected 9 measures of domestic conflict and 13 measures of foreign conflict for 77 countries in 1955–1957. Three dimensions of domestic conflict behavior ("turmoil," "revolution," and "subversion"), together accounting for 71 per cent of the total foreign conflict variance, emerged from his factor analysis. Among his findings, four points stand out: (1) "foreign conflict behavior is generally completely unrelated to domestic conflict behavior"; (2) "a *war* dimension is more important than any other dimension of foreign conflict behavior in accounting for the variation in conflict behavior between nations"; (3) "foreign conflict behavior is not a necessary and sufficient condition for domestic peace"; and (4) "the acts or occurrences of conflict behavior within and between nations are not sporadic—unpredictable—but are patterned and can be predicted on the basis of their history of such conflict behavior" (p. 24). Subsequent replications for the 1955–1960 period (Tanter, 1965), for 1958–1960 (Tanter, 1966), and for 1946–1959 (Rummel, 1966) validated Rummel's original findings. And Rummel (1965, 1969), in integrating the findings of 12 such studies of conflict within nations into a field theory of social action, has discovered that the three dimensions of turmoil, revolution, and subversion recur persistently.

Bruce M. Russett (1967) factor analyzed 54 social and cultural variables from the files of the Yale Political Data Program (Russett, Alker, Deutsch & Lasswell, 1964) for 82 countries in an effort to delineate empirically homogeneous regions in the world of the late 1950s. He reduced these 54 variables to 5 (orthogonally rotated) dimensions that accounted for 60 per cent of the total variance: economic development, communist influence, size, "Catholic culture," and intensive vs. extensive agriculture. After eliminating the size dimension for reasons of parsimony and factor analyzing a matrix based on the "socio-cultural distance" scores (stemming from the countries' factor loadings in the earlier factor analysis), Russett found regions that were in one respect similar to those discovered by Berry but that allowed more differentiation than was possible in Berry's model.

To these must be added two factor analyses using some judgmental variables. In one of these, Phillip M. Gregg and Arthur S. Banks (1965) used data from the Cross-Polity Survey (Banks & Textor, 1963) discussed earlier. Altogether they found seven factors, accounting for 72 per cent of the total variance among the 68 variables. Their first factor (accounting for 24.6 per cent of the variance) reflects "the degree of access to political channels"; their second (13.5 per cent) "differentiation of political institutions within former colonial dependencies"; their third (13.2 per cent), "the degree of consensus and cooperation among participants"; and others, "sectionalism," "legitimation," "interest circulation," and "leadership." Irma Adelman and Cynthia Taft Morris (1965; 1967), in examining the interrelationship between social and political variables and per capita gross national product, focused upon 74 "less-developed countries" during the period 1957–1962. Among their 23 variables were some that were statistical in nature, such as their index of the "extent of mass communication," which was based upon newspaper circulation and radios in use. Others, such as "extent of nationalism and sense of national identity," were judgmental. Their analysis generated four major factors that, together, accounted for 66 per cent of the variance on the per capita gross national product variable (1965, p. 577):

> The relationship expressed in Factor I indicates a strong tendency for levels of economic development to be positively correlated with the extent of functional differentiation and integration of diverse social units. A similarly significant positive association is evident in Factor II between income levels and the degree of articulation and Westernization of political systems. In contrast, a rather weak relationship appears between broad levels of development and indicators summarizing the character of leadership and the degree of social and political stability in the past decade (Factors III and IV).

Separate analyses of three different regions—Africa, the Near East and the Far East, and Latin America—produced substantially the same results. These findings, the authors conclude, lend "support to the views, long held by development economists, that, in the last analysis, the purely economic performance of a community is strongly conditioned by the social and political setting in which economic activity takes place" (p. 578).

The findings outlined above only scratch the surface of the rich lode currently being probed. What makes this particularly felicitous is the very newness of approaches to cross-national research using aggregate data. Scarcely a decade ago, politically relevant studies using such data on a comparative basis could practically be counted on the fingers of one hand. By now, special research centers in five continents are generating and analyzing aggregate data, both for cross-national and within-nation comparisons. This is not to say that these scholars have resolved all or even most of the intellectual and technical problems confronting them. As this chapter has made abundantly clear, there are many areas in which our knowledge is severely limited. In other cases there is dispute about the meaning of indicators, or about the efficacy of particular techniques for analysis. But, if the coming decade enjoys the rate of progress attained during the past one, then the future of cross-national research using aggregate data is bright indeed.

REFERENCES

Adelman, Irma, and Cynthia Taft Morris. "Factor Analysis of the Interrelationship between Social and Political Variables and Per Capita Gross National Product," *The Quarterly Journal of Economics.* 79:4 (November 1965), 555–578.

Adelman, Irma, and Cynthia Taft Morris. *Society, Politics, and Economic Development: A Quantitative Approach.* Baltimore, Md.: The Johns Hopkins Press, 1967.

Alker, Hayward R., Jr. "The Comparison of Aggregate Political and Social Data: Potentialities and Problems," *Social Science Information.* 5:3 (September 1966), 1–18.

Alker, Hayward R., Jr. "Dimensions of Conflict in the General Assembly," *The American Political Science Review.* 58:3 (September 1964a), 642–657.

Alker, Hayward R., Jr. "Regionalism Versus Universalism in Comparing Nations" [1964b]. In Russett, Alker, Deutsch & Lasswell (1964), pp. 322–340.

Alker, Hayward R., Jr., and Bruce M. Russett. "Multifactor Explanations of Social Change." In Russett, Alker, Deutsch & Lasswell (1964), pp. 311–321.

Alker, Hayward R., Jr., and Bruce M. Russett. *World Politics in the General Assembly.* New Haven and London: Yale University Press, 1965.

Almond, Gabriel A. "A Functional Approach to Comparative Politics." In Almond & Coleman (1960), pp. 3–64.

Almond, Gabriel A., and James S. Coleman, editors. *The Politics of the Developing Areas.* Princeton, N.J.: Princeton University Press, 1960.

Almond, Gabriel A., and Sidney Verba. *The Civic Culture: Political Attitudes and Democracy in Five Nations.* Princeton, N.J.: Princeton University Press, 1963.

Anonymous. "What Indicates What?" *The American Behavioral Scientist.* 8:4 (December 1964), 29–31.

Banks, Arthur S., and Robert B. Textor. *A Cross-Polity Survey.* Cambridge, Mass.: The M.I.T. Press, 1963.

Bauer, Raymond A. "Detection and Anticipation of Impact: The Nature of the Task" [1966a]. In Bauer (1966b), pp. 1–67.

Bauer, Raymond A., editor. *Social Indicators.* Cambridge, Mass.: The M.I.T. Press, 1966b.

Berry, Brian J. L. "Basic Patterns of Economic Development." In Ginsburg (1961), pp. 110–119.

Biderman, Albert D. "Social Indicators and Goals." In Bauer (1966b), pp. 68–153.

Buchanan, William, and Hadley Cantril. *How Nations See Each Other: A Study in Public Opinion.* Urbana: University of Illinois Press, 1953.

Cattell, Raymond B. "The Dimensions of Culture Patterns by Factorization of National Characters," *The Journal of Abnormal and Social Psychology.* 44:4 (October 1949), 443–469.

Cattell, Raymond B. *Factor Analysis: An Introduction and Manual for the Psychologist and Social Scientist.* New York: Harper & Brothers, 1952.

Cattell, Raymond B. "The Principal Culture Patterns Discoverable in the Syntal Dimensions of Existing Nations," *The Journal of Social Psychology.* 32:2 (November 1950), 215–253.

Cattell, Raymond B., H. Bruel, and H. Parker Hartman. "An Attempt at More Refined Definition of the Cultural Dimensions of Syntality in Modern Nations," *The American Sociological Review.* 17:4 (August 1951), 408–421.

Coale, Ansley J., and Frederick F. Stephan. "The Case of the Indians and Teen-Age Widows," *The Journal of the American Statistical Association.* 57:298 (June 1962), 338–347.

Cutright, Phillips. "National Political Development: Its Measurement and Social Correlates." In Polsby, Dentler & Smith (1963), pp. 569–582.

Deutsch, Karl W. "Social Mobilization and Political Development," *The American Political Science Review.* 55:3 (September 1961), 493–514.

Deutsch, Karl W., and Richard L. Merritt. "Effects of Events on National and International Images." In Kelman (1965), pp. 132–187.

Dogan, Mattei, and Stein Rokkan, editors. *Quantitative Ecological Analysis in the Social Sciences.* Cambridge, Mass., and London: The M.I.T. Press, 1969.

Eckstein, Harry. "Internal War: The Problem of Anticipation." In Pool et al. (1963).

Feierabend, Ivo K., and Rosalind L. Feierabend. "Aggressive Behaviors within Polities, 1948–1962: A Cross-National Study," *The Journal of Conflict Resolution.* 10:3 (September 1966a), 249–271.

Feierabend, Ivo K., and Rosalind L. Feierabend. "The Relationship of Systemic Frustration, Political Coercion, International Tension and Political Instability: A Cross-National Study." Paper prepared for delivery at the Annual Meeting of the American Psychological Association, New York City, 2–6 September 1966b.

Feierabend, Ivo K., Rosalind L. Feierabend, and Betty A. Nesvold. "Social Change and Political Violence: Cross-National Patterns." In Graham & Gurr (1969), pp. 632–687.

Fitzgibbon, Russell H., and Kenneth F. Johnson. "Measurement of Latin American Political Change," *The American Political Science Review.* 55:3 (September 1961), 515–526.

Ginsburg, Norton Sydney. *Atlas of Economic Development.* Chicago: University of Chicago Press, 1961.

Graham, Hugh Davis, and Ted Robert Gurr, editors. *Violence in America: Historical and Comparative Perspectives.* A Report Submitted to the National Commission on the Causes and Prevention of Violence. New York, Toronto, and London: Bantam Books, 1969.

Gregg, Phillip M., and Arthur S. Banks. "Dimensions of Political Systems: Factor Analysis of *A Cross-Polity Survey,*" *The American Political Science Review.* 59:3 (September 1965), 602–614.

Gross, Bertram M. "The State of the Nation: Social Systems Accounting." In Bauer (1966b), pp. 154–271.

Gurr, Ted. "A Causal Model of Civil Strife: A Comparative Analysis Using New Indices," *The American Political Science Review.* 62:4 (December 1968), 1104–1124.

Gurr, Ted. *New Error-Compensated Measures for Comparing Nations: Some Correlates of Civil Violence.* Princeton University, Center of International Studies, Research Monograph No. 25, May 1966.

Gurr, Ted, with Charles Ruttenberg. *The Conditions of Civil Violence: First Tests of a Causal Model.* Princeton University, Center of International Studies, Research Monograph No. 28, April 1967.

Harman, Harry H. *Modern Factor Analysis* (2d ed.). Chicago and London: University of Chicago Press, 1967.

Kelman, Herbert C., editor. *International Behavior: A Social-Psychological Approach.* New York: Holt, Rinehart and Winston, 1965.

Lasswell, Harold D., and Abraham Kaplan. *Power and Society: A Framework for Political Inquiry.* New Haven: Yale University Press, 1950.

Lasswell, Harold D., Daniel Lerner, and Ithiel de Sola Pool. *The Comparative Study of Symbols: An Introduction.* Hoover Institute Studies, Series C: Symbols, No. 1. Stanford, Calif.: Stanford University Press, 1952.

Lazarsfeld, Paul F. "Evidence and Inference in Social Research." In Lerner (1959), pp. 107–138.

Lazarsfeld, Paul F., and Morris Rosenberg. *The Language of Social Research: A Reader in the Methodology of Social Research.* Glencoe, Ill.: The Free Press, 1955.

Lerner, Daniel, editor. *Evidence and Inference: The Hayden Colloquium on Scientific Concept and Method.* Glencoe, Ill.: The Free Press, 1959.

Linz, Juan J. "Ecological Analysis and Survey Research." In Dogan & Rokkan (1969), pp. 91–131.

Lipset, Seymour Martin. *Political Man: The Social Bases of Politics.* Garden City, N.Y.: Doubleday & Company, 1960; copyright © by Seymour Martin Lipset; reprinted by permission of Doubleday & Company, Inc.

MacRae, Duncan, Jr., and James A. Meldrum. "Factor Analysis of Aggregate Voting Statistics." In Dogan & Rokkan (1969), pp. 487–506.

McClelland, David C. *The Achieving Society.* Princeton, N.J.: D. Van Nostrand Company, 1961.

Merritt, Richard L. "The USIA Surveys: Tools for Policy and Analysis." In Merritt & Puchala (1968), pp. 3–30.

Merritt, Richard L., and Donald J. Puchala, editors. *Western European Perspectives on International Affairs: Public Opinion Studies and Evaluations.* New York: Frederick A. Praeger, 1968.

Merritt, Richard L., and Stein Rokkan, editors. *Comparing Nations: The Use of Quantitative Data in Cross-National Research.* New Haven and London: Yale University Press, 1966.

Morgenstern, Oskar. *On the Accuracy of Economic Observations* (2d ed.). Princeton, N.J.: Princeton University Press, 1963.

Nesvold, Betty A. "Scalogram Analysis of Political Violence," *Comparative Political Studies.* 2:2 (July 1969), 172–194.

Neubauer, Deane E. "Some Conditions of Democracy," *The American Political Science Review.* 61:4 (December 1967), 1002–1009.

Osgood, Charles E. "On the Strategy of Cross-National Research into Subjective Culture," *Social Science Information.* 6:1 (February 1967), 5–37.

Polsby, Nelson W., Robert A. Dentler, and Paul A. Smith, editors. *Politics and Social Life: An Introduction to Political Behavior.* Boston: Houghton Mifflin Company, 1963.

Pool, Ithiel de Sola, et al., editors. *Social Science Research and National Security: A Report Prepared by the Research Group in Psychology and the Social Sciences.* Washington, D.C.: Smithsonian Institution, 5 March 1963.

Rokkan, Stein. "Comparative Cross-National Research: The Context of Current Efforts." In Merritt & Rokkan (1966), pp. 3–25.

Rummel, Rudolph J. "Dimensions of Conflict Behavior Within and Between Nations." In *General Systems: Yearbook of the Society for General Systems Research,* Volume VIII, 1963, editors Ludwig von Bertalanffy and Anatol Rapoport. Ann Arbor, Mich.: Society for General Systems Research, 1964a. Pp. 1–50.

Rummel, Rudolph J. "Dimensions of Conflict Behavior Within Nations, 1946–59," *The Journal of Conflict Resolution.* 10:1 (March 1966), 65–73.

Rummel, Rudolph J. "Dimensions of Error in Cross-National Data." Yale University, Dimensionality of Nations Project, mimeographed, 21 December 1964b.

Rummel, Rudolph J. "A Field Theory of Social Action with Application to Conflict Within Nations." In *General Systems: Yearbook of the Society for General Systems Research,* Volume X, 1965, editors Ludwig von Bertalanffy and Anatol Rapoport. Ann Arbor, Mich.: Society for General Systems Research, 1965. Pp. 183–211.

Rummel, Rudolph J. "Indicators of Cross-National and International Patterns," *The American Political Science Review.* 63:1 (March 1969), 127–147.

Rummel, Rudolph J. "Understanding Factor Analysis," *The Journal of Conflict Resolution.* 11:4 (December 1967), 444–480.

Russett, Bruce M. *International Regions and the International System: A Study in Political Ecology.* Chicago: Rand McNally & Company, 1967.

Russett, Bruce M. "A Note on the Evaluation of Error and Transformation in Data Analysis," *The American Political Science Review.* 59:2 (June 1965), 444–446.

Russett, Bruce M., and Hayward R. Alker, Jr., Karl W. Deutsch, and Harold D. Lasswell. *World Handbook of Political and Social Indicators.* New Haven and London: Yale University Press, 1964.

Scheuch, Erwin K. "Cross-National Comparisons Using Aggregate Data: Some Substantive and Methodological Problems." In Merritt & Rokkan (1966), pp. 131–167.

Tanter, Raymond. "Dimensions of Conflict Behavior Within Nations, 1955–60: Turmoil and Internal War." In Peace Research Society (International): *Papers,* Volume III, 1965 (Chicago Conference, 1964), editors Walter Isard and Julian Wolpert. Pp. 159–183.

Tanter, Raymond. "Dimensions of Conflict Behavior Within and Between Nations, 1958–1960," *The Journal of Conflict Resolution.* 10:1 (March 1966), 41–64.

Taylor, Charles Lewis, editor. *Aggregate Data Analysis: Political and Social Indicators in Cross-National Research.* Paris and The Hague: Mouton & Co., 1968.

Usui, Mikoto, and Everett E. Hagen. *World Income, 1957.* Cambridge, Mass.: Massachusetts Institute of Technology, Center for International Studies, 1959.

Vincent, Jack E. "National Attributes as Predictors of Delegate Attitudes at the United Nations," *The American Political Science Review.* 62:3 (September 1968), 916–931.

3

CROSS-NATIONAL
CONTENT ANALYSIS

Systematic content analysis as a tool for political research is not particularly new. In primitive form it flourished during the 1930s. Students of journalism and others ascertained attention patterns, as indicated by column inches or occasionally by word counts, for wide varieties of newspapers and other publications; they compared patterns of attention to political events over time in the same publications; they contrasted political interest in large metropolitan dailies to that in small-town weeklies; they spent much time with questions of appropriate sampling and validation techniques.

It remained for Harold D. Lasswell and his colleagues, however, to develop content analysis as a tool specifically for comparative political research. Their studies of attention patterns in the "prestige papers" of five countries set standards of precision, clarity, and objectivity that students of comparative political behavior have sought to emulate (Lasswell, Lerner & Pool, 1952). Since then numerous scholars have undertaken substantial content analyses of aspects of the communication process relevant for the cross-national study of politics.

The communication process, in a slight modification of Harold D. Lasswell's (1948, p. 37) phrase, deals with *why who* says *what* to *whom* and with *what effect*—expressed schematically in Figure 3.1. Content analysis focuses on the message, or the *what* in Lasswell's formulation. It is the systematic, objective, and quantitative characterization of content variables manifest or latent in a message (Berelson, 1952, p. 18; see also, Budd, Thorp & Donohew, 1967; Holsti, 1969; Gerbner *et al.*, 1969). In principle, any type of message may be content analyzed: interesting cross-national work has been performed on movies by Martha Wolfenstein and Nathan Leites (1950), on plays by Donald V. McGranahan and Ivor Wayne (1948), on pictures in popular American and Soviet magazines by Wayne (1956), on doodling and designs on vases by Elliot Aronson (1958), on the film hero by Colum-

SYSTEMATIC APPROACHES TO COMPARATIVE POLITICS

FIGURE 3.1
The Communication Process

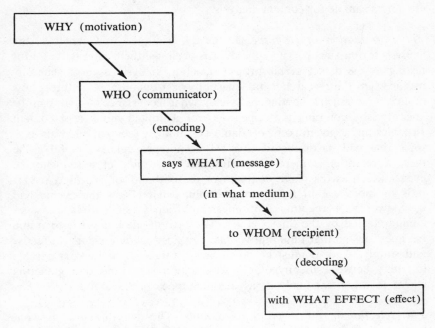

WHY (motivation)

WHO (communicator)

(encoding)

says WHAT (message)

(in what medium)

to WHOM (recipient)

(decoding)

with WHAT EFFECT (effect)

Source: Adapted from Lasswell (1948), p. 37.

bianum in Genoa (1963), and on children's drawings by Wayne Dennis (1966). To date, however, most cross-national research using content analysis has dealt with written messages, and it is with such research that this chapter will be primarily concerned. Before discussing the place of content analysis in systematic, cross-national research, a brief outline of some of its procedures and problems is required.

Research Design: Some Preliminary Considerations

As a research technique, content analysis entails a number of distinct but interrelated steps. In sorting out these steps for discussion, it should be borne in mind that the type of sample depends upon the nature of the material to be analyzed, the decision about the unit of analysis intertwines with the procedure to be used for processing the data, reliability varies with the unit of analysis as well as the data-processing procedure, and so forth. This section, after a brief discussion of the formulation of hypotheses, will pay particular attention to problems of creating a sample for content analysis.

The Formulation of Hypotheses. Ideally, as noted in Chapter 1, the analyst formulates his hypotheses (as well as their alternatives) for testing at the outset of his project. Content analysis is most generally useful when the researcher has questions of a quantitative nature—how often? how much? how many? with what covariance?—that can be answered by counting the appearance of a limited number of content variables in a given body of data. (Qualitative content analysis is a topic that will be discussed later.) It is not particularly helpful if the task of research is merely to determine the timing of a sequence of events (such as the death of Stalin or the outbreak of World War II); it is of more use in trying to determine what effects the events had upon people's perceptions, attitudes, and values (such as in messages communicated by the Soviet elite). The task of the analyst is to frame his questions so that quantitative data can answer them clearly, directly, and simply. And, it must be noted again, there is usually considerable interplay between the hypothesis-formulation stage and data-gathering stages in a content analysis, as in other types of research.

The Selection of an Appropriate Sample. The determination of what body of material could be used to test the hypotheses rests upon both the availability of data and the nature of the inferences to be drawn from the analysis. To get an idea of values current among Soviet elites, for instance, it would be ideal if we had access to the minutes of Presidium meetings. But such data are not at our disposal. In their absence, will the news columns of *Pravda* or *Izvestia* give us the information we want? Similarly, if our files of the most nearly ideal body of material are incomplete, it may be necessary to work out a compromise: accepting the information loss due to missing data, estimating the nature of the missing data through statistical techniques already developed, selecting a second-best source of data, possibly even using available files of the first choice as a check on trends present in the second choice. Such problems of the "representational model" will be discussed at greater length later.

Confronted with the task of analyzing a set of messages, such as editorials in the prominent newspapers of several countries, the researcher could follow one of two different procedures. He could, first of all, examine each item individually; or, alternatively, he could use some sort of sampling method to select a few representative items for close examination. The appropriateness of either procedure rests primarily upon the amount and type of information needed to answer his questions about the class of items, as well as the opportunity cost of securing a certain amount of information. If he were interested in press reactions to specific events, such as the Baruch Plan or the test-ban treaty of 1963, then he would most likely have to analyze every issue of a given number of newspapers for a certain, limited time period. But searching for long-run trends in press attitudes would pose an entirely different research task.

One means of analyzing long-run trends in newspaper editorials would be to read through every issue published (or extant) for the years in question. This is the time-honored historical method, and has much to commend it. In this manner the alert and insightful scholar can often spot significant relationships in the data that enable him to formulate interesting research problems and to reach useful conclusions.

That his results are important, however, is no guarantee that they adequately represent the actual content of the editorials. Three critical types of error might have crept into his findings. We may, first of all, ignore the type of error produced by a writer merely searching for statements fitting his preconceived notions about the content of the press. Charlatanism is possible regardless of the research method used. The occurrence of such instances is nonetheless frequent enough to make us wary. A second and more important type of error occurs when the researcher searches through the newspapers for different points of view. It is sometimes difficult to assess the importance of certain ideas or symbols without some sort of frequency count or other measure of intensity. To ignore this is to run the risk of evaluating widely differing ideas or symbols on a par, assigning equal weights to an argument appearing only occasionally and to one appearing constantly (Goodman, 1941). The third type of error falls into the category of simple human failings. To scrutinize every issue of the modern European press for a period of perhaps a dozen years would assume an inordinate amount of time. The researcher cannot read every word with equal care. He is generally able to do little more than scan the newspapers, looking for key words or concepts. Even as Homer nodded, so too the modern scholar occasionally slips, momentarily gliding by a few words or even paragraphs as the library grows dimmer, the microfilm copy grows fuzzier, or the hour grows later. He may judge certain items to be of only marginal interest when in fact their inclusion would be necessary to give a rounded aspect to his final conclusion. Or, still more likely, the categories of items or concepts he considers of marginal interest may vary from day to day.

The alternative is to utilize some method of sampling. The detailed examination of every nth issue of a newspaper, or of a certain number of newspapers selected at random for each year, is as useful in measuring long-run trends in attitude changes as a sampling process is in testing blood or in controlling quality on an assembly line. Such a procedure eliminates the necessity of scanning large quantities of newsprint as well as errors of the type mentioned in the previous paragraph. The more we can stratify the sample according to some characteristic of the media— according to political sympathies, for instance, or place of publication, or popularity as indicated by circulation—the more refined it will be. But, at the same time, with increasing refinement comes the need for larger sample sizes and hence added expense in terms of the time and money available for research. Ideally, the sample should be small enough to be manageable, yet large enough to answer the most important questions about the total class of items (Mintz, 1949).

Whether or not a sample is appropriate also rests upon certain empirical tests. One test for a random sample compares the distribution of content variables in the sample with that in the larger set from which the sample was drawn. Since such a procedure would obviate the need for a sample, it would be efficient only if the sampling technique were to be used in analyzing additional bodies of similar data. More frequently it is sufficient to compare the random sample with a second sample drawn independently from the same data. If the variation between the two independent samples is not statistically significant, then either could be used within certain limits of probability in analyzing the data. If the variation is significant, then a larger sample, or perhaps one stratified differently, must be used. An alternative procedure (the "split-halves" technique) divides a random sample into two equal subsamples and tests for the degree of variation (for example, Namenwirth & Brewer, 1966).

Often in political research, however, we cannot be quite· certain of the randomness of the sample. Published foreign office documents, for instance, are clearly not exhaustive of all documents in the archives of a country's foreign office. Compilers of such documents necessarily use some criteria of relevance in deciding which items to include and which to exclude. In such cases the problem of validating the sample is difficult indeed. And yet, the extent to which a random sample of the published collection actually approximates the distribution of documents in the entire files is a question that demands an answer if we are to credit any content analysis of the sample (North, Holsti, Zaninovich & Zinnes,

1963, pp. 17–36). Statistical techniques will tell us whether or not the sample is representative of the published documents, but correction factors are necessary to answer the more difficult question. Otherwise, some serious digging must be done in the particular country's foreign office files.

Translation. In any cross-national content analysis using materials written in different languages, the issue of translation is crucial. Traditional types of analyses, that is, those not using automatic (computerized) techniques for processing the data, have been able to utilize coders fluent in the languages in which the documents being analyzed were written. In such cases, the problem is one of the functional equivalence of the categories being coded. Given a list in English of symbols of democracy, for example, what words or concepts will be truly comparable in the German language?

With computerized content analysis, however, the task is considerably different. One such approach is the General Inquirer (Stone, Dunphy, Smith & Ogilvie, 1966), to be discussed in greater detail later in this chapter. It requires the analyst to transfer his communications content to IBM punchcards or magnetic tape, which in turn the computer is programmed to read and sort out the content into specified categories for further, primarily statistical analysis. The General Inquirer is presently equipped to handle textual material in the English language only. Efforts to make the system operational in German have to date not proved successful. Consequently, if the analyst wants to study American, British, French, and West German newspaper editorials (Namenwirth & Brewer, 1966), he must have the latter two sets of editorials translated into English.

Translation entails several problems, not the least of which is its cost. Also there is the question of the accuracy of the translation, by which is meant two things. The less important of these—less important because it can be checked by an independent translator rather than because it is less problematic—is content accuracy. Is what is being written on the manifest level in a German editorial reflected accurately by the translation? More important is the problem of translation on the latent level. This is what translators refer to as the problem of style. If the content analyst is interested in examining the communicator's psyche as indicated by the subtle phraseology of his writings, he must be reasonably certain that the translator has caught this level of meaning. Again, this is the question not of literalness but of functional equivalence. In actual practice—since as yet no one has concentrated upon this immense problem for computerized content analysis—investigators using the General Inquirer for cross-national research (such as Namenwirth & Brewer, 1966) have preferred functionally equivalent and literal to literary translations, fully aware that they were automatically cutting down on the richness of the language used by the original writer. (Anyone who has read a college freshman's literal translation of a portion of Goethe's *Faust* will appreciate this point.) However painful this choice may be from an aesthetic point of view, it seems imperative for scientific reasons.

Simplification of Syntax. A special problem that arises with some kinds of content analysis is the need to transform existing material into a less complicated text. In the case of the General Inquirer, this requires a certain amount of editing: breaking "complex sentences down into simple thought-sequence units" (Stone, Bales, Namenwirth & Ogilvie, 1962, p. 492); adding information not normally found in the computer's memory drum (for example, adding parenthetically "warm vacation place" to references to Florida); clarifying the referent of ambiguous words (references to the singer George London and the city of London); and, as will be discussed more fully later, "tagging" some words or combinations of words relevant to concepts in which the analyst is interested (for example, "ideal-value," "emotion," "European economic integration"). The Stanford project on conflict and integration utilized "evaluative assertion analysis" (Osgood, Saporta & Nunnally, 1956) to translate messages into a "simple, three-element assertive format" (North, Holsti, Zaninovich & Zinnes, 1963, p. 91). Thus the sentence, "The treacherous American aggressors are abetting the corrupt ruling circles of Japan," taken from a Communist Chinese newspaper, becomes:

1. Americans are treacherous.
2. Americans are aggressors.
3. Americans are abetting Japanese ruling circles.
4. Japanese ruling circles are corrupt.

(It will be noted that, if we follow the normal canons of logic, the four assertions are most assuredly *not* a reasonable restatement of the original sentence, but they do facilitate the evaluative analysis of the original sentence.) Merritt's study (1970) of history textbooks used in East Berlin and West Berlin high schools reduces complex sentences to sets of action-oriented assertions comprising a subject or actor, an action verb, and an object of action. Such transformations, although seemingly simple, may contribute significantly to the level of error in any content analysis.

The Process of Content Analysis

Having formulated his hypotheses and organized his sample of material to be analyzed, the content analyst must then establish his procedures for tabulating and processing the data. The discussion in this chapter, as noted earlier, focuses upon quantitative methods of approaching these issues, but "qualitative" or nonfrequency approaches must also be noted. In either case, if the procedures are sufficiently well spelled out in a coding manual, well-trained coders should be able to process the selected material with a high degree of reliability.

The Selection of Units of Analysis. Content analysts of written communications have generally used four types of analytical units: space, symbols, specific concepts, and underlying themes. Determining the relative amount of space devoted in a set of messages to particular topics is often a good indicator of the communicator's concern with those topics. An excellent example of this is the International Press Institute's study (1953) of the flow of international news among the United States, eight Western European countries, and India. In the case of Western Europe, the IPI analyzed the distribution of space in 48 daily newspapers (p. 199):

> This was admittedly a small sampling, but was designed to reflect not merely circulation but the individual variations characteristic of the European press —metropolitan papers, "national dailies," regional papers, morning and evening provincials, papers with and without foreign correspondents, papers taking only the national [news] agency, papers taking others, so-called "quality" papers, "popular" papers and papers whose political identifications lead to particular interests in foreign news coverage.

As shown in Table 3.1, interest in foreign news (defined as the percentage of foreign material to total nonadvertising text) varied widely among the eight countries as well as among the individual newspapers in each country. "Quality" newspapers were more inclined (except in the cases of Italy and Holland) to pay attention to foreign news than were others, and newspapers with high circulation rates were more likely to cover foreign events than were those with low circulation. "Limitations on space may prevent extensive daily coverage of even the most important countries," the IPI concluded on the basis of both its quantitative analysis and reports from numerous editors and journalists (p. 170); "but the aim can yet be for greater balance, more depth and greater continuity within the necessary limits."

Since man enshrouds so much of his behavior and thinking in symbolism, it only makes good sense to analyze his use of *symbols*. In brief,

TABLE 3.1
Western European Press Interest in Foreign News[a]
For Four Separate Weeks from October 1952 through January 1953
(in per cent)

Country	"Quality" Newspaper	High Circulation Newspaper	Low Circulation Newspaper	Average[e]
Switzerland	41.8[b]	27.0	22.8	30.5
Italy	30.3	34.4[b]	15.6[c]	26.8
Belgium	22.1[bd]	22.1[bd]	19.1	21.1
France	31.8[b]	18.5	11.1[c]	20.5
Holland	22.0	24.8[b]	12.2[c]	19.7
West Germany	25.1[b]	14.9	13.4	17.8
United Kingdom	25.2[b]	16.4	10.1	17.2
Sweden	15.0[b]	14.8	7.5[c]	12.4
Average	26.7	21.6	14.0	20.8

[a] Percentage of foreign material to total nonadvertising text.
[b] Indicates top percentage among the newspapers examined in this country in 48-papers sample.
[c] Indicates bottom percentage among the newspapers examined in this country.
[d] The same paper.
[e] Average only of the three figures listed in this table, not of all newspapers for each country.

Source: Adapted from International Press Institute (1953), p. 250.

---

symbols constitute "orders to recall something from memory" (Deutsch, 1955, p. 24). What is recalled may be referential, in the sense of denoting particular objects, or condensative, in the sense of evoking "the emotions associated with the situation" (Edelman, 1964, p. 6). Flags, emblems, badges, anthems, names assigned to groups, nicknames, crucifixes, diction, paintings, gestures, tones of voice, as well as such phrases as "King and Country" and such words as "liberty," "equality," "capitalism," and "communism" may be politically relevant symbols, both referential and evocative (Gerth & Mills, 1953). And of particular importance for the political analyst, of course, are words used as symbols. As Deutsch (1955, p. 23) writes:

> Viewed as indicators, political symbols and their statistical distribution can tell us something about the flow of messages between political groups and organizations, such as states, countries, regions, peoples, special interest groups, or particular institutions, such as governments, foreign offices, legislatures, newspapers, and other media of mass communication or control.

Such flows of messages can tell us something, in turn, about the distribution of attention of the individuals, groups, and organizations concerned. By noting which symbols are frequently associated with each other, we may learn something about the context in which political messages are perceived, remembered, and recalled on later occasions. Thus they help us understand political meaning and political perception at different times and in different communities.

To use words as symbolic indicators, however, raises the important question of validity.

Symbol analysis rests on the assumption that the words a person uses in communicating are indicative of or symbolize his perspectives. To some extent the selection of words by a communicator is a conscious process. Novelists frequently seek to describe characters in their stories in a way that will give their readers a set of vivid images. One thinks of Dickens' Mr. Micawber, always painted in gray tones, or Uriah Heep, who everlastingly sought to impress his 'umility upon one and all. Similarly, much as the villain in a nineteenth-century melodrama wore (and was expected to wear) a black hat and a moustache, so villains in modern-day propaganda are clothed in "appropriate" garb. It is not the United States that communist newspapers discuss, but rather the monopolistic or imperialistic United States. And not infrequently do American politicians and writers preface the term communism with adjectives bearing a pejorative connotation in American symbol usage, such as atheistic or totalitarian. By the same token, the patriot is the people's hero, the friend of peace, or the red-blooded American.

In contrast to this deliberate use of language, designed to create a particular image for its audience, is what might be termed the style of a communication—"the subtle *unconscious* patterning of speech, handwriting, posture, and involuntary movements" (Lasswell, Lerner & Pool, 1952, p. 21). Certain stylistic elements creep into a person's communication regardless of how hard he may try to exclude them. The passion for anonymity and unity of style that attended the writing of the *Federalist* papers have not been completely successful in disguising their authorship (Mosteller & Wallace, 1964). Similarly, matters of style are very significant in differentiating literary, musical, and artistic masterpieces from copies or imitations.

But what is meant by the phrase "unconscious patterning of speech"? In one sense the analysis of such unconscious patterns resembles the psychoanalyst's search for the *lapsus linguae,* the "slip of the tongue" that has become such a prominent aspect of the folklore of psychoanalysis. And yet, quantitative symbol analysis does not place much emphasis upon such speech blunders. The intentional or accidental use of a word, such as immortality or immorality, in a speech or in a diary of such a man as Woodrow Wilson may mean nothing in itself. It would be, we might say, a random element in an otherwise patterned context, a word that might appear once or perhaps twice in any similar speech or diary. (As we shall see later, qualitative content analysis pays more attention to the unexpected appearance of key words and phrases.)

The symbol analyst most often focuses upon the regularities of speech usage. If a word or phrase is used constantly in some form of communication, it ceases to be a random occurrence and becomes a stylistic pattern itself. In extreme cases, using the example from above, we would say that the speech or diary was preoccupied with immortality or immorality. The songs that Hitler's Stormtroopers sang as they marched through the streets of Weimar Germany, for example, dwelled on death and the dead; similarly, such concepts as nullification and abolition find as prominent a place in American writing of the mid-nineteenth century as international communist conspiracy did in the utterances of John Foster Dulles when he was secretary of state (Holsti, 1967).

The symbol analyst is interested less in whether a particular message represents the communicator's style or his deliberate manipulation of symbols than in the frequency with which certain items appear, in frequency changes over time, in the extent to which the direction and intensity of valences attached to the symbols change, in variations in frequency patterns in different communication media or in the same media in different geographic or political areas. (See, however, Mahl's [1959] use of content analysis to differentiate between a patient's "instrumental" and "representational" use of speech.) He is concerned not with what the message was intended to communicate (the encoding problem) but with what its content is perceived to be (the decoding problem), which in turn depends far less upon the subtle psychological processes operating on the communicator than upon the qualities of the audience. Taking an example from American colonial history, if a Tory newspaper, such as the *Massachusetts Gazette,* devoted an increasing share of its news columns to American events and symbols as the colonial years passed, or if with increasing frequency it identified its readers as Americans rather than His Majesty's subjects or even colonists, then we might say that, despite its pro-British point of view, the latent content of its symbol usage encouraged its readers to think of themselves as members of a distinctly American community and to turn their thoughts inward toward that American community (Merritt, 1966b).

If we view words as symbols for content analysis purposes, then establishing a list of relevant symbols is a crucial step. The experience of the Hoover Institute's study of Revolution and the Development of

International Relations (the RADIR Project), which concentrated on "symbols supposed to reflect trends in world politics with particular reference to changing attitudes toward the values of democracy, fraternity, security, and well-being," is instructive in this regard. Pool, Lasswell, and Lerner (1952a, pp. 16–17) write:

> Our own procedure in attempting to draw up a relatively valid list was to draw upon the best knowledge available and to use a long enough list so that the arbitrary decisions about inclusion or exclusion would affect the relatively infrequent terms in the tails of the word usage distribution, rather than more common words. To draw up the list we called upon Harold D. Lasswell, for thirty years one of the leading students of political movements and propaganda. The list he drew up consisted of nouns, although the listed words were also counted when they appeared in other forms. The list was then subjected to the test of use. Any expert, by pure oversight, might omit some symbols of obvious importance. Our readers were, therefore, instructed to note and report any additional symbols that seemed appropriate to the list.

A survey of the terminology of democracy, for instance, produced the list of democratic and antidemocratic symbols shown in Table 3.2. In summarizing the attention paid to symbols of democracy in American,

TABLE 3.2
Democracy-Relevant Symbols

Freedom	Tyranny of majority	Leadership
Liberty	Syndicalism	Etatisme
Free elections	Labor unions	Corporation state
Right to vote	Agrarianism	Feudalism
Suffrage franchise	Masses	Trusts
Civil rights	Labor	Usurer
Freedom of speech	Working-class	Plutocracy
Freedom of press	Proletariat	Authority
Freedom of assembly	People	Clericalism
Freedom of religion	Constitutionalism	Discipline
Bill of Rights	Parliamentarism	Fascism
Freedom of movement	Popular sovereignty	Nazism
Freedom of choice	Majority rule	Aryan
of occupation	Dictatorship	Blood
(right to work)	Absolute monarchy	States rights
Totalitarian	Caeserisme	Self-determination
Authoritarian	Censorship	Equality
Military state	Government use of force	Individualism
Police state	Centralization	Anticlericalism
Tyranny	Leader	Classless society

Source: Pool, Lasswell & Lerner (1952b), p. 75.

British, French, German, and Russian newspaper editorials during the period 1890–1949, Pool found not only that references increased markedly and that such symbols appeared in increasingly positive contexts, but also that the countries had different views of the content of democracy (Pool, Lasswell & Lerner, 1952b, p. 69):

> The difference in conceptions of democracy becomes clear when we look separately at each of the main components of the democratic ideology. Since De Tocqueville, the dilemma of democracy has often been seen as a conflict between the goals of mass rule and freedom. These two elements have been stressed differently in the Eastern and Western theories of democracy. The ratio of symbols of freedom to symbols of mass orientation was highest in those papers in which the tradition of classical liberalism was strongest—*Le Temps,* the London *Times,* and the *New York Times.* It was lowest in *Izvestia,* in which mass symbols dominated. With time, however, all the papers assumed a more positive orientation toward the masses. The highly critical tone which prevailed everywhere before World War I has given way either to praise or to neutrality, and attention to mass symbols has been growing.

The fact that another component of democracy, a system of representative government, found little attention in the press of any country led Pool to conclude that "representative government seems to be the sort of practice that is discussed mainly when it is under attack and is taken for granted otherwise."

Other symbol analysts have developed different lists. Karin Dovring (1956) searched ten documents on land reform in Europe for symbols of identification, of demands for certain values, and of resistance to other values. She tabulated the frequency of the symbols, grouped into themes; determined their function (that is, whether they were symbols of identification, demand, or resistance); and noted whether their contexts were favorable or unfavorable. More recently, in his examination of the colonial American press, Merritt (1966b) tabulated the frequency with which place-name symbols occurred. His concern was twofold: to determine when the eighteenth-century Americans began to pay more attention to local events than to European wars and English court gossip, and to find out when they began to refer to themselves more often in an American than in an Anglo-American or even British frame of reference.

The computerized General Inquirer views the denotative or connotative meanings of words as symbolic of *concepts* (Stone, Dunphy, Smith & Ogilvie, 1966). The system starts with an a priori dictionary of terms (subsequently modified or expanded empirically after examination of samples of the data to be analyzed) useful for the researcher's theoretical framework. The dictionary labels or "tags" the terms as first-order or second-order concepts. Each word appearing in a text can be categorized under one and only one *first-order tag*, according to the word's denotation in natural language. The main categories of first-order tags are objects, processes, and qualifiers. Objects appear in either the social realm (comprising persons, roles, collectivities), the cultural realm (cultural objects, cultural settings, cultural patterns), or the natural realm. Six tagged concepts comprise the subcategory "cultural patterns": ideal-value, deviation, action-norm, message-form, thought-form, and nonspecific objects. Examples of words tagged with the concept ideal-value, which includes "culturally defined virtues, goals, valued conditions and activities," are ability, able, beauty, and bold (p. 174).

The second main category of first-order tags contains psychological processes (emotions, thought, evaluation) and behavioral processes (social-emotional actions, impersonal actions). One type of emotion, affection (defined as "incidents of close positive, interpersonal relationships"), finds expression in such words as admire, affection, charm, dear, and flirt. Finally, qualifiers have either temporal, spatial, quantitative, or qualitative (sensory) reference.

The General Inquirer also categorizes words according to *second-order tags,* which "are designed to identify pervasive qualities of the text and thus to indicate significant generalized concerns with the external or internal worlds" (p. 183). Unlike first-order tags, second-order tags rest upon both the denotative and connotative meanings of words, and individual words may have two or more second-order tags. The main categories of second-order tags are institutional contexts (academic, artistic, community, economic, and so forth), status connotations (higher, peer, or lower status), and psychological themes (including overstatement, sex theme, authority theme, and death theme). Thus such terms as business, cost, debt, and finance suggest a context of economic institutions; aunt, analyst, doctor, devil, and opera connote higher status; and emphatic or exaggerated words such as gratefully, terrible, badly, and hopelessly indicate the defensive style of overstatement. It should be clear by now that the General Inquirer dictionary described here rests upon current theory in both psychology and sociology. Researchers in other disciplines, such as political science (see Namenwirth & Brewer, 1966; Holsti, 1966; Namenwirth & Lasswell, 1969; Pirro, forthcoming), have had to modify it to suit their own needs.

Robert C. Angell (1964) delineated 40 value dimensions relevant for Soviet and American ideology, and coded "elite" publications in the two countries according to several possible positions along each dimension. (See also Singer, 1964; for a related approach applied soley to the Soviet Union, see Lodge, 1968.) Angell's interest in values is an input in the policy-making process. "The values men cherish," he writes (p. 330), ". . . are influential in the making of choices and the determination of policies." The particular values upon which he focuses concern the economy ("Mode of ownership of property," "Structure of economic incentives"), social and internal political affairs ("Integration or separation of political functions," "Indoctrination of youth"), and external relations ("Civil-military relations," "War as a means of national policy"). The possible value positions that a newspaper or magazine could take on the dimension "Mode of ownership of property," for instance, were three in number (p. 342):

a. Socialization of property should be the norm. Exceptions should be very few.
b. Our society has been too dogmatic in its property principles. We should accept some modifications that will bring us nearer a mixed system of private and public ownership.
c. Private property should be the norm with only rare exceptions, e.g., the postal service.

Soviet publications, without exception, took the first position; American journals were divided between (b) and (c), with about three quarters of the references opting for the latter alternative. Less clear-cut are the positions these publications took on the value dimension "Ends of the society" (p. 368):

a. Increase in mastery over nature and technological power is emphasized. (42 per cent of American references and 30 per cent of Soviet references took this position.)
b. Increase in mastery over nature and technological power, and increase in the immediate standard of living are emphasized. (1 per cent American and 41 per cent Soviet)
c. Increase in the immediate standard of living is emphasized. (6 per cent American and Soviet)
d. Increase in intellectual, artistic, or spiritual achievement is emphasized. (51 per cent American and 23 per cent Soviet)

Noting the American emphasis on intellectual, artistic, or spiritual achievement and the Soviet concern with production and distribution, Angell suggested (p. 369): "This is perhaps natural since the United States is more mature as an industrial society, while the Soviet Union still tends to stress the importance of material progress. Materially, Americans tend to feel they have arrived."

Analysts of cross-national communications are increasingly looking at the *themes* appearing in their material. David C. McClelland (1961) analyzed children's stories from 23 countries for the period 1920–1929 (centering around 1925) and from 40 countries for the period 1946–

1955 (centering around 1950), using the analytical framework developed for projective tests of an individual's "need" for achievement, affiliation, and power (McClelland, Atkinson, Clark & Lowell, 1953; Atkinson, 1958). The themes selected to indicate the extent to which the stories dealt with a need to achieve were:

1. *Imagery:* whether or not an image of achievement—success in competition with some standard of excellence—appears in the story;
2. *Need:* a statement of a positive need for achievement on the part of a character in the story (in the sense that he "dreams of" achieving something);
3. *Instrumental Activity:* a statement in the story indicating that a character actually acts to achieve something; such instrumental activity may be successful $(I+)$, unsuccessful $(I-)$, or of doubtful outcome (Io);
4. *Goal Anticipation:* anticipations of successful outcomes $(Ga+)$, unsuccessful outcomes $(Ga-)$, or outcomes that are neither successful nor unsuccessful $(Ga\ o)$;
5. *Block:* the perception of environmental obstacles (Bw) or personal obstacles (Bp) hindering successful achievement;
6. *Nurturant or Hostile Press:* if a character in the story is standing behind or helping the person who wants to achieve, nurturant press (Nup) is scored; if the character is actively hindering (as opposed to being a static block to) the achievement-oriented person, hostile press (Hop) is scored;
7. *Affective Goal State:* a statement indicating that a character is emotionally involved with the goal that he is trying to achieve, showing positive effect $(G+)$ if he attains it or negative affect $(G-)$ if he fails to attain it;
8. *Thema:* if the major theme of the entire story deals directly with achievement, thema (Th) will be scored.

"To get a total score for a country, each achievement-related story is given a score of $+2$, each further subtype of imagery in such a story a score of $+1$ (with the limitation that each subtype of imagery can be scored only once per story), each possibly achievement-related story a score of $+1$, and each unrelated story a score of 0" (McClelland, 1961, p. 74). The eight subtypes of imagery that may be scored are: need (N), instrumental activity successful, unsuccessful, or doubtful $(I+, I-,$ or $Io)$, anticipations of success or failure $(Ga+$ or $Ga-)$, obstacles in the self or the world $(Bp$ or $Bw)$, help or hindrance by another person $(Nup$ or $Hop)$, positive or negative emotions $(G+$ or

$G-$), and themas (Th). The maximum score of the need for achievement for any single story is, therefore, 10 points. (It turns out that the mean score for all 1925 stories is 1.52 and, for all 1950 stories, 2.00—a conclusion to which I shall return later in this chapter.)

Procedures for Processing the Data. Perhaps the simplest type of content analysis tabulates the frequency with which specified content variables appear in the text being analyzed. We have already seen examples of this: Merritt (1966b), for instance, in his examination of the colonial American press, counted the appearance of place-name symbols. Among other things he found that the colonists' interest in things and places American grew markedly, as did the colonists' perception of themselves as Americans rather than as members of a British political community, long before the occurrence of such dramatic events as the Stamp Act Congress of 1765 or the outbreak of revolution a decade later. It was the changed perceptual ecology of the colonists that produced a willingness to react to such events as the Stamp Act and that contributed most to the emergence of an American sense of community. Angell (1964) counted the frequency with which Soviet and American publications took positions along his 40 value dimensions; in 31 of these instances the positions taken varied significantly from the one country to the other. In the case of Merritt's investigation, each reference to a unit of analysis was recorded; for the Angell study, no content variable could be coded more than once in any single communication.

It is also possible to add vectors to frequency counts. These may indicate the direction and intensity of attitude. The analyst interested solely in frequencies might find that the relative share of space devoted by newspaper editorials to a particular symbol, such as nationalism, remains constant over time, and conclude that the newspapers' attitudes toward that symbol have also remained constant. Closer examination might reveal, however, that the term appears in an increasingly positive (or negative) context, or that the level of emotion enshrouding the symbol is increasing (or decreasing). Indications of these latter changes would be crucial in examining the newspapers' changing attitudes toward nationalism. The RADIR studies (Lasswell, Lerner & Pool, 1952) noted whether the context of the tabulated symbols was positive, neutral, or negative. The Stanford project on conflict and integration (Holsti, 1966) coded communications along three dimensions—good-bad, active-passive, and strong-weak—derived from Osgood's study of the semantic differential (Osgood, Suci & Tannenbaum, 1957). The Yale Arms Control Project (Merritt & Pirro, 1966) coded French, West German, British, and American editorial responses to arms control proposals along 5-point or 7-point scales according to the perceived specificity or diffuseness of the proposal, its perceived operationality or nonoperationality, the level of affect displayed, and so forth.

Of increasing concern to content analysts is the context within which units of analysis appear. "Contingency analysis asks not how often a given symbolic form appears in each of several bodies of text, but how often it appears in conjunction with other symbolic units" (Pool, 1959, p. 196). Charles E. Osgood (1959, pp. 69–71) gives an example of contingency analysis based upon the wartime diaries kept by Nazi propaganda minister Joseph Goebbels (Lochner, 1948). A frequency count yielded 21 key content categories. The next step was to construct contingency matrices showing the probability that each pair of content cate-

FIGURE 3.2
A Contingency Analysis of Goebbels' Diaries

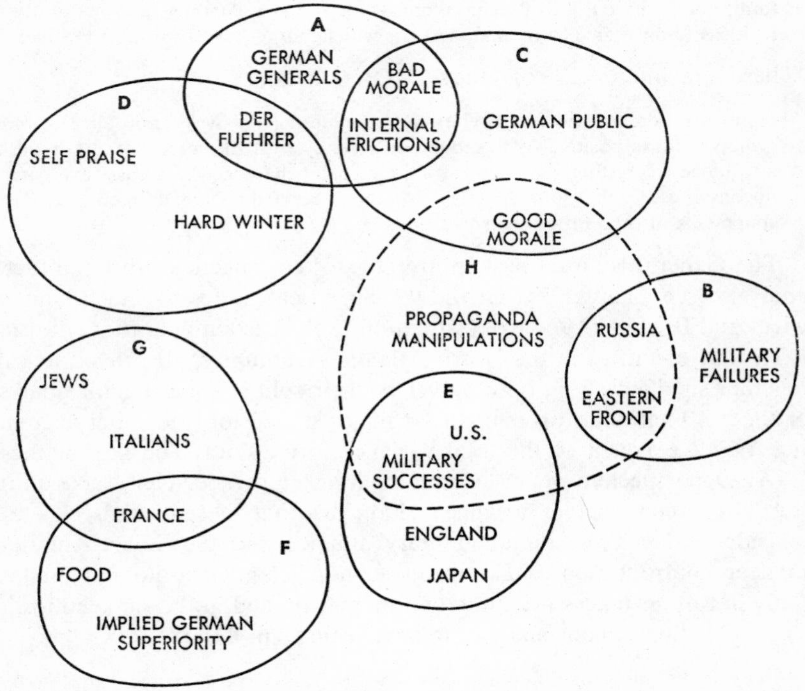

Source: Osgood (1959), p. 70.

gories would appear in the same passage selected from the diaries. From the (positive) contingencies, Osgood performed a cluster analysis, with the results shown in Figure 3.2. "Numerous inferences," he writes (pp. 70–71), "might be made from this chart":

> For example: (D) that Goebbels defends himself from thoughts about the HARD WINTER with SELF PRAISE and thoughts about his closeness to DER FUEHRER; (A) that ideas about BAD MORALE lead promptly to rationalizations in terms of the INTERNAL FRICTIONS brought about by GERMAN GENERALS, which in turn bring up conflicts between himself and others in securing the favor of DER FUEHRER; (C) that thoughts about his job of maintaining GOOD MORALE among the GERMAN PUBLIC lead to thoughts about BAD MORALE and INTERNAL FRICTIONS; (H) that his problem-solving ideas about PROPAGANDA MANIPULATIONS may lead him alternatively to the GOOD MORALE cluster of associations, to the dismal RUSSIA-EASTERN FRONT-MILITARY FAILURES cluster, or to the more encouraging cluster in which his ally, JAPAN, is having MILITARY SUCCESSES against ENGLAND and the U.S.; and finally (G and F), that when he thinks about the subject peoples, JEWS and ITALIANS, and FRANCE, he tends also, particularly in the case of FRANCE, to think about difficulties of maintaining FOOD supplies, leading quite naturally to ideas about GERMAN SUPERIORITY in withstanding hardships, and the like.

"These are inferences, of course," Osgood adds;

> there are alternative interpretations possible as to why any cluster of symbols shows positive or negative contingency. But the inferences have the advantage of resting on demonstrable verbal behavior which may even be unconscious to the source. They do not necessarily depend upon explicit statements of relation by the source.

The General Inquirer system investigates contingencies through factor analysis (see Chapter 2). Of the 99 tagged categories to which Namenwirth and Brewer (1966) pay attention in their examination of editorials from four countries in the North Atlantic community, 40 proved to vary together significantly in both halves of their split sample. Factor analysis of these 40 variables produced four major dimensions, together accounting for 42 per cent of the total variance in the data. The first of these, "NATO perspective versus Common Market perspective" (accounting for 16 per cent of the variance) "indicates that the editorials generally consider *either* the Atlantic military alliance and the Soviet-American nuclear confrontation *or* European economic and institutional matters. Only in rare instances are these two themes treated in the same editorial" (p. 143). Subsequent analysis indicated that (p. 414):

> there is a significant difference between the *New York Times* and the three European papers. While the *New York Times* has increased [from 1953 to 1963] its already high concern with ATLANTIC and MILITARY solutions to world problems, the Europeans have moved away from these concerns,

toward EUROPEAN ECONOMIC and INSTITUTIONAL problems. In particular, *Frankfurter Allgemeine Zeitung* increased its already high concern with European matters. *Le Monde* reversed its position from a high concern with Atlantic issues to a substantial interest in European matters. The *Times* (London) maintained a rather low contribution to the Atlantic aspect of the dimension, with a slight decline over the decade.

These data, together with other findings, lead Namenwirth and Brewer to conclude (pp. 423–424):

> The increased European interest in the European institutions and their policies reflects the growing penetration of supranational activities into the domestic scene. Hence the editorial commentators have been forced to discuss European unification more and more in terms of practical, day-to-day politics, rather than in terms of utopian expectations. Meanwhile, the *New York Times* has continued to discuss Atlantic unification in utopian terms.

Consequently, the authors suggest "that there has not only been a change in the *nature* of the European concern with integration but that this change implies in turn a greater *extent* of European integration."

Qualitative Content Analysis. The slowness and clumsy rigidity of early quantitative procedures led some researchers to seek systematic methods of qualitative content analysis. "Inferences from content to noncontent variables . . . need not always be based on the frequency values of content features," Alexander L. George (1959b, pp. 9–10) pointed out, on the basis of his wartime experience with propaganda analysis. "The content term in an inferential hypothesis or statement relationship may consist of the mere *presence* or *absence* of a given content characteristic or content syndrome within a designated body of communication." What was advocated was a flexible technique, at once responsive to the analyst's intelligence and insight and yet subject to the same methodological constraints as is the quantitative variety of content analysis—the careful formulation of hypotheses, selection and sampling of a set of communications, specification of content variables, strict adherence to analytic procedures.

Qualitative content analysis has in fact found many uses. The psychiatrist may search for the revealing *lapsus linguae* in the comments of his patient, or watch for stuttering, incomplete sentences, and other patterns of jumbled speech that indicate personal anxiety (Mahl, 1959). The political historian trained in psychology may read through the public and private statements of a prominent politician to find clues to his personality structure that explain his political actions (Garraty, 1959); (see Chapter 4). The social scientist may search through the writings of Lenin and Stalin to decipher the cardinal principles governing the behavior (the "operational code") of Soviet Leaders (Leites, 1951, 1953), or examine the public statements by the accused in the Moscow trials of the late 1930s to delineate the key elements of "the ritual of liquidation" (Leites & Bernaut, 1954). Or the propaganda analyst may study the speeches of the enemy, looking for phrases that indicate a shift in the enemy's policies (George, 1959a). An interesting example stems from the wartime propaganda analyses of German communications made by a branch of the Federal Communications Commission (George, 1959b, p. 14):

> Following the German disaster at Stalingrad, domestic morale sank in Germany; and rumblings of discontent with the Nazi regime were heard. In this crisis German leaders addressed the nation. Goebbels, in one of his speeches, used the word "counterterror." From the context in which this word was used, and taking into account the situation itself, the F.C.C. analyst inferred that Goebbels had in mind pogroms against the Jews. The inference rested upon the mere presence of the word "counterterror" in a particular context. The word may or may not have appeared several more times in Goebbels' speech or in other propaganda materials at the time; the F.C.C. analyst was interested only in the presence of the word in a particular linguistic and situational context.

Subsequent analysis of Goebbels' wartime diaries (Lochner, 1948, pp. 177, 261–262, 290) provided "indirect support for the correctness of the inference."

And yet qualitative content analysis is not so different from the quantitative variety as it might seem at first blush. First of all, all content analysis ultimately rests upon qualitative distinctions. The analyst must recognize the existence of a content variable before he can code it, and he must be able to decide into which of alternative categories of content variables he must place it. Quantitative content analysis merely aggregates numerous qualitative decisions of this sort into frequency distributions that show changes in the usage of content variables over time or in different regions, no less than into contingency tables that tell us something about the context of these content variables. Second, qualitative content analysis is not unlike deviant case analysis in other forms of social research. In approaching a body of communications, the analyst has either in his mind or in his research design a model of the situation that interests him. This model rests upon norms of relationships or interactions that find their basis in quantities: Listening to the speech of many individuals enables the analyst to delineate less or more systematically a "normal" speech pattern; studying many propaganda messages from an enemy communicator tells us what patterns to expect. Only with these quantitative or quasi-quantitative norms in mind can the analyst spot deviations in the subsequent communications stemming from any particular source. Third, in the not too distant future, the development of computerized routines will doubtless make quantitative content analysis a rapid and flexible procedure. The realization of this goal will obviate the analyst's fear that inundation in large quantities of "normal" data will render him insensitive to important deviations. Rapid manipulation of large quantities of data will only serve to make deviant case analysis more efficient and effective (Pool, 1969).

Coding Reliability. As in other areas of social research, the reliability of coding procedures is a critical problem. If the investigator is processing his own material, then he usually has a good idea of what his content variables are and how to locate an observed variable into one of his categories. If, however, his project is large, then he will doubtless employ assistants to perform the often tedious task of coding. In both cases the problem of reliability crops up. How likely is it that a single coder (even the major investigator himself) will process his data in the same way at the beginning and at the end of his project? How likely is it that two or more coders working independently will produce similar results?

Very little experimental information exists on the determinants of high-quality coding (see Kaplan & Goldsen, 1949; and Feld & Smith, 1958). Common sense tells us that reliability increases with the explicitness of the coding manual (but surely a point of diminishing returns for explicitness exists). When the analyst who originated the project is performing the coding, there is a marked temptation to postpone any effort to formalize the techniques by writing them down in detail. But if he employs assistants to do the coding, or if students and scholars at other universities are to be able to use the procedures, then explicit and precise coding manuals are imperative (see, for example, Smith & Feld, 1958; Stone, Dunphy, Smith & Ogilvie, 1967). Again, there is general agreement that coders need training. But what type of training and practice procedures are most likely to enhance coder reliability? Does the difficulty of securing high intercoder reliability coefficients increase if themes rather than symbols are coded? What impact does the intelligence and educational level of the coder have upon his performance? Clearly, both are important, but it may well be that persons who can adjust to routine work are better coders than are quick-thinking intellectuals. For the future development of content analysis, attention must be paid to some of these basic issues.

Actually, error can occur at several stages in the coding process. Klaus Krippendorff (1966), in his summary of the literature, rightly distinguishes among six types of coding problems: the reliability of the data, individual judges, single categories, sets of categories, instructions, and the units of analysis. For the purpose of this chapter, however, it is sufficient to treat all these potential sources of error as aspects of a total process and to look at the reliability of net outcomes rather than of individual coding stages. We shall also pay attention only to cases where two judges are processing independently the same body of data. The principles entailed when three or more judges are coding this material are the same, but the procedure for computing indices of intercoder reliability are more complicated (see Schutz, 1958–1959; Krippendorff, 1966).

The simplest, and perhaps most often used, test of reliability is the percentage agreement test:

$$P_o = \frac{2r_{ab}}{r_a + r_b}, \tag{3.1}$$

where P_o is the percentage of intercoder agreement, r_a is the number of units of analysis recorded by judge A, r_b is the number of units of analysis recorded by judge B, and r_{ab} is the number of units of analysis recorded by both judges A and B. The hypothetical data presented in Table 3.3 show that each judge coded a total of 100 units ($r_a = r_b = 100$). Of the 33 items that judge A put into category 1, judge B recorded 28 of them in the same category ($r_{a1b1} = 28$); of the 13 items that judge A put into category 2, judge B recorded 11 of them in the same category ($r_{a2b2} = 11$); and so forth. Therefore:

$$P_o = \frac{2(28 + 11 + 15 + 21 + 3)}{100 + 100} = \frac{156}{200} = .78.$$

TABLE 3.3
Hypothetical Table of Agreement Between Two Judges
(100 content variables coded into five categories)

	Category	Judge A 1	2	3	4	5	Total
	1	28	1	1	2	1	33
	2	0	11	0	0	0	11
Judge B	3	2	1	15	2	2	22
	4	2	0	3	21	2	28
	5	1	0	1	1	3	6
	Total	33	13	20	26	8	100

We would say that the level of intercoder agreement was 78 per cent in this case. A problem with the percentage agreement test is that it does not take into account chance factors in coding. Given the constraints of

Table 3.3 (that is, 100 items to be placed into five discrete categories), even a random distributing procedure on the part of both judges would produce a certain amount of agreement. The question, then, is the extent to which the observed agreement is an improvement upon the amount of agreement produced by chance alone. As it stands, the percentage agreement test introduces an upward bias in scores (1) the smaller the number of categories into which the content can be coded (Scott, 1955), and (2) the greater the amount of material to be coded (Angell, 1964).

William A. Scott (1955) has developed a reliability index for nominal scales (that is, where the categories cannot be ordered along a dimension of "more-or-less") that takes chance agreement into account. Scott's measure, π, is "the ratio of the actual difference between obtained and chance agreement to the maximum difference between obtained and chance agreement":

$$\pi = \frac{P_o - P_e}{1 - P_e}, \tag{3.2}$$

where P_o is the observed percentage agreement (as indicated by formula 3.1 above) and P_e is the expected percentage agreement on the basis of chance alone. The calculation of P_e rests upon the assumption that the ultimate distribution of responses to a particular question is also the most probable and hence the "truest" distribution. (It should be added that the assumption is not absolutely necessary: "P_e can be calculated from the actual distributions of each pair of coders, but the procedure is more complicated." Cohen [1960] presents such a procedure based upon the joint probabilities of the marginal proportions, that is, cross-multiplication of the distributions made by judges A and B in Table 3.3.) By way of example, we may first of all secure the total marginal proportions for Table 3.3. Since judge A put 33 observations into category 1 and judge B did the same, a total of 33 per cent of the observations were in category 1; since judge A put 13 and judge B put 11 observations into category 2, a total of 12 per cent of the observations were in that category; and so forth. "The expected per cent agreement for the dimension is the sum of the squared proportions over all categories (since the categories are mutually exclusive, and the two coders' probabilities for using any one of the categories are assumed equal)." The formula for ascertaining P_e, therefore, is:

$$P_e = \sum_{i=1}^{k} p_i^2, \tag{3.3}$$

where k is the total number of categories and p_i is the proportion of all content variables falling into the ith category. Hence, for Table 3.3:

$$P_e = (.33)^2 + (.12)^2 + (.21)^2 + (.27)^2 + (.07)^2 = .25.$$

Given the fact that the level of observed intercoder agreement is 78 per cent ($P_o = .78$), then Scott's index of intercoder reliability yields:

$$\pi = \frac{0.78 - 0.25}{1.00 - 0.25} = \frac{0.53}{0.75} = .71.$$

What this means is that the level of agreement after the removal of chance factors is 71 per cent.

For equal-interval scales (such as the degrees of a thermometer, or a 7-point friendliness-hostility scale ranging from $+3$ = extremely friendly through 0 = neutral to -3 = extremely hostile), a Pearson product-moment correlation coefficient is the most appropriate test for intercoder reliability (Scott, 1955). If we assume that the five categories of Table 3.3 comprise such an equal-interval scale, then the correlation coefficient r is .72, which explains slightly over half ($r^2 = 51.8$ per cent) of the total variance in the data. Without going into details (see Blalock, 1960), we might note that this test takes account of the degree to which the entire set of data varies from the cells on the main diagonal in Table 3.3 ($r_{a1b1} = 28$; $r_{a2b2} = 11$; etc.). It indicates that, if we know how judge A coded a set of messages, we can predict with 72 per cent accuracy how judge B will code the same set of messages.

It should be clear by now that the type of reliability statistic that will be most useful to the researcher depends upon the type of data he has. More troublesome is the fact that there is no common agreement upon the level of reliability that is needed for content analysis. Almost two decades ago Berelson (1952, p. 172) wrote: "Whatever the actual state of reliability in content analysis, the published record is less than satisfactory. Only about 15–20% of the studies report the reliability of the analyses contained in them." In fact, the most important cross-national analyses of recent years have been quite careful to discuss their problems of reliability. In the absence of standards upon which there is agreement, the best that the reader of these studies can do is to take into account in evaluating them the data on reliability given by their authors.

Inferences from Content Analysis

As suggested earlier, content analysis focuses on the message—or the *what* in Lasswell's formulation. Our reasons for wanting to know the substance or form of the message may be various. On the most trivial level, the message may merely be of intrinsic interest to us. We may be curious to know, for instance, what the Western European press says about a particular arms control proposal, or the frequency of certain types of word usage in the editorials of the "elite" newspapers. More frequently, however, we are interested in the message because we think it contains clues about other, less directly observable, aspects of the communication process (see Merritt, 1966a; Mitchell, 1967).

Consequent Aspects: Recipients and Effects. Sometimes the content analyst is interested in the recipients of a set of messages—the *whom* of the earlier formulation. Part of the justification for using prestige papers to estimate the mood of elites is, according to Pool, that these newspapers are read by the elite (Pool, Lasswell & Lerner, 1952a, p. 7). The question of readership posed by Pool's assertion may be looked at in two ways. On the one hand, we would like to know who the actual, as opposed to the intended, recipients of the message are. Who in fact reads the *New York Times?* What percentage of those readers properly constitutes the elite of the United States? Of those, how many read the editorials—that portion of the prestige papers to which most content analysts direct their attention? What percentage of the reader's total time spent each day in gaining new information is devoted to perusal of the *Times?* On the other hand, what in fact do the intended recipients of the message in elite publications read (see Nafziger, MacLean & Engstrom, 1951–1952)? What percentage of those comprising the American political elite reads the messages in the *New York Times?* Which of them also read other (and possibly contradictory) messages as well? The answers to such questions lie neither in a content analysis itself nor even in the force of logic. Questions of actual as opposed to intended readership lie more properly with various types of media analysis through survey research.

The issue of *what effect* the message has upon its recipients is thornier still. Pool's assertion that the prestige newspapers are not only read by elites but also influence them raises unanswered questions about attitudes, attitude change, and decision-making processes (Pool, Lasswell & Lerner, 1952a, p. 7). Actually, information has a variety of possible effects upon the recipient's images (Deutsch & Merritt, 1965, pp. 139–140; see also Klapper, 1960):

> Messages about external events . . . may (a) reinforce the image, much as a message about British or Russian misdeeds in the international arena strengthens the image that we may already have of a perfidious Albion or Soviet Union; (b) produce no significant change in the image, either if the messages are not relevant to the image or if the person holding the image does not or chooses not to receive the messages; (c) add explicit information, perhaps of the sort that only extends or fills out the image without altering it in any significant way; (d) clarify the image by reducing un-

certainty and thus adding information implicitly; (e) reorganize the image, increasing its internal consistency, perhaps, or making it more understandable by relating it to a context of other cues or images; or (f) change the importance of the image, that is, the dependence of other images upon it.

The same is true of behavior. Suppose, for instance, that a person reads a message telling him to vote for a particular candidate in an election, and then goes out to vote for him. Can we infer a causal relationship between the message and the ballot? It may be that the person happened to pick up the message as he was already on his way to vote for the candidate. Or it may be that persons likely to vote for the candidate are more likely than others to happen upon such literature. Or it may be that the message did indeed persuade the voter to opt for the candidate. The point is that, although to be sure it is important to know what information is made available to a decision-making system, it is even more important to know what is assimilated or accepted for use by the system. At this stage in political research, determining the effect of communication upon attitudinal and behavioral change is simply not a function of content analysis itself (unless the analyst has independent validating evidence, such as that produced by experimental psychology, in which case the content analysis may be superfluous).

Antecedent Aspects: Communicators and Their Motivation. Sometimes we are interested in determining *who* the communicator is. This is the case in propaganda analysis where we assume that if we know the source of a message we shall also know the extent to which it is likely to contain biased information. "When the vigilant citizen sees that he depends upon a limited or biased source, he may be expected to look for other sources capable of providing a more balanced picture of reality on the basis of which action may be taken" (Lasswell, 1949, pp. 174–175). Thus Lasswell used content analysis techniques during World War II with great effectiveness to determine the extent to which certain American publications contained news and editorial comment stemming from Nazi sources. The Department of Justice subsequently used the results of this research in prosecuting several foreign agents who had failed to register as such with the State Department. Discovering who the author of a message is has also been important in some types of literary detective work. Recent efforts by Mosteller and Wallace (1964), using electronic computers, to infer who wrote which of the *Federalist* papers are exemplary in this regard.

In cross-national political research it is usually clear who the communicator is. Sleuthing is generally directed to other ends. The question of who the communicator is nonetheless raises in elementary form two other basic issues. One is the question of individual motivation: *Why* does the communicator transmit a particular message? The other asks why we are interested in his messages: Are we interested in the communicator himself, because of his personal attributes? Or do we examine his messages because he seems to be speaking for some other group, such as the organization or culture of which he is a member?

Individual motivation rests upon a variety of subtly operating factors in the human psyche. Not the least of these is the nature of the *information* an individual has at his disposal when he makes decisions. The amount of information available to the individual is limited by both chance and choice. He does not see, for instance, most newspapers published in the United States, nor is it likely that he could manage to read them were they all delivered on his doorstep. Every individual consciously and unconsciously screens out certain types of information. He may deliberately choose to skip some sections of his morning newspaper, such as the women's page or the financial section; if he reads the paper when he is tired he may miss some of the more subtle points expressed by editorial writers; moreover, experimental evidence indicates that some people literally do not see certain items that disagree with their preconceptions. In contrast to the input of current information—values, attitudes, beliefs—there is also information stored in *memory*. In the individual's active memory is much information that can be readily recalled, information ranging from the date of his birth to his perception of the course of events in Vietnam. More deeply stored information includes items of very low salience, such as the telephone number of his childhood residence, as well as such repressed data as painful emotional experiences in childhood. Individual motivation also rests upon a person's *perception of alternative courses of action* as well as their likely outcomes. Some behavior is purposeful. A person postulates a set of goals and then implements them as best he can. At the same time it must be added that random or habitual behavior often plays a role in the communication process, in determining what things a person will communicate and how he will communicate them.

In short, individual motivation is at best a complex mix of both current and stored information, perceptions of modes of behavior, and some nonrational factors such as chance and habit; and when the individual does communicate, his message may be either representational or instrumental—that is, on a warm day he may either ask the hostess directly for a glass of water or exclaim, "My, but it is warm today!" in the hope that the hostess will take the hint and offer him something to drink (Mahl, 1959; Osgood, 1959; Pool, 1959b). If the task of content analysis is to infer a person's motivations from his messages, then what is needed is a sound theory bridging the gaps among motivation, verbal behavior, and other forms of behavior. Freudian psychology presents one possible bridge. The goal of the psychoanalyst is frequently to try to account for individual behavior through the examination of a wide range of the individual's messages. Some scholars have even tried to "psychoanalyze" historical personages by content analyzing their verbal messages and comparing these messages with those produced by people, now alive and possessing specific personality types, the characteristics of which have been analyzed clinically (for example, George & George, 1956).

The Communicator as Representative. The problem of motivation becomes still more complex as soon as we move from the personal to the public realm. Political psychology aside, content analysis generally deals not with the private utterances of a man lying on a psychoanalyst's couch but with his public message—the speeches he delivers, the pictures he paints, the position papers and memoranda he drafts, the editorials he writes, and so forth. If we are looking for the reason—or motivation—for such communications, then we may examine either the man's personality structure or his relationship with the environment, or both. The question to be asked is, whom or what does the individual represent when he communicates?

One possible answer is that he represents himself and no one else. He is seeking to express his own mind rather than pretending to be the spokesman for any group or culture. Such an answer, however, poses new questions: (1) How accurately does the message reflect his "true" feelings? (2) Why did he choose the particular mode of communication that he did? (3) Why did others permit the article to be published or the speech to be delivered publicly? To what extent were they in agreement with the values, attitudes, and beliefs expressed in the message? If the level of agreement is high, then we might argue that the communicator, regardless of his intentions and preferences, may be perceived to be representing someone else (such as those in control of the means of communication). (4) What influence did the communicator's group memberships have on the substance and form of his message? To what extent was the communicator aware of such group influences? Did he seek to counteract them? Again, regardless of intention or preference, the extent to which the message reflects the actual constellation of group values, attitudes, and beliefs may be taken as an indication of the extent to which the communicator represents the group. The task, however, is to discover the degree of congruence.

An alternative answer is that the communicator is in fact representative of some other group. Thus we may be less interested in the remarks of a specific general as an indicator of his personal views than as an indicator of what generals or even the military elite think. Among the significant questions that arise if we take this position are the following: (1) How accurately does the communicator's message reflect the true feelings of the group? (2) To what extent is the linkage perceived or consciously sought by either the individual or the represented group? The previous paragraph suggested that representation might be inferred in certain circumstances despite specific disclaimers on the part of the communicator that he does or is seeking to speak for the particular group. The other side of this coin is the extent to which a communicator may be said to speak for a group even though the group disavows him and openly rejects his views. (3) In the presence of a clear link between communicator and group, how can we tell whether the communicator is consciously trying to mirror group attitudes or whether he is writing to persuade the group to adopt new attitudes? In the latter case the manifest content of the message might deviate substantially from group norms. (4) Given the fact that most people are members of more than one social group, what is the mix of different group influences that is relevant for any single individual's messages? When a doctor, who happens also to be a Catholic and of Italian extraction, writes an editorial in the *Journal of the American Medical Association,* how sure can we be that his views represent those of the rest of the medical profession, which comprises by and large Protestants of Anglo-Saxon origin? (5) To what extent is *any* message that a person communicates influenced by the overall culture of which he is a member? That is, how much by way of group or cultural values creeps autonomously into every message?

If the purpose of content analysis, then, is to extrapolate from observed variables in messages to non-observed motivational variables, two interrelated questions are crucial. First, is the communicator perceived or assumed to be representing his own views, those of the group or groups to which he belongs, or those of his overall culture? And, second, what mix of conscious and unconscious elements goes into the formulation of his message? Let us turn to a couple of major cross-national content analyses to see how such questions have been treated.

The RADIR Project analyzed symbols of democracy and internationalism in newspapers from five countries, covering the years from 1890 to 1949 (Pool, Lasswell & Lerner, 1951, 1952a, 1952b):

Great Britain	*Times* (1890–1949)
Russia	*Novoe Vremia* (1892–1917); *Izvestia* (1918–1949)
United States	*New York Times* (1900–1949)

France	*Le Temps* (1900–1942;) *Le Monde* (1945–1949)
Germany	*Norddeutsche allgemeine Zeitung* (1910–1920);
	Frankfurter Zeitung (1920–1932); *Völkischer*
	Beobachter (1933–1945)

As justification for the decision to examine editorials in these news-papers, Pool writes (Pool, Lasswell & Lerner, 1952a, pp. 1, 7):

> In each major power one newspaper stands out as an organ of elite opinion. Usually semiofficial, always intimate with the government, these "prestige papers" are read by public officials, journalists, scholars, and business leaders. They seldom have large circulations, yet they have enormous in-fluence. They are read not only in their own countries, but also abroad by those whose business it is to keep track of world affairs. They differ among themselves, but, despite national and temporal differences, they are a distinct species. It is generally possible to name with fair confidence one paper in any given country which plays the role of prestige paper at any given time. . . .
> . . . The prestige paper is in some respects a good index of elite behavior. It is read by the elite and influences them. In addition, it is produced by men who have themselves become part of the elite and share the typical life pattern of the elite.

The argument is plausible, but is it true? We know that the prestige papers are representative of something or someone. But of what or of whom? To take a recent example, editorials in the *New York Times* on the issue of American participation in the Vietnam struggle, prior to the Tet offensive of early 1968 at least, could scarcely be called indicative of government policy or even of informed opinion among American elite groupings. It is doubtless true that, over the long run, and given a wide range of issues, the *New York Times* is closer to official or elite opinion than any other single publication in the United States. Despite the fairness of this assumption, it cannot be a fully satisfactory answer to the question raised above until empirical tests can show an actual (as opposed to an imputed) relationship between the distribution of attitudes in *Times* editorials and policies pursued or attitudes held in official or elite quarters (see also Merrill, 1968).

A second set of questions was raised earlier: Does the elite in fact read the prestige papers, either in the United States or elsewhere? And how can we verify whether or not the editorials influence those who read them? In these regards intensive interviews with samples of elite groupings might give us relevant answers (see Rosenau, 1963).

A third question is the extent to which the prestige papers compare in their expressed values, attitudes, and beliefs with the other newspapers in their own countries. Two projects currently under way are seeking clues to resolve this problem. One, under the direction of J. Zvi Namenwirth, is content analyzing three elite and three mass newspapers in the United States, using the General Inquirer procedure; the other is investigating editorial attitudes in a wide variety of British, French, West German, and American journals toward specific arms control events and proposals (Merritt & Pirro, 1966). A comparison of the prestige papers with the others will at least give us an idea of how typical they are of the press of the different countries (see, for example, Bush, 1954–1955; Coddington, 1965; Galtung & Ruge, 1965).

Finally, the study of elite newspapers poses a problem similar to that faced by students of community power structures who concentrate upon community influentials. A newspaper may enjoy a reputation for influence when in fact it is not influential. Other newspapers, although perhaps somewhat less intellectual than the prestige papers, may be widely read by elite groupings. Or it is possible that a newspaper loses whatever influence among the elite it once had. If we continue to concentrate upon attention and value patterns in newspapers after they have passed their zenith, we may be deluding ourselves about actual trends in the country. But, then, how do we know when the star of an elite journal is falling and that of another publication is taking its place?

Among other projects that have analyzed prestige papers (see Schramm, 1959; Markham, 1961; Abu-Lughod, 1962; Namenwirth & Brewer, 1966), one of the more elaborate extensions is Robert C. Angell's study (1964) of social values held by Soviet and American elites. One of his interests was to differentiate the values held by subelites. Thus, for the American provincial elite he examined *Nation's Business* and the *American Bar Association Journal;* for the American labor elite, the *American Federationist;* for the Soviet economic elite, *Voprosy Ekonomikii, Sovetskaia Torgovlia,* and *Planovoe Khozaistvo;* and so forth. In a sense this procedure merely compounds the problem faced by Pool. Even if we were willing to accept the *New York Times* as indicative of American elite attitudes, we may well be unwilling to agree that the *American Bar Association Journal* is indicative of any attitudes other than those of the men writing its editorials. It may still be possible to view the distribution of values in all the American publications taken together as somehow an indicator of values held by a broad stratum of American elite groupings; similarly, the entire collection of 13 Soviet journals examined by Angell may give us a better idea of Soviet elite values than would one prestige paper by itself. (It is interesting in this regard that Angell devotes less space to intracountry than to intercountry variations; his data nonetheless present interesting possibilities for the analysis of within-nation differences.)

Particularly problematic is David C. McClelland's analysis (1961) of achievement orientations in children's readers from 23 countries in 1925 and from 41 countries in 1950. For one thing, sampling biases of several types reduce sharply the value of any data stemming from his content analysis of these readers (see Merritt [1966a] for a discussion of these biases). For another, not even McClelland is sure that the readers are appropriate for a study of societal values. He rejects the simple notion that the stories in the readers "represent" solely characteristics of their authors' personalities. While recognizing that this may be true in part, he sees the author not as a creator but as a mediator. The author transmits aspects of the culture to a particular audience— "children and the adults having to do with the education of children who will decide whether their stories will be included in the textbooks or not" (p. 75). (This position raises two problems that cannot be discussed here: errors that creep into the process of transmitting values; and traps created by marketing considerations, into which the reader most representative of cultural values can easily fall. See Merritt [1966a].) Even if we assume that the author has played the role of cultural bridge properly, we must ask, along with McClelland, of what or of whom the values are typical. Do they represent values typical of the culture as a whole or of specific subcultures (for example, the intellectual elite)? Do they represent the values actually held by most of the people in the culture or just the "best" values that they wanted transmitted to their children?

McClelland's efforts to answer such questions have not been very satisfactory. A national sample survey of Catholic and Protestant students in the United States offered some confirmation of the thesis that values in readers are typical of more generally held cultural values. Less representative but cross-national surveys, however, have held out less hope. In countries where readers were low on the n Achievement scale, students scored high in projective tests for levels of n Achievement, and vice versa. McClelland rejects the conclusion that such findings cast doubt upon the validity of reader n Achievement scores as indicators of cultural values. Instead, he suggests (p. 79) that these findings show that

> reader scores may not reflect n Achievement levels in any group of individuals in the country: in this sense any comparison with individual scores is invalid or unrepresentative. Rather, the reader stress on achievement may represent something more like "national aspirations"—the tendency of people in public (e.g., in children's textbooks) to think about achievement.

In short, after data or their absence have failed to confirm other interpretations of the representativeness of the readers, McClelland falls back upon the conclusion that they must represent the totality of the culture that produced them.

But McClelland is obviously not happy with this conclusion. His final statement on representativeness is illuminating (p. 79):

> Comparison of reader n Achievement levels with levels obtained from individuals has raised some interesting questions as to just what the readers are measuring. It has even thrown some doubt on whether they are measuring anything of importance, but in the end, the proof of the pudding is in the eating: do they enable us to predict which countries will develop more rapidly economically?

That the readers do enable such predictions—at least to McClelland's satisfaction, if not always to that of others (Brown, 1965)—does not get around the fact that his argument begs the key question of representativeness.

In concentrating upon the weaker aspects of some of the recent cross-national content analysis, I do not mean to suggest that the analyses themselves have been without merit. But the fact that their results have been both interesting and fruitful in terms of generating hypotheses about political behavior should not hide the fact that their theoretical underpinnings have often been insufficiently examined. Perhaps the time has come for content analysts to look again at their research tools, just as survey researchers in the 1940s and early 1950s turned their attention to some procedures that many of them had come to take for granted.

The Future of Content Analysis

A decade ago the prospects for content analysis as a tool for political research did not seem very bright. For one thing, it is a lengthy process, costly both in time and research money; and, even worse for the person who is doing the actual counting, an extensive project could become rather tedious. Moreover, like any form of systematic research, content analysis is beset with major problems: What procedure will produce the most appropriate sample of the body of material to be analyzed? Are the sources of data, units of analysis, and analytic categories functionally equivalent over time or across a set of different countries? Is the set of messages to be analyzed actually representative of the group or culture in which the analyst is interested (source validity)? Will the analytic categories produce the statistic that he wants, that is, will his measures indicate what they are supposed to indicate (instrument validity)? Are his processing procedures reproducible by trained coders (reliability)?

And, of course, how does one interpret the data emanating from content analysis?

The development of computerized procedures for content analysis—initially the General Inquirer (Stone, Dunphy, Smith & Ogilvie, 1966) but later other systems as well (see IBM, 1967)—was a quantum leap in the direction of greater feasibility and wider applicability. (Eventually, optical scanners will even eliminate the need to punch the material first onto IBM cards.) Programs can be written to retrieve whatever data the analyst needs for his specific project. This in turn permits him to be more flexible. A revision of his dictionary, for instance, no longer means that the researcher must recode his original materials by hand; hence, the cost of late innovations and second thoughts is no longer as prohibitive as it once was. Similarly, the speed and accuracy with which computers can process the data have made content analysis more attractive.

These technological advances notwithstanding, the future of content analysis continues to demand substantial intellectual contributions (Lasswell, 1966). To be sure, computer routines for the storage, retrieval, and processing of data are important, and we can hope and expect to see marked advances in the years to come. But more important are intellectual tasks—the development of conceptual frameworks to guide our research, and the elaboration of procedures for making inferences from a message to antecedent or consequent aspects of the communication process.

REFERENCES

Abu-Lughod, Ibrahim. "International News in the Arabic Press: A Comparative Content Analysis," *The Public Opinion Quarterly*. 26:4 (Winter 1962), 600–612.

Angell, Robert C. "Social Values of Soviet and American Elites: Content Analysis of Elite Media," *The Journal of Conflict Resolution*. 8:4 (December 1964), 330–385.

Aronson, Elliot. "The Need for Achievement as Measured by Graphic Expression." In Atkinson (1958), pp. 249–265.

Atkinson, John W., editor. *Motives in Fantasy, Action, and Society: A Method of Assessment and Study*. Princeton, N.J.: D. Van Nostrand Company, Inc., 1958.

Berelson, Bernard. *Content Analysis in Communication Research*. Glencoe, Ill.: The Free Press, 1952.

Bernd, Joseph L., editor. *Mathematical Applications in Political Science, II*. Dallas, Texas: Southern Methodist University Press, 1966.

Blalock, Hubert M., Jr. *Social Statistics*. New York, Toronto, London: McGraw-Hill Book Company, Inc., 1960.

Brown, Roger. *Social Psychology*. New York: The Free Press, 1965.

Bryson, Lyman, editor. *The Communication of Ideas: A Series of Addresses*. New York and London: Harper & Brothers, 1948.

Bryson, Lyman, Louis Finkelstein, Hudson Hoagland, and R. M. MacIver, editors. *Symbols and Society: Fourteenth Symposium of the Conference on Science, Philosophy and Religion*. New York and London: Harper & Brothers, 1955.

Budd, Richard W., Robert K. Thorp, and Lewis Donohew. *Content Analysis of Communications*. New York: The Macmillan Company, 1967.

Bush, Henry C. "The United Nations as a Norm in British Opinion," *The Public Opinion Quarterly*. 18:4 (Winter 1954–1955), 427–429.

Coddington, Alan. "Policies Advocated in Conflict Situations by British Newspapers," *Journal of Peace Research*. 2:4 (1965), 398–404.

Cohen, Jacob. "A Coefficient of Agreement for Nominal Scales," *Educational and Psychological Measurement*. 20:1 (Spring 1960), 37–46.

Columbianum (Genoa). "An International Survey on the Film Hero," *International Social Science Journal*. 15:1 (1963), 113–119.

Dennis, Wayne. *Group Values Through Children's Drawings*. New York, London, Sydney: John Wiley & Sons, Inc., 1966.

Deutsch, Karl W. "Symbols of Political Community." In Bryson, Finkelstein, Hoagland & MacIver (1955), pp. 23–54.

Deutsch, Karl W., and Richard L. Merritt. "Effects of Events on National and International Images." In Kelman (1965), pp. 132–187.

Dovring, Folke. *Land and Labor in Europe, 1900–1950: A Comparative Survey of Recent Agrarian History*. The Hague: Martinus Nijhoff, 1956.

Dovring, Karin. "Land Reform as a Propaganda Theme." In F. Dovring (1956), pp. 261–348, 432–438.

Edelmann, Murray. *The Symbolic Uses of Politics*. Urbana: University of Illinois Press, 1964.

Feld, Sheila, and Charles P. Smith. "An Evaluation of the Objectivity of the Method of Content Analysis." In Atkinson (1958), pp. 234–241.

Finlay, David J., Ole R. Holsti, and Richard R. Fagen. *Enemies in Politics*. Chicago: Rand McNally & Company, 1967.

Galtung, Johan, and Mari Holmboe Ruge. "The Structure of Foreign News: The Presentation of the Congo, Cuba and Cyprus Crises in Four Norwegian Newspapers," *Journal of Peace Research*. 2:1 (1965), 64–91.

Garraty, John A. "The Application of Content Analysis to Biography and History." In Pool (1959a), pp. 171–187.

George, Alexander L. *Propaganda Analysis: A Study of Inferences Made from Nazi Propaganda in World War II*. Evanston, Ill.: Row, Peterson & Company, 1959a.

George, Alexander L. "Quantitative and Qualitative Approaches to Content Analysis" [1959b]. In Pool (1959a), pp. 7–32.

George, Alexander L., and Juliette L. George. *Woodrow Wilson and Colonel House: A Personality Study*. New York: The John Day Company, 1956.

Gerbner, George, Ole R. Holsti, Klaus Krippendorff, William J. Paisley, and Philip J. Stone. *The Analysis of Communication Content: Developments in Scientific Theories and Computer Techniques*. New York: John Wiley & Sons, Inc., 1969.

Gerth, Hans, and C. Wright Mills. *Character and Social Structure: The Psychology of Social Institutions*. New York: Harcourt, Brace and Company, 1953.

Goodman, Warren H. "The Origins of the War of 1812: A Survey of Changing Interpretations," *The Mississippi Valley Historical Review*. 28:2 (September 1941), 171–186.

Holsti, Ole R. "Cognitive Dynamics and Images of the Enemy: Dulles and Russia." In Finlay, Holsti & Fagen (1967), pp. 25–96.

Holsti, Ole R. *Content Analysis for the Social Sciences and Humanities*. Reading, Mass.: Addison-Wesley Publishing Company, 1969.

Holsti, Ole R. "External Conflict and Internal Consensus: The Sino-Soviet Case." In Stone, Dunphy, Smith & Ogilvie (1966), pp. 343–358.

IBM. *IBM System/360 Document Processing System: Application Description*. Publication H20-0315-0. White Plains, N.Y.: International Business Machines Corporation, Data Processing Division, 1967.

International Press Institute. *The Flow of the News: A Study by the International Press Institute, In Cooperation with Editors, Agency Executives and Foreign Correspondents in Ten Countries*. Zurich: International Press Institute, 1953.

Kaplan, Abraham, and Joseph M. Goldsen. "The Reliability of Content Analysis Categories." In Lasswell, Leites & Associates (1949), pp. 83–112.

Kelman, Herbert C., editor. *International Behavior: A Social-Psychological Approach*. New York: Holt, Rinehart and Winston, 1965.

Klapper, Joseph T. *The Effects of Mass Communication*. Glencoe, Ill.: The Free Press, 1960.

Krippendorff, Klaus. "A Coefficient of Agreement for Situations in Which Qualitative Data are Categorized by Many Judges." Philadelphia, Penna.: University of Pennsylvania, The Annenberg School of Communications, 1966 (mimeographed).

Lasswell, Harold D. "Detection: Propaganda Detection and the Courts." In Lasswell, Leites & Associates (1949), pp. 173–232.

Lasswell, Harold D. "Foreword." In Stone, Dunphy, Smith & Ogilvie (1966), pp. vii–ix.

Lasswell, Harold D. "The Structure and Function of Communication in Society." In Bryson (1948), pp. 37–51.

Lasswell, Harold D., Nathan Leites, and Associates. *Language of Politics: Studies in Quantitative Semantics.* New York: George W. Stewart, Publisher, Inc., 1949; Cambridge, Mass.: The M.I.T. Press, 1965.

Lasswell, Harold D., Daniel Lerner, and Ithiel de Sola Pool. *The Comparative Study of Symbols: An Introduction.* Hoover Institute Studies, Series C: Symbols, No. 1. Stanford, Calif.: Stanford University Press, 1952.

Leites, Nathan. *The Operational Code of the Politburo.* New York, Toronto, London: McGraw-Hill Book Company, Inc., 1951.

Leites, Nathan. *A Study of Bolshevism.* Glencoe, Ill.: The Free Press, 1953.

Leites, Nathan, and Elsa Bernaut. *Ritual of Liquidation: The Case of the Moscow Trials.* Glencoe, Ill.: The Free Press, 1954.

Lochner, Louis P., editor and translator. *The Goebbels Diaries, 1942–1943.* Garden City, N.Y.: Doubleday & Company, Inc., 1948.

Lodge. Milton. "Soviet Elite Participatory Attitudes in the Post-Stalin Period," *The American Political Science Review.* 62:3 (September 1968), 827–839.

Mahl, George F. "Exploring Emotional States by Content Analysis." In Pool (1959a), pp. 89–130.

Markham, James W. "Foreign News in the United States and South American Press," *The Public Opinion Quarterly.* 25:2 (Summer 1961), 249–262.

McClelland, David C. *The Achieving Society.* Princeton, N.J.: Litton Educational Publishing, Inc., by permission of Van Nostrand Reinhold Company, 1961.

McClelland, David C., and John W. Atkinson, Russell A. Clark, and E. L. Lowell. *The Achievement Motive.* New York: Appleton-Century-Crofts, 1953.

McGranahan, Donald V., and Ivor Wayne. "German and American Traits Reflected in Popular Drama," *Human Relations.* 1:4 (August 1948), 429–455.

Merrill, John C. *The Elite Press: Great Newspapers of the World.* New York: Pitman Publishing Company, 1968.

Merritt, Richard L. "Perspectives on History in Divided Germany." In Small (1970).

Merritt, Richard L. "The Representational Model in Cross-National Content Analysis" [1966a]. In Bernd (1966), pp. 44–71.

Merritt, Richard L. *Symbols of American Community, 1735–1775.* New Haven and London: Yale University Press, 1966b.

Merritt, Richard L., and Ellen B. Pirro. *Press Attitudes to Arms Control in Four Countries, 1946–1963.* New Haven: Yale University, Political Science Research Library, 1966 (mimeographed).

Mintz, Alexander. "The Feasibility of the Use of Samples in Content Analysis." In Lasswell, Leites & Associates (1949), pp. 127–152.

Mitchell, Robert Edward. "The Use of Content Analysis for Explanatory Studies," *The Public Opinion Quarterly.* 31:2 (Summer 1967), 230–241.

Mosteller, Frederick, and David L. Wallace. *Inference and Disputed Authorship: The Federalist.* Reading, Mass., Palo Alto, Calif., London: Addison-Wesley, 1964.

Nafziger, Ralph O., Malcolm MacLean, Jr., and Warren Engstrom. "Who Reads What in Newspapers?" *International Journal of Opinion and Attitude Research.* 5:4 (Winter 1951–1952), 519–540.

Namenwirth, J. Zvi, and Thomas L. Brewer. "Elite Editorial Comment on the European and Atlantic Communities in Four Countries." In Stone, Dunphy, Smith & Ogilvie (1966), pp. 401–427.

Namenwirth, J. Zvi, and Harold D. Lasswell. "Changing Language in American Party Platforms: A Computer Analysis of Political Values." New Haven: Yale University, 1967 (mimeographed).

North Robert C., Ole R. Holsti, M. George Zaninovich, and Dina A. Zinnes. *Content Analysis: A Handbook with Applications for the Study of International Crisis.* Evanston, Ill.: Northwestern University Press, 1963.

Osgood, Charles E. "The Representational Model and Relevant Research Methods." In Pool (1959a), pp. 33–88.

Osgood, Charles E., Sol Saporta, and Jum C. Nunnally. "Evaluative Assertion Analysis," *Litera.* 3 (1956), 47–102.

Osgood, Charles E., George J. Suci, and Percy H. Tannenbaum. *The Measurement of Meaning.* Urbana: University of Illinois Press, 1957.

Pirro, Ellen B. *African Political Ideology: A Comparative Analysis of Three Nations.* Forthcoming.

Pool, Ithiel de Sola. "Content Analysis and the Intelligence Function." In Rogow (1969).

Pool, Ithiel de Sola, editor. *Trends in Content Analysis.* Urbana: University of Illinois Press, 1959a.

Pool, Ithiel de Sola. "Trends in Content Analysis: A Summary" [1959b]. In Pool (1959a), pp. 189–233.

Pool, Ithiel de Sola, with the collaboration of Harold D. Lasswell, Daniel Lerner, et al. *The "Prestige Papers": A Survey of Their Editorials.* Hoover Institute Studies, Series C: Symbols, No. 2. Stanford, Calif.: Stanford University Press, 1952a.

Pool, Ithiel de Sola, with the collaboration of Harold D. Lasswell, Daniel Lerner, et al. *Symbols of Democracy.* Hoover Institute Studies, Series C: Symbols, No. 4. Stanford, Calif.: Stanford University Press, 1952b.

Pool, Ithiel de Sola, with the collaboration of Harold D. Lasswell, Daniel Lerner, et al. *Symbols of Internationalism.* Hoover Institute Studies, Series C: Symbols, No. 3. Stanford, Calif.: Stanford University Press, 1951.

Rogow, Arnold A., editor. *Politics, Personality and Social Science in the Twentieth Century: Essays in Honor of Harold D. Lasswell.* Chicago, Ill.: The University of Chicago Press, 1969.

Rosenau, James N. *National Leadership and Foreign Policy: A Case Study in the Mobilization of Public Support.* Princeton, N.J.: Princeton University Press, 1963.

Schramm, Wilbur. *One Day in the World's Press: Fourteen Great Newspapers on a Day of Crisis, November 2, 1956, with Translations and Facsimile Reproductions.* Stanford, Calif.: Stanford University Press, 1959.

Schutz, William C. "On Categorizing Qualitative Data in Content Analysis," *The Public Opinion Quarterly.* 22:4 (Winter 1958–59), 503–515.

Scott, William A. "Reliability of Content Analysis: The Case of Nominal Scale Coding," *The Public Opinion Quarterly.* 19:3 (Fall 1955), 321–325.

Singer, J. David. "Soviet and American Foreign Policy Attitudes: Content Analysis of Elite Articulations," *The Journal of Conflict Resolution.* 8:4 (December 1964), 424–485.

Small, Melvin, editor. *Public Opinion, Foreign Policy, and the Historian.* Detroit, Mich.: Wayne State University Press, 1970.

Smith, Charles P., and Sheila Feld. "How to Learn the Method of Content Analysis for *n* Achievement." In Atkinson (1958), pp. 685–818.

Stone, Philip J., Robert F. Bales, J. Zvi Namenwirth, and Daniel M. Ogilvie. "The General Inquirer: A Computer System for Content Analysis and Retrieval Based on the Sentence as a Unit of Information," *Behavioral Science.* 7:4 (October 1962), 484–498.

Stone, Philip J., Dexter C. Dunphy, Marshall S. Smith, Daniel M. Ogilvie with Associates, editors. *The General Inquirer: A Computer Approach to Content Analysis.* Cambridge, Mass., and London: The M.I.T. Press, 1966.

Stone, Philip J., Dexter C. Dunphy, Marshall S. Smith, and Daniel M. Ogilvie. *User's Manual for The General Inquirer.* Cambridge, Mass., and London: The M.I.T. Press, 1967.

Wayne, Ivor. "American and Soviet Themes and Values: A Content Analysis of Pictures in Popular Magazines," *The Public Opinion Quarterly.* 20:1 (Spring 1956), 314–320.

Wolfenstein, Martha, and Nathan Leites. *Movies: A Psychological Study.* Glencoe, Ill.: The Free Press, 1950.

4

THE COMPARATIVE
STUDY OF ELITES

Elites play a key role in the political process. It is they who at once shape and reflect the values, attitudes, and beliefs of a society, who set the standards of taste and elegance, who are most instrumental in molding the public institutions that are the framework for our lives. It is they who, individually or collectively, formulate or articulate demands within the political system, who maintain the flow of communications within the system, and who enact, interpret, and enforce the rules that govern us.

But who are these elites? The answer to this question rests upon a pair of well-founded assumptions. First, societies are organized around a set of values, such as power, wealth, prestige, skill, and other valued resources (Lasswell & Kaplan, 1950, pp. 55–57). Human societies are multivalued, that is, no single value is so important that it overrides all the others. Within the society, of course, individuals may have differing views about which concatenation of values is the most important, and some people may even behave (or say that they are behaving) as if they considered a single value to be peremptory. Second, "every complex society known to scholarship has been stratified" (Kahl, 1961, p. 14). The resources valued in a society are distributed unequally among its members. Viewed on a continuum, some individuals possess more and others less of any particular value. Thus, in the United States at least, senators have more political power than do college students, financiers are wealthier than college professors, judges enjoy greater prestige than do stenographers, clerics have more of a reputation for righteousness than do butchers. To assert that societies are stratified, it must be added, does not imply that the student of elites approves either of stratification itself or of any particular form of stratification. It is possible to recognize the existence and importance of elites without adopting anti-democratic notions (Bottomore, 1964/1966, pp. 18–20).

Given the fact of stratification, it is tempting to say that those who

SYSTEMATIC APPROACHES TO COMPARATIVE POLITICS

possess the greatest amount of any single value—the most powerful, the wealthiest, the most prestigious—comprise the elite as far as that particular value is concerned (Pareto, 1935, iii, pp. 1422–1423). In a single-valued society, this may be an adequate definition of elite status: For example, the most righteous constitute the elite in the society of saints, and, in a society concerned solely with height, the tallest members are the elite. As indicated earlier, however, the organizational basis of human society is an n-dimensional field of values. In principle, it is possible to locate each individual in terms of his position on each of these n dimensions; after properly weighting the role of the n dimensions in the society as a whole, vector analysis could yield the individual's position in the overall field of values. But is this what we want to know? Of more importance than a person's position in an n-dimensional field of values is the likelihood that he will be influential with respect to the distribution of any single one or a set of these values.

An elite comprises those who participate in decisions affecting the distribution of valued resources in a society. The nature of this participation may vary. On the one hand, an individual may be quite active, making his views known during the process of decision-making, acting in the role of a communicator, organizing support, and so forth. On the other hand, he may be a passive participant, in the sense that his perspectives are taken into account in the process of decision-making even though he himself may never lift a finger or be consulted by those making the decision (Sereno, 1962, p. 102). The question is the extent to which the individual *behaves* or *is seen to behave* in a way that makes a difference in the outcomes of decision-making. Legislators influence the distribution of power in a society, not because they themselves can enforce their will upon a population with respect to a range of issues, but because they can enact legislation that brings into play institutionalized or informal elements of voluntary compliance and enforcement in the control of human behavior. Legislators, then, are among a society's elite in regard to the distribution of power. Similarly, bankers influence the distribution of wealth, not because they themselves possess vast sums of money but because they control institutions entrusted with these vast sums to invest or otherwise manipulate. The influence of individual legislators or bankers, we must note, is a function of their position in the society's n-dimensional field of values. That is, to achieve their influential status, they usually have to demonstrate at least a modicum of administrative or oratorical skill, education, reputation for honesty, wealth, prestige, and ability to control people's behavior.

Underlying this view of elites is a probability concept of participation in decision-making. First of all, there is the probability that the individual's activity will affect an outcome in decisions about the distribution of a value. A problem here is finding a cutting-off point to separate more marginal participants from those whose behavior is decisive. Even what the district tax collector does ultimately affects the federal budgeting process, but does it make sense to say that the district tax collector is a major decision-maker in this process? Second, there is the probability that the outcome will affect the reference group, that is, those holding the value the distribution of which is in question. Again, since presumably all decisions affect this distribution in one way or another, it is necessary to differentiate between less and more relevant outcomes. With Suzanne Keller (1963, p. 20) we may define strategic elites in modern society as "those whose judgments, decisions, and actions have important and determinable consequences for many members of society." But selecting the various cutting-off points on these continua (decisive vs. marginal participants, more vs. less relevant, "important" consequences "for many members") imposes a task that will vary from one research project to the next; at present we have no adequate criteria that are universally applicable. This viewpoint of probability also makes clear the fact that elites are not the sole groups of importance in the political process. To the contrary, elites must be considered in their larger societal context, which includes the mobilized as well as the underlying masses, structural elements such as political parties and a formal division of power, the values and other perspectives inherent in the society, and even the international environment (Sereno, 1962; Greenstein, 1967). To say that elites are an important element in the political process is not to adopt the elitist notion that such elites are (or should be) all-important.

Other functional approaches to the study of elites focus upon different conceptualizations of the societal division of labor. Talcott Parsons, for instance, lists four functional imperatives of such systems of action as a society: adaptation, goal gratification, integration, and latent-pattern maintenance and tension management (Parsons & Smelser, 1956). The social structures performing these functions are, respectively, the economy (which produces wealth), the polity (power), the integrative subsystem (solidarity), and the cultural-motivational subsystem (prestige). In this view the elites are those individuals most instrumental in the performance of these functions. Gabriel A. Almond (1950/1960, p. 138) has proposed a set of functional categories which, although considerably less precise, has achieved more widespread acceptance because of its congruence with institutions in society. Among his policy and opinion elites—"the articulate policy-bearing stratum of the population which gives structure to the public, and which provides the effective means of access to the various groupings" within the society—are political, administrative or bureaucratic, interest, and communications elites. Each of these categories may in turn be subdivided. Thus it is possible to speak of business, military, trade union, and still other elites. Similarly, Raymond Aron (1950, p. 9) delineates five elite groups which correspond to essential functions in modern society: political leaders, government administrators, economic directors, leaders of the masses, and military chiefs.

The Structural Characteristics of Elites

What all these views postulate is a plurality of elite groupings operating with respect to different values. They talk of *elites* rather than *the elite*. Characteristic of industrial and most transitional societies is the diffuse interaction of several elite groupings within the societal context as a whole. It is nonetheless possible to think of societies, past and present, with a highly unified elite structure. If the multiplicity of elites comprises an integrated group—integrated in the sense both of their consciousness of a common set of interests and of their ability to coordinate their behavior in the effective pursuit of these interests—that controls all the crucial aspects of the society, then we may speak of a ruling elite. (That such a power elite was emerging in the United States during the late 1950s was a main argument of C. Wright Mills [1956], an argument, by the way, that other scholars have seriously disputed [Dahl 1958].) It may even be a ruling class if considerations of social class (for example, a hereditary nobility) intervene to determine membership in this group (see Mosca, 1939). If, as political scientists, we are especially interested in the shaping and sharing of power within a community, then we may want to direct our attention to political elites and others whose behavior affects political values (Lasswell & Kaplan, 1950, p. 201; Bottomore, 1964/1966, p. 14). But this is a far cry from asserting either that political values are the only ones that count in a society or that the political elite constitutes some sort of tightly knit ruling class with a high degree of collective consciousness. Usually we are dealing with that middle range described by Aron (1950, p. 143):

A unified élite means the end of freedom. But when the groups of the élite are not only distinct but become a disunity, it means the end of the State. Freedom survives in those intermediate regions, which are continually threatened when there is moral unity of the élite, where men and groups preserve the secret of single and eternal wisdom and have learnt how to combine autonomy with co-operation.

An issue related to the overall unity of a society's elites is the extent to which individual functional elites are unified. In contrast to Great Britain, for instance, where most labor union members belong to a single organizational structure with a common set of national representatives, at least five alternative sets of elites compete to represent trade union interests in the French political process. We might hypothesize that the effectiveness of a functional elite in a society's politics varies with its level of internal cohesiveness (Lasswell & Kaplan, 1950, p. 200).

Second, and particularly important in assessing the unity or pluralism of elites, is the nature of the cleavages (in the sense of highly salient divergencies) separating them from one another. In some societies these cleavages are cumulative, that is, regional, ethnic, economic, and other cleavages combine in dividing one portion of the population and its leaders from other segments. Imagine a country composed of two different ethnic groups, the one living in the industrialized and urbanized valleys of the north, fairly well-to-do, Catholic, and overrepresented in the national parliament, and the other living in the mountainous south, at a subsistence level in a backward economy, Protestant, and underrepresented in the national legislature. Potentially, at least, such a situation is explosive, for cumulated cleavages decrease a polity's effectiveness and increase its instability. And this is particularly the case if both groups are led by articulate and strong-willed men. Although cleavages exist in most modern, industrialized states, rarely are they so cumulated as in this hypothetical example (Linz & de Miguel, 1966, pp. 278–279). More frequently, cleavages cut across other cleavages, mitigating some of their divisive effects.

A third structural aspect of elites that merits consideration is the extent to which they are, as groups, permeable. The hardness of the boundaries between such groups is a function of the specificity of a society's division of labor. In the last century and a half at least, the world has seen a trend toward growing specificity. One manifestation of this is an increasing compartmentalization of knowledge, with a concomitant departmentalization of universities which in turn produce an ever larger number of experts on ever smaller areas of knowledge. Another is the multiplication of elite groups, more or less autonomous and yet instrumental in the allocation of social values (Keller, 1963, p. 5). On the basis of such trends, we should hypothesize that elite groups are becoming increasingly impermeable. What this means in terms of political stability is suggested by Lasswell and Kaplan (1950, p. 36; see also Pareto, 1935, iii, p. 1431). "Conflict among given groups," they write, "varies inversely with . . . their mutual permeability" by which they mean that "conflict will be minimized by expectations of possible membership in the other group."

And yet a number of other developments mitigate these trends toward a collision course. Although roles within society may be growing increasingly specific, society itself remains a totality of these roles. The implications of this are several. For one thing, roles are multifunctional. Since decisions made by one elite group affect a broad area of societal life, it is in the interest of the other elite groups to prevent excessive compartmentalization that could eliminate their own influence over such decisions. Patterns of interaction, if frequent and persistent enough and covering a wide range of interests, may blur the boundaries separating members of different elites from one another. If the degree of overlap is significantly great, we may speak of an interlocking elite—a small coterie of men who control several key aspects of the political life of a nation—or, in extreme cases, of a ruling elite (Mills, 1956; Dahl, 1958). Second, individuals may perform several (formal as well as informal) roles in society. Thus Dwight D. Eisenhower, as a former five-star general and as president of the United States, spanned two elite groups, as did Secretaries of Defense Charles E. Wilson under President Eisenhower and Robert S. McNamara under Presidents Kennedy and Johnson, who were able to move from the business to the political elite without encountering insuperable obstacles. The probability of moving successfully from one elite area to another varies with the degree to which the skills entailed in the two areas (for example, articulation of values, management) are comparable. Third, with increasing specificity comes the emergence of new roles at the interstices: individuals who are themselves expert in two separate areas, or who have skills enabling them to mediate between these two areas. Whether such developments affect the permeability of elite groups rests upon the societal style of recruitment into elite roles.

Recruitment patterns in turn are a function of the way in which a society distributes its valued resources. At one end of the continuum, ascriptive criteria apply. Either an individual is "born to the purple" or he is not. More prosaically, racial or ethnic tests still find use in determining whether an individual even has the rights of full membership in a community. At the other end of the continuum, achievement criteria govern possession of the society's main values and hence the attainment of elite status. In this case, the individual's status at birth is far less important than what he has accomplished in life. Most societies, of course, are mixed types. Even the most humble farmer of ancient Egypt could rise to courtly status, although not to the kingship, which bore the ascriptive attributes of divinity. Wealthy bourgeoisie in more recent feudal societies have been able to buy their way into the nobility. Societies, such as that of the United States, that stress achievement as the key to upward social mobility have nonetheless bestowed favors now and then upon individuals who have had the good fortune to have been born into the "right" families (the First Families of Virginia, for example). Access to the opportunity to rise is distributed unequally among the population in even the most egalitarian societies known to scholars. The probability that a child of the slums, born to poverty and raised in an atmosphere of cultural deprivation, will rise to attain elite status is considerably less than the probability that a son of the New England Brahmins will gain such a position. The other side of this coin is that knowledge of an individual's social background has sometimes been used to predict aspects of his future. At this juncture in our society, for instance, the best single predictor of whether an American college student will attend law school is the simple question of whether one of his parents is a lawyer (Zelan, 1967). Finally, achievement of elite status with respect to one value may be a sufficient basis for elite status with respect to other values to be ascribed to an individual. This can be true even though the skills involved vary widely. Thus a movie actor can use the prestige he has earned in the public's eye as a springboard into politics, however much he happens to know about the latter field.

It should be added that, together, the permeability of elite groups and patterns of recruitment constitute a more general phenomenon which Vilfredo Pareto (1935, iii, p. 1419–1432) has termed the circulation of elites. As elaborated by one of his students, Marie Kolabinska (1912), the concept implies three types of circulation (in Bottomore, 1964/ 1966, p. 49):

> There is, first, the circulation which takes place between different categories of the governing elite itself. Secondly, there is the circulation between the elite and the rest of the population, which may take either of two forms: (i) individuals from the lower strata may succeed in entering the existing elite, or (ii) individuals in the lower strata may form new elite groups which then engage in a struggle for power with the existing elite.

Harold D. Lasswell, Daniel Lerner, and C. Easton Rothwell (1952, p. 8) make a similar distinction when they differentiate *personal* circulation from *social* circulation. Writers on elites, from Pareto to the present, have sensed the importance for the study of political processes of the concept of elite circulation, pointed to the need for finding measures of circulation rates, and formulated hypotheses relating political instability to low levels of elite circulation. But, as T. B. Bottomore (1964/1966, p. 61) has observed:

Not one of these studies makes it possible to establish that there is, or is not, a constant connexion between the amount of circulation of individuals and groups in society and the extent of changes in the economic, political and cultural system: first, because they present no systematic comparisons between societies, and secondly, because they provide no exact measurement of the phenomena with which they deal.

Fortunately, however, these are not problems inherent in the comparative study of elites, and indeed, although this sometimes seems to be small consolation, beginnings are being made in contemporary research (for example, Zapf, 1965) that may ultimately enable us to specify more precisely the relationship of levels of elite circulation to such characteristics of political systems as stability and conservatism.

All the points discussed above—unified vs. pluralistic elites, cumulative or cross-cutting cleavages, permeability, and recruitment—are only aspects of the central issue: the structure of the country's elites and their relationship to other groups. On the one hand this entails the elites' position in the decision-making system of the country. Which elites actually participate in making what sorts of decisions? How important are the elites as a whole in the decision-making process? It also refers, on the other hand, to the relationship of elites with subgroups. As an example, we may hypothesize that one segment of the American elite comprises influential labor leaders, that is, the top-level officers of the

FIGURE 4.1
Relationships Among Elites, Constituencies, and Masses: A Paradigm

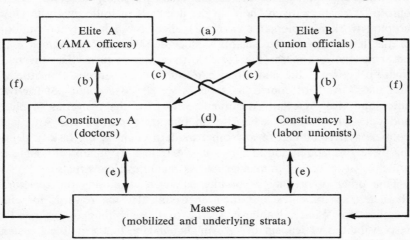

American Federation of Labor–Congress of Industrial Organizations. The constituency of this elite in the most direct sense is the body of members of the AFL-CIO, which in turn is only a part of the entire American population. Similarly, we may consider the leaders of the American Medical Association to be an elite in American society, with a constituency (doctors) and some sort of contact with the mass of Americans. (It should be added here that, from the point of view of their political behavior, the masses may be subdivided further into those who are mobilized—that is, those who have some knowledge of and interest in political events, who follow, even if not participating actively in, elections, and who vote—and the underlying population which has few such attributes; for our present purposes, however, we can ignore the distinctions between these two subcategories.) We may diagram the possible intergroup relationships as shown in Figure 4.1. In our concern with elites, the types of relationships that are of particular interest are (a), (b), (c), and (f), the first of which has been discussed at some length in preceding paragraphs. Regarding the linkage between the elite and its constituency (b), the degree of unity in each group plays a role, as do the mode of selection of elites, the differentiation of elite from nonelite groups on other (for example, class) grounds, the type of communication channels open between them, the nature of their transactions, and so forth. Similar considerations are important when examining the relationship between an elite group and the constituency of another elite group (c). In what respects does the leadership of the AMA have an impact upon members of trade unions? On what types of issues are union members likely to credit AMA officers? Or, alternatively, how do the demands of trade unionists (in a hospital workers' union, for example) affect the behavior and outlook of the leadership of the doctors' association? Finally, what ties exist between elite and mass (f)? How do these ties in turn affect the relationship between elite and direct constituency, or between constituency and mass? And, of course, as soon as we try to account not for two elites and their relevant constituencies but for the congeries of elites and constituencies that comprise an important part of the American political system or that of any other modern country, the task of defining these various relationships becomes extremely complex (although, in principle at least, not unmanageable as theoretical constructs).

One other point may be of interest when examining the structural characteristics of elites and their environments: the rewards for elite membership. What advantages accrue to those willing to assume the responsibilities of leadership? We might imagine that a political system that accords its political elites high social status but low salaries would

SYSTEMATIC APPROACHES TO COMPARATIVE POLITICS

attract a different type of aspirant to political leadership than would the system offering little prestige but an opportunity to amass considerable wealth. Note that we are not asking here what motivates the aspirant. This is a question that must be considered later in our discussion of the personality characteristics of elites. What is important here is the other side of the coin: What rewards and penalties for leaders are built into the political system?

Statements about the structural characteristics of elites lie at the heart of elite studies. It is not always the case that these studies make such statements explicit—in the form, perhaps, of propositions for testing. The conceptual disarray that frequently results prevents some of these studies from contributing to our cumulative knowledge about elites in society. The task of this chapter, after discussing ways to identify the elites of a country, is to cut a path through the dense and bewildering thicket of empirical elite studies—dense, because of the sheer numbers of these studies; bewildering, because, much more so than the other techniques analyzed in this book, systematic approaches to the study of elites are intimately tied to their theoretical frameworks, however well or poorly articulated these may be.

Identifying Members of the Elites

Suppose that, in our analysis of a country's political system, we want to determine who the members of the various elite groupings are. How do we go about this task? The simplest way, of course, is for the researcher to identify them himself. And it is true that a keen-witted observer of a country's politics may well be able to draft a fairly comprehensive list. (This has frequently been a successful journalistic approach; for a recent discussion of West Germany's political elite, see Henkels, 1968.) From the point of view of systematic political science, however, it is subject to the limitations of such unconscious and conscious factors as forgetfulness and lack of specific knowledge about some groups within the society. If a second and equally keen-witted observer were to draw up his own list of elite group members, how could differences between the two lists be arbitrated?

In this possibility of differing perceptions lies the basis of a second approach to our task. The researcher may ask several knowledgeable informants to identify elite members and then select as his final list those individuals on whom there is the greatest degree of agreement among the informants. To date, the best known applications of this technique have been studies of American communities, such as that of

Atlanta by Floyd Hunter (1953). One advantage of this reputational approach is that the researcher can select informants who are especially well informed about specific aspects of the society. Another is that it is useful for identifying the *éminences grises* of the society, those "powers behind the throne" who participate in decision-making in a very real but nonofficial capacity. But, when used alone, the limitations of the reputational approach often outweigh its advantages. On a trivial level, but one that is sometimes forgotten by researchers, there is the problem of regression. How does the researcher determine who his knowledgeable informants should be? If he relies solely upon his own colleagues or the people with whom he has personal contact, then the degree of congruence of their choices may belie the true situation. Their similar perspectives may lead them to apply principles of selection that turn out to be nearly alike and that build systematic biases into the elite sample. Second, in asking the judges for their estimates of who the elite members are, should the researcher give them open- or closed-ended ballots? The former type increases the likelihood that particular names will be forgotten by informants, but closed-end ballots prejudice somewhat the responses that will be obtained. Third, to raise again the question asked earlier, how do we decide who is correct when the experts disagree? Several answers to this question have been suggested, none of them, however, wholly satisfactory. One way might be to rank the elite members according to the number of informants listing them and then select for the sample to be analyzed those ranking at the top of the list; another might be to permit the informant to rank each of his selections on a scale from 0 (= least important) to 10 (= most important), and then select the sample according to the average ranking of the various candidates (for some other variations see Dick, 1960; Bonjean, 1963; Freeman, Fararo, Bloomberg & Sunshine, 1963; and Ehrlich & Bauer, 1965). A more important limitation of the reputational approach is that it is likely to produce lists of people who enjoy the reputation for wielding influence but who in fact may not be influential at all (Wolfinger, 1960; D'Antonio & Erickson, 1962; and Danzger, 1964). The relationship between reputation for and actual possession of influence is a question that can be answered empirically and hence cannot be discussed here except to point out the possibility for discrepancy. Moreover, a reputation for power may influence the behavior of other persons toward the reputed elite member, producing a kind of self-fulfilling prophecy. In this sense, for some types of studies the analysis of persons perceived to be elite members may be of considerable value; for these the perceived role may be of more interest than the actual role that putative elite members play in the political process.

If a list of members of various elite groupings is already available, the researcher can sometimes find it of immense value. Best known of these is the Who's Who type of publication, which today appears in many countries and contains biographical data about large numbers of prominent people. One of the more interesting of recent studies to use this approach was Wendell Bell's analysis of Jamaican leaders (1964). His first step was to draw a random sample comprising one-fourth of the names listed in *Who's Who, Jamaica 1957*. Then, after removing from the initial sample of 598 the names of seven persons who had either died or left the island or who were seriously ill, Bell added 212 additional names from the "King's House Invitation List, which was a ranking of persons in Jamaica according to their official status, be they elected political leaders, civil servants, religious leaders, bank officials, foreign trade commissioners, or what" (p. 181). This adjustment had the effect of weighting the top Jamaican leaders in the sample.

Bell's procedure suggests some of the difficulties of the elite directory approach. For one thing, most Who's Who publications are large enough to require the researcher to limit himself to a sample of the names listed. And yet any method of sampling raises new questions and problems. A random sample of entries in such a general publication is likely to contain a fairly large proportion of cultural, athletic, scientific, and other prominent individuals who, we may assume, know little about and have even less interest in politics. (Note, however, the assumptions about the political process implicit in such a statement.) For analysts interested in general perspectives, such a broad sample may be appropriate; for those interested in the perspectives of individuals likely to be important for the political process, many of the personages in a sample this broad would be of only marginal interest. To sort the many entries into various elite categories for the purpose of drawing a stratified random sample might nonetheless be a task too enormous for him to contemplate. (This will be facilitated, of course, and compilation, updating, and printing costs doubtless reduced when publishers of such compendia adopt a format using electronic data-processing equipment.) Bell's solution, as we have seen, was to supplement his random sample from an elite directory with names drawn from a special list of politically relevant elites. Other studies have disregarded general lists at the outset, opting instead for special lists. One of the best known of these is Daniel Lerner's study of Nazi elites (1951), based on samples drawn from the *Führerlexikon,* published in 1934, which contained biographies of the most important Nazi leaders. But, whether he is using a general or a specialized list as a basis for his systematic sampling of elites, the researcher must recognize that he is throwing himself upon the mercy of the compilers of the publication and their criteria for selection, and, for some purposes, these criteria (if specified) may be far from ideal in the researcher's view. Those performing cross-national research using such compendia must also be aware of differences from one country to the next in the means used to select names and gather data.

Another approach that reduces subjective judgments about who should be included among the elite focuses on the occupants of the most important positions in the society's politics. A definitional problem does arise in the question, What are the most important positions (or roles)? And the answer to this rests, of course, on the theory of decision-making underlying the researcher's analysis. Most analysts avoid answering the question, however, by limiting their studies to specific types of decision-making—parliamentarians, supreme court justices, cabinet members, bureaucrats, union officials, military leaders, or other elite groupings whose members are listed in official handbooks. Of these studies, most have dealt with parliamentarians. They include the analysis of attitudes of legislators in the United States, Great Britain, France, West Germany, Italy, Japan, and India by Lloyd A. Free (1959), the social background and perspectives of United States senators by Donald R. Matthews (1960), attitudes of Israeli Knesset members by Lester G. Seligman (1964), characteristics of Ceylonese legislators by Marshall R. Singer (1964), and the views and attributes of Turkish parliamentarians by Frederick W. Frey (1965).

The positional approach nonetheless raises two serious problems. First, by looking solely at a narrowly circumscribed group of men, such as members of the Fourth Bundestag, the researcher has no way of knowing a priori which members of that body are in fact influential as far as national decision-making is concerned and which are merely "serving time," having received the nomination for faithful service to a particular political party. Equating one member of the body with another may be acceptable for some studies; for others it may cast spurious elements into the findings. Second, concentration upon formal positions of power may mean that the researcher excludes influential elite members merely because they hold no such formal position (Clifford-Vaughan, 1960; Sereno, 1962, p. 97). The importance of such informal presidential advisers as Colonel Edward M. House, Bernard Baruch, and Harry Hopkins cannot be assessed properly merely by listing their official titles. Finally, for cross-national research, the positional approach poses a trap for the unwary researcher. It may not be immediately obvious that formal bodies bearing the same name may serve different functions in different political systems, but we might legitimately ask what relationship a rubber-stamp parliament in a dictatorship bears to the House of Commons in the United Kingdom or to the Bundestag in West Germany, or whether, given differences in their electoral systems, British members of parliament and American congressmen can be compared meaningfully.

The multitude of problems posed by these various approaches to elite studies has led some scholars to seek empirical means to delineate the members of elite groupings. In one such a posteriori effort, Robert A. Dahl (1957) used as an indicator of power among United States senators (to determine the more influential or elite senators) the probability that they would vote on the majority side in certain committees. He found, however, that this method did not enable him to differentiate between those senators who had in fact exercised influence in committee voting patterns and the "chameleons" who happened to vote consistently with the majority. A more elaborate study by Dahl (1961) tried to determine who had and who had not participated in making key decisions on several issue areas in the municipal politics of the southern New England city of New Haven. In answering the question "Who governs?" he found a plurality of elites, with only a minor degree of overlapping membership among them. What this approach may ignore are those persons who are implicitly taken into account when decisions are made but who may themselves not participate in making these decisions. Thus a decision to initiate urban renewal in downtown New Haven will implicitly or explicitly consider the interests of the Downtown Businessmen's Association, whether or not its representatives sit on the committee deliberating the course of action. A more general concern regarding such empirical approaches is that any study trying to determine who the elite of a community or nation are may have little time left over to examine closely the characteristics of these elite groups themselves.

No one of these various approaches—the intuitive, reputational, elite directory, positional, or empirical—is completely satisfactory for the comparative study of elites. Indeed, there is some evidence (Walton, 1966a, 1966b) suggesting that the means used to delineate the members of a community's elite or the researcher's academic discipline may prejudice systematically the sorts of conclusions reached about the structure of the elite in that community. Perhaps the best procedure for the researcher who wants to go beyond merely determining who the elites are, and into an analysis of their attributes or behavior, is a combination of the positional and reputational approaches. In a recent study of elite attitudes in France and West Germany (Deutsch, Edinger, Macridis & Merritt, 1967), the investigators first determined which groups in the two countries they wanted to examine. They then requested knowledgeable informants in the countries to suggest the names of influential persons in each of the elite categories. The next step was to go through official handbooks to make certain that no person holding a position above a certain level in any of the elite categories was omitted from the sample. Since the resulting lists of about 450 French leaders and 650 West Germans were too long for the interview project at hand, a sampling procedure was used to select respondents. Another recent study by Charles C. Moskos, Jr., used another combined approach—a modified "snowball" technique— as a basis for interviews with 111 top leaders in Jamaica, Trinidad and Tobago, British Guiana, and in Barbados, Grenada, and Dominica (1967a, p. 52; see also Moskos, 1967b; and Oxaal, 1968):

> Initially, persons in a cross-section of institutional sectors were selected who, on the basis of their formal roles or institutional positions, were likely to be top leaders. They were asked to identify individuals whom they considered to wield national influence. As the nominations of the national leaders accumulated, the most frequently mentioned persons were in turn asked to identify other influentials. In this way, the original positional approach gave way to a reputational approach, and the list of reputed leaders was increasingly refined. The same procedure was used in each of the territories, so that comparability between the units was insured.

In short, however complex the task of identifying members of the elites, it is far from hopeless. And, as we shall see, scholars have produced interesting and fruitful results from elite studies using each of the approaches described above. It nonetheless seems clear that, like the use of multiple indicators to test political propositions, combined means to identify elites are the most satisfactory in securing representative samples.

The Focus of Elite Studies

What do we want to find out about elite groups and their members once we have identified them? What sorts of data about elites would be of value in understanding political structures and processes? Moving from the general to the particular—and, incidentally, from the area with the most to that with the least readily accessible information about elites— major points of concern include the external characteristics of elite members, that is, their social background; their behavioral patterns, particularly as they concern political decision-making; their perspectives, or values, attitudes, and beliefs; and their personality attributes.

Social Background. When we look at the individual members of an elite grouping, we frequently want to ask questions about their background.

The following items of information, by no means an exhaustive list (Hanhardt & Welsh, 1964, are gathering data on no less than 126 variables!), are among those often of use:

Traits acquired at birth
 date of birth
 place of birth: size and location of town of birth
 sex
 nationality
 ancestral background (e.g., aristocracy)
 caste, race, ethnicity, tribe, clan
Socialization
 religion
 political affiliation and activity of parents
 education
 rural vs. urban upbringing
 membership in youth organizations (religious, sports,
  patriotic, etc.)
 apprenticeships and other occupational training
Adult career pattern
 first occupation or profession
 length of time spent in various occupations
 length of time spent in main occupation
 marital status; age and sex of children
 record of military service; wartime duty; service awards
 foreign contacts (travel, correspondence, family members who
  emigrated)
 membership in organizations
 political participation (level of participation, political party
  identification, nomination for or service in public or party
  office)
 participation in specific events (e.g., for Chinese communists,
  the "long march"; for Italian Fascists, the march on Rome;
  jail sentences for American civil rights leaders)
 honors (medals, civic awards, honorary degrees)

Some scholars have based their research on the assumption that aggregated data about the social background of elite groupings as a whole would help to explain significant aspects of their perspectives and behavior.

Collecting such data poses several research problems. In principle, of course, at least for areas and times that have kept written records, it should be possible to locate such information for any member of any elite grouping. What limits the amount of information to be gained for any particular study is what economists call the opportunity cost of getting each additional bit. The biographer of a prominent political figure may spend years gathering such an array of information about his subject. The political scientist interested in comparable data about large numbers of elite members, however, must weigh the costs as well as the benefits of tracking down fugitive data. Second, standard sources of biographical information sometimes contain inaccuracies or, what is more problematic, the Who's Who entrant filling out his own questionnaire may suppress or recast aspects of his own past. Then, too, for comparative studies we must search for variables that are functionally equivalent. To what extent are we justified in equating the university training of a citizen in a developing country in which only a small minority of the population is even literate with that of a modern American or Western European? Though in both cases the training may have been identical, the function that it serves for the individual in his own country varies vastly.

Social background data serve a variety of purposes. Alone they can give us an idea of recruitment patterns within a society, that is, the groups from which the various elites are drawn, and they can tell us something about the typical career patterns of these elites. Speaking of the Nazi propagandists as a group, for instance, Daniel Lerner notes that its "distinctive character . . . was its recruitment from among the alienated young intellectuals of the upper middle classes who had formed the elite of pre-Nazi Germany" (1951/1965, p. 230). Nazi administrators provide a contrast: "Born largely in rural places and smaller towns, of parents with little income and less prestige, they acquired little formal education and, after military service, found themselves confronting a life filled with hard and unrewarding labor in jobs that offered them, like their fathers, little income and less prestige" (p. 251). Such findings are by themselves interesting; they may even suggest explanatory propositions about differences among the various Nazi elites or, more generally, about elites in coercive ideological movements; but until they are put together with other data they remain *descriptive* rather than *explanatory*. The same is true of George K. Schueller's finding (1951/1965, p. 142) that, for members of the Soviet Politburo, "foreign contacts, particularly with the Western World, for the most part took place before 1930; since then the foreign contacts of the Politburo have been few and far between." Intuitively, however, we suspect that the finding is directly relevant to the changed behavior of these Soviet elites after the early 1930s vis-à-vis the outside world.

If we have time-series data about the occupants of specific roles, we can determine something about trends in recruitment and career patterns (or, to use the term of Lasswell, Lerner, & Rothwell [1952, p. 8], "social circulation") no less than personal circulation, that is, the turn-over rate over time as discussed in a previous section. Again, such data enable us to examine descriptive propositions, such as that formulated by Aron (1950, p. 129): It is characteristic of "the revisionist or western type of socialism" that "company directors are replaced by managers, trade union leaders are introduced into councils of government and public affairs, the political power of the capitalist economic leader is reduced and that of the leaders of the masses is increased." Lewis J. Edinger (1961, p. 36; see also Edinger, 1960), by way of contrast, has discovered that "despite drastic and sudden changes in political systems, there appears to have been a great deal of continuity and only a limited amount of slow change in the background of German decision-makers over the last half century, and over the last two or three decades in particular." Gabriel A. Almond's study (1939) of holders of important governmental posts in New York City gives a good example of flexibility in recruitment patterns. During times of crisis, such as a war, these high officeholders were chosen from wealthy circles, but from among the poorer classes during noncritical periods. But it is a long distance from this type of descriptive proposition to explanatory propositions such as "the stability of a polity increases (or decreases) with the degree of flexibility in the recruitment of its elites," or "the stability of a polity increases with the ability of the elites to adapt their perspectives to correspond to popular demands." The point is not that descriptive propositions are useless. This is far from the truth. Rather, the question is the extent to which we can generalize such findings. To answer this question, we need considerable data besides the biographical characteristics of elite members.

Together with information about the demographic characteristics of the population, it is possible to determine the representativeness of its elite groupings. By itself, representativeness or nonrepresentativeness is doubtless of little importance. Most populations are led by elites who are in some way or another unrepresentative of the masses: Elite members are generally older than a random sample of the entire population, better educated, higher in terms of socioeconomic status, male rather than female, and come from larger towns. The important question is when this degree of differentiation begins to matter in the country's political process. Harry J. Benda (1960, pp. 208–209), for instance, asserts that, because they are "a product of alien education more or less precariously grafted on indigenous non-western societies, . . . non-western intellectuals are very frequently an isolated social group in indigenous society," a fact that affects their control over the masses. More generally, however, and particularly for countries that are not going through the upheavals of modernization, it would seem that representativeness in terms of traits acquired at birth (such as ethnicity) is more important than that in terms of characteristics acquired subsequently (such as education) in determining the effectiveness of an elite group. The leopard cannot change his spots, but he can adapt himself to the demands of his environment. Similarly, elite members can learn new skills, change their (publicly expressed) perspectives, and adopt new ways of speaking or new styles of dress. All this leads us to ask what the circumstances are in which a population will accept the leadership of a nonrepresentative elite, and when they will insist upon a "man of the people" in a leadership position. But, to answer such a question, we need information about the perspectives of both the population and its elites.

Together with information about elite perspectives, biographical data can be useful for testing conflicting propositions about social background vs. role in society as key determinants of perspectives and behavior (Rosenau, 1967). One of these proceeds from the assumption that origins are explanatory or, in the words of Donald R. Matthews (1954, p. 2), "the conviction that the political decision-maker's behavior and decisions are influenced by his personal life experiences." If you would know the man, these theories seem to say, then look at his parents, the environment in which he grew up, his life experiences. Carried to an extreme, we might formally assert that homogeneous backgrounds produce homogeneous perspectives. To be sure, there were differences of opinion among the nineteenth-century English political elite —men of a common social heritage, products of a handful of private schools and universities, members of the same clubs. But the differences among elite members were as molehills next to the mountains that differentiated the elites from the masses or even the middle classes (see, for example, Wilkinson, 1962). The counterproposition is that the role played by the individual is of equal if not greater importance in understanding the perspectives and behavior of elites. Accordingly, the constraints imposed upon the individual when he assumes a public office— traditions, bureaucratic framework, decision-making procedures—are strong enough that he follows particular patterns regardless of what his social background may have been. That there are more lawyers than any other occupational group as members of American state legislatures is by itself interesting, but this may or may not be a significant variable for explaining their actions as legislators (Wahlke, Eulau, Buchanan & Ferguson, 1962; Barber, 1965).

Although we are confident that there is some truth in the assumption that origin and life experiences are explanatory of later behavior, the extent to which the assumption holds true is still indeterminate. Is it greater or lesser or about the same for aggregates of individuals as it is for single individuals? Are there realms of experience for which it is more appropriate than for others, such as for personal rather than for political life? In the most significant study to date of the relationship between social background characteristics and perspectives, using a multivariate approach to analyze data about French and West German elites, Lewis J. Edinger and Donald D. Searing (1967, p. 445) conclude: "(1) some background variables are considerably better predictors than are others of attitudes within a single national system; (2) some elite attitudes in a particular national polity are more frequently related to background variables than are others; and (3) relationships between social background and attitude vary from one national political system to another even within the same supranational culture area." It is clear, however, that considerable work on this relationship between background and perspectives remains to be done before any satisfactory theory will result (see also Searing, 1969).

In sum, catalogues of biographical characteristics are important for the systematic study of elites. Alone, however, they are not likely to answer most of the politically relevant questions that we might want to ask. They are most useful in conjunction with other sorts of information about the elites and their environment.

Behavior. Of manifest importance are the ways in which elites actually behave, whether consciously or unconsciously. Even apparently trivial aspects of behavior frequently symbolize underlying perspectives that are politically relevant (Edelman, 1964). Those indulging consciously in such symbolic behavior are usually seeking to solidify a population behind them. In modernizing countries, it may make a difference what types of clothes elite members wear in parliamentary sessions or while taking a Sunday morning walk. Mustapha Kemal Atatürk went so far as to forbid certain garments associated with Turkey's traditional culture in order to emphasize his country's drive toward modernity (Frey, 1965). In other countries, such as Ceylon, wearing traditional costumes is a sign of solidarity with the nationalist movement, an implied sign of rejection of Western ways of life forced upon a people during its colonial days (Singer, 1964). Another form of symbolic behavior is diet. Nationalist leaders publicize their preference for the simple diet of the "people," while ostentatiously eschewing imported luxuries. And mayoralty candidates of such polycultural cities as New York run the risk of severe indigestion to make certain that they are photographed while eating various local specialties. The appointment of political associates, such as campaign advisers or cabinet members, also assumes symbolic proportions, as do such devices as ticket-balancing, to ensure that most major groups within the population find representation on a slate of candidates for political office. Victor A. Thompson's comments (1961) about the role of dramaturgy in administration are applicable to a broad range of elite behavior. And, similarly, what Felix M. and Marie M. Keesing (1956, p. 68) point out about Samoan elites—"Important interaction among elite persons is carried on, if at all possible, in a formal setting, and publicly recognized and made memorable by elaborate paraphernalia and ceremonial behavior"—is also characteristic of national party meetings and summit conferences of heads of state.

Forms of communication behavior are especially relevant. Where do various elites normally get the information upon which they base their decisions? If it turns out that most of the elites of a particular country read a given newspaper or news magazine, then a systematic analysis of this publication could give us clues about the perspectives held by these elites (Rosenau, 1963; Merritt, 1966). We might hypothesize, for example, that they comprise a community of information, which in turn implies an ability to communicate with one another on a wide range of issues. If, however, it turns out that half the elite members read one set of publications and the other half read another set with sharply differing foci of attention and views, then communication between the two groups may be more difficult and misunderstandings are more likely to arise. How extensive are the face-to-face communication networks linking the elites together (Katz & Lazarsfeld, 1955)? Rarely, in a mass society, anyway, do we find the type of network of familial associations and business partnerships that characterized the American elites at the time of the Revolution (Lamb, 1966). Most such networks rest upon more diffuse bases. But even now, as the recent cases of the Kennedy family in the United States and the Ngo family in South Vietnam testify, special circumstances sometimes give rise to particularly closely knit face-to-face communication networks at high levels in government. Indeed, for C. Wright Mills (1956, p. 281), viewing what he termed the American power elite of the mid-1950s, "their continued association further cements what they feel they have in common." He added:

> Members of the several higher circles know one another as personal friends and even as neighbors; they mingle with one another on the golf course, in the gentleman's clubs, at resorts, on transcontinental airplanes, and on ocean liners. They meet at the estates of mutual friends, face each other in front of the TV camera, or serve on the same philanthropic committee;

and many are sure to cross one another's path in the columns of newspapers, if not in the exact cafes from which many of these columns originate.

Other scholars, however, have disputed Mills's inference that such associations produce a class consciousness that in turn leads to highly coordinated political decisions made solely in the interests of these elites (Dahl, 1958).

Still another aspect of the behavior of elites is the decision-making process. This encompasses not only the way in which elites reach decisions but also their strategies for implementing them: how they go about getting the specific information they require for making decisions; the degree to which they are receptive to new and possibly contradictory information; their techniques for handling the flow of information, particularly that which is apparently contradictory; their procedures for outlining possible solutions as well as their preferences for certain types of decisions (for example, preferences for military as opposed to economic solutions in conflict situations); their willingness to experiment with novel solutions (creativity); their flexibility in adapting to new situations or to refutation of preconceived notions; the mechanisms and techniques by which they maintain themselves in their elite positions; the means by which they seek to secure support for their decisions; their choice of modes of implementation. Fortunately enough, for those pursuing systematic analyses of elites, various models of decision-making processes exist (Dahl & Lindblom, 1953; Lasswell, 1956; Deutsch, 1962; Snyder, Bruck & Sapin, 1962). And in some instances scholars have initiated empirical studies of actual leadership groups in small-group settings (Barber, 1966). More generally, hypotheses about decision-making processes abound in the literature. An example is the well-known view that, in a modern industrialized society, political decision-making is the outcome of competition among shifting coalitions formed around various policy issues. Keesing and Keesing (1956, p. 87) show that this is also the case in the more primitive society of Samoa: "The binding of groups and individuals in an equivalent network of mutual rights and obligations contributes strongly to social integration and provides a kind of 'insurance' system in terms of economic and political securities." Robert E. Lane (1958, p. 433), in affirming the aptness of this proposition for American society as well, concludes that " 'log-rolling' and 'back-scratching' know no boundaries."

Elite behavior at the interface of national and international systems poses a special topic for research. At one level is the extent to which elite groupings entertain contacts with foreigners, whether through visits to foreign countries or through their reception of foreign visitors (Kelman, 1965; Merritt, 1967). How frequently do various elite groupings have contacts with foreigners? How frequently do they travel abroad? To what extent are political leaders and businessmen willing to learn the language and customs of the countries they visit? How willing are business firms to employ nationals of the countries in which they have subsidiaries? How willing are they to put these nationals into leadership positions? How willing are they to bring in foreigners to direct their operations at home? At another level is the extent to which different elite groupings pay attention to foreign as well as to domestic inputs into the decision-making process. Most countries by now have embassy or consular officials who report on events and attitudes in the countries to which they are accredited. Some even conduct public opinion surveying. But how likely is it that political leaders at home will take account of this information in planning their own operations (Merritt & Puchala, 1968)? Does the American president pay as much attention to foreign press comment as he does to that appearing in American newspapers? Are domestic political considerations likely to prevail over the realities of the conflict situation itself in his conduct of a foreign war? At still another level is the extent to which such elite groupings pay attention to the impact of their own decisions upon the international system as a whole. The decision in 1933 by President Roosevelt and his advisers to take the United States temporarily off the gold standard had worldwide repercussions, as have had other, supposedly purely domestic actions.

Perspectives. The perspectives—that is, their beliefs about themselves and the world around them, their attitudes toward these events and processes, and their basic values—of the broad stratum of politically relevant elites in a national system are indicative of those that go into the making of policy. Whether the perspectives of representative officials at the British Foreign Office or at the Quai d'Orsay stem from common social backgrounds or stem from similar socialization processes, information about these perspectives would tell us much about the environmental framework of a particular policy—even if we are unable to get comparable information about the people who actually formulated that policy. It is also possible to infer, although with considerably less confidence about the accuracy of the inference, the values, beliefs, and attitudes that went into that foreign policy measure if we merely have access to the broader stratum of individuals from whom Foreign Office or Quai d'Orsay officials were recruited or with whom they consort in their hours of leisure.

Moreover, today's elites are largely responsible for recruiting and promoting tomorrow's elites into positions of power, and men tend to put their trust in their own kind. In a stable society, we can fairly safely predict that the basic perspectives of the leaders of the 1960s will be carried over to the leaders of the 1970s, albeit with some modifications. (The volatile politics of a state in which elites have provided education for the lower classes without commensurate opportunities for social mobility might, by way of contrast, pave the way for a sudden overthrow of established elites by an alignment of counterelite leaders.) Despite political shifts, postwar society in most of the major countries of the world has been fairly stable. The phenomenon of the self-perpetuation of elites together with the fact that today's younger leaders will spend long years being socialized into positions of power suggest that we may expect a reasonable degree of stability in elite perspectives during the years to come, although of course not on all issues.

For "dual politicians," those whose concerns bridge the national and international systems, some types of perspectives are of special interest (see Lerner & Gorden, 1969; Deutsch, Edinger, Macridis & Merritt, 1967). What are their images of the international environment? Do they see it as an anarchic conglomeration of sovereign states battling one another for positions of power, prestige, and wealth? Or is it a system with some generally accepted (if often unspoken) rules of behavior and some predictable patterns? Do they feel their national security threatened by the constellations in the current international system? What are the attitudes of these elites toward other states, toward international institutions, toward measures designed to enhance the area of regularity and predictability in the international system? Do they value the predominance of the nation-state over continued stability in the international arena? How do they feel about the use of force as a means of resolving different types of international conflicts? Do they favor forms of international cooperation likely to lead to a regional or worldwide division of labor, or is national autarchy more important to them?

A standard method for investigating elite perspectives has been the examination of the elite's public and private statements: speeches, press conferences, books and articles, letters, diaries, and so forth. Such a procedure requires the assumption that the perspectives presented in the individual's messages actually represent his "true" perspectives. In many instances, of course, this is not the case: Individuals sometimes communicate, whether deliberately or unconsciously, in a way that covers up their consciously held perspectives. Particularly useful for resolving this problem are content analytic methods that stress less the manifest content of a person's communications than their underlying dimensions of expression (see Stone, Dunphy, Smith & Ogilvie, 1966; Leites, 1951; Leites, 1959).

Interviewing highly placed persons in public and private life also has a long and honorable tradition. Only recently, however, have social scientists sought to do this on a systematic basis cross-nationally, using more careful sampling techniques to decide who their respondents should be, using schedules of questions to ensure that all respondents are asked the same set of questions in roughly the same order and manner, and using questions that can be scaled to give us additional clues about the latent or underlying attitudes of the respondents. Any such undertaking raises immediately a number of problems.

Some of these relate to the very nature of elite interviews (Lerner, 1956; Robinson, 1960; Hunt, Crane & Wahlke, 1964). Members of elite groups are almost by definition busy. Some are simply unwilling or unable to give up the amount of time that the interviewer needs; or the interview, when granted, may be short or frequently interrupted by telephone calls and messages from the respondent's secretary; or the questions may be so searching or require so much thinking that the respondent contents himself with giving the shortest answers that seem to satisfy the interviewer. In some areas and among some elite groups, still other resistances to interviews crop up: Potential respondents resent the researcher who pokes his nose into what they consider to be their personal affairs; they fear their responses might fall into the hands of political opponents; the promise of anonymity is unappealing because they want publicity for their views; they resist tightly structured interviews that do not present them with sufficient chances to demonstrate the individuality of their views, or they resent the fact that the interviewer will ultimately want to classify and categorize them into empirical pigeonholes; or elite groups may by now be "over-researched," that is, they may feel they have spent too much time answering too many questions from too many academicians interested in elite perspectives (see, for example, Dexter, 1964). Resourceful scholars have proved, however, that with ingenuity and persistence they can frequently get useful results from even the most reluctant respondents.

Another important question pertains to the truthfulness of elite respondents in an interview situation: Do they tell the interviewer what they really believe? Whether or not the respondent accurately indicates his attitudes to the interviewer is, of course, impossible to determine with certainty in each individual case. By explaining fully the scholarly nature of his inquiry and by guaranteeing the confidential nature of the interview the researcher may enhance the likelihood that the respondent will express his true feelings. And, by and large, a competent interviewer can judge the openness of the respondent on the basis of his mannerisms, the logical consistency of his responses, and the relationship between his responses in the interview and his remarks published elsewhere. In the last analysis, only a close watch on other indicators of the respondent's perspectives can tell us something about the extent to which his expressed attitudes represented his real attitudes; but, even then, since a man may change his mind, future behavior may be misleading about that man's current views.

In some instances scholars investigating elite perspectives have sent questionnaires to members of elite groupings, asking that they be filled out and returned. The rate of return is rarely very great—25 per cent or less. Quasi-governmental sponsorship helped Rosenau (1963) get 61 per cent of his respondents to fill out questionnaires, and Mark Abrams (1965) got a return rate of 62 per cent, but these are exceptions rather than the rule. A comparison of the attributes of those individuals returning questionnaires with the attributes of the entire sample to whom questionnaires were sent permits an assessment of the representativeness of the respondents. Bell (1964), for instance, found that the 30 per cent of his Jamaican leaders who returned questionnaires differed significantly from the 70 per cent who did not on only two of 13 variables (education and occupational mobility), a fact that gave him a good basis to extrapolate his findings to the larger elite population. Another problem, probably less serious than it might seem, is that the researcher has no control over the way the questionnaire is completed. Is it filled out by the respondent himself or by his secretary? Is it clear that the respondent has interpreted the questions in the way the investigator intended? Has he given complete answers? Singer (1964) provided a unique, albeit risky, solution to a complex of such problems. After finding that neither he nor his Ceylonese assistants could arrange interviews with Ceylonese elites, he made contact with a well known and knowledgeable Ceylonese who agreed to send out questionnaires under his own name and, for those elite members who did not return the questionnaires (more than 500, as opposed to about 70 who did), to fill them out himself. The key question here, as in some other type of research in the social sciences, is the reliability of the informant. Whatever the problems, mail questionnaires can nonetheless be of considerable value, particularly if used in conjunction with interviews or other methods to get at the respondents' perspectives.

Personality. Doubtless the most difficult task of research into the role of elites in the political process is the investigation of personality characteristics that contribute to behavior. Considerable agreement stands behind the assertion by Fred I. Greenstein (1967, p. 629; see also Greenstein, 1969) that "there is a great deal of political activity which can be explained adequately only by taking account of the personal characteristics of the actors involved." He goes on to note that "the impact of an individual's actions varies with (1) the degree to which the actions take place in an environment which admits of restructuring, (2) the location of the actor in that environment, and (3) the actor's peculiar strengths or weaknesses" (pp. 633–634). Greenstein then lists eleven propositions (pp. 635–639) about conditions permitting greater or lesser variability in personal behavior, such as:

1. There is greater room for personal variability in the "peripheral" aspects of actions than in their central aspects.
2. The more demanding the political act—the more it is not merely a conventionally expected performance—the greater the likelihood that it will vary with the personal characteristics of the actor.
10. The more emotionally involved a person is in politics, the greater the likelihood that his personal characteristics will affect his political behavior.

Asking, "Under what circumstances are ego-defensive needs likely to manifest themselves in political behavior?" Greenstein adds three general propositions (pp. 639–641):

1. Certain types of environmental stimuli undoubtedly have a greater "resonance" with the deeper layers of the personality than do others.
2. The likelihood that ego-defensive needs will affect political behavior also is related to the degree to which actors "have" ego-defensive needs.
3. Finally, certain types of response undoubtedly provide greater occasion for deep personality needs to find outlet than do others.

When we turn from general propositions to specific research, however, the level of agreement drops off sharply.

Analytic procedures for the study of personality and politics vary widely, and none is entirely satisfactory. Psychoanalysis of leaders, however ideally suited to this purpose it might be, is not possible technically. For one thing, there is no universally accepted theory of personality or even agreement about methods. For another, even if there were agreement on means and goals, it is highly doubtful that busy elites would submit themselves to any such procedure. Hence, other means must be sought.

Some ways of approaching dimensions of personality have been hinted at before: (1) Content analysis of an individual's communications of all sorts, including doodling and mannerisms as well as written and oral messages, can provide clues to his personality structure. (2) For those researchers using paper-and-pencil tests or mail questionnaires, it is usually possible to include some psychologically oriented questions and scales, such as the authoritarianism scales developed by Adorno and his associates (1950), Rokeach (1960), and Roghmann (1966), or Osgood's semantic differential (Osgood, Suci & Tannenbaum, 1957), or various forms of the Thematic Apperception Test (see, for example, Atkinson, 1958). (3) Similar and more discriminating types of indicators can be used in personal interviews. And, of course, the trained researcher who interviews elite leaders "in depth" has that much more opportunity to utilize such measures (Lane, 1962).

A second kind of approach is the developmental biography. It most frequently concentrates upon the structure of an individual's personality to explain (that is, account for) his behavior. Scholars have examined the life and career patterns of such individuals as Martin Luther (Erikson, 1958), Woodrow Wilson (George & George, 1956), Kurt Schumacher (Edinger, 1965), and revolutionary personalities such as Lenin, Trotsky, and Gandhi (Wolfenstein, 1967a). In brief the research task is to compare all available information on the verbal and physical behavior of the individuals with models of behavior that have emerged from clinical studies by modern psychologists and psychoanalysts. The assumption is that, if the available data about the leader's behavior conform in the main to the behavioral patterns typical of the models, there are grounds for inferring a degree of similarity in the underlying personality structures. Such studies cannot, of course, "prove" that any elite member acted from any particular set of psychological factors; and there is always the danger that the information available to the researcher is incomplete or, still worse, systematically biased in one direction or another. But they are nonetheless useful for posing hypotheses about political behavior and perspectives.

Only recently have there been serious efforts to expand the biographical approach for comparative purposes, either through the development of a systematic framework "to trace the dynamic patterns of interaction between personality, role, and setting" (Edinger, 1964, p. 670) or through the analysis of a variety of leaders in a search for common variables. One major project by E. Victor Wolfenstein (1967b) rests upon psychoanalytic theory. According to this model of personality, the demands of the superego (an individual's set of internalized moral standards) coincide only more or less with those of the ego ("the relatively rational, reality-oriented part of the personality which must try to satisfy not only the dictates of the superego but also the instinctual demands of the id"); and "when the superego can be brought into close accord with the ego, the individual feels a minimum of guilt and depression and a maximum of strength and self-sufficiency as well as moral righteousness." His examination of the biographies of Churchill,

Gandhi, Hitler, and Lenin leads Wolfenstein to hypothesize: "Crisis leaders have usually well-developed and ego-supportive superegos." Elaborating, and drawing out the implications of this hypothesis, he notes (pp. 163–164):

Their ideologies and ideological gods would then be viewed as the conscious and articulated manifestations of the superego, and hence are indeed an integral part of the individual's personality, a sincere object of reverence. It is also clear, however, that even for these men the psychic distance between ego and superego is highly variable. At almost no time is the unity between the two so great that a state of genuine mania results, and rarely do the men tend to the other extreme of a truly pathological melancholia. But within these limits the number of possible positions is great. . . .

What is distinctively political about this psychodynamic configuration is not its form but its content. The mood swings are in response to variations in political circumstance (although the overt content of the changes may not be what is critical to the individual) and are usually manifested in ideological pronouncement. For example, after the attempted and unsuccessful Bolshevik uprising during July of 1917, Lenin found it necessary to go into hiding to avoid what he felt would be an impending death blow to his movement and himself from the Provisional Government. During this time he was evidently quite depressed, and this depression resulted in fevered and desperate notes to those Bolsheviks still active in the capital, imploring them to take care and strike quickly if and when the opportunity presented itself. Lenin's mood was thus not a reaction to a private difficulty but a political distress politically expressed.

In subsequent pages Wolfenstein hypothesizes that "for crisis leaders generally, adolescence brings with it a psychic crisis whose solution serves as a model for the individual in his attempts to cope with the political crises of his adult life" (p. 173; see also Erikson, 1963), and relates levels of emotional independence, world views, and degrees of single-mindedness to alternative modes of resolving adolescent identity crises.

Still another kind of approach rests upon the creation of typologies. On the one hand, it has frequently been observed that specific occupations seem to attract certain personality types. To the extent that this is true, typologies of personalities—generated either through projective tests or even developmental biographies—may serve a predictive function. The biographies, by focusing upon interaction between personality and situational factors, can also tell us how individuals go about choosing their roles. As Alexander L. and Juliette L. George (1956, p. 319) write:

It is in interaction with his milieu that the individual "finds himself" and learns ways of expressing himself in a satisfying manner. It is from this standpoint that the biographer examines the development of the subject's interest in politics and in leadership, and attempts to account for the subject's selection of a particular political role for himself. It is from this standpoint, too, that he studies the subject's efforts to develop the skills appropriate to the political role which he has chosen.

In their study of President Woodrow Wilson and his adviser, Colonel Edward M. House, they examine in great detail the sequences of man-milieu interactions that led the one to choose an active career that culminated in his quest for public office and the other to opt for an advising role behind the scenes of public politics.

On the other hand, some studies view occupants of a particular role in the aggregated terms of a multidimensional personality type that links formative experiences to subsequent perspectives and behavior. Any single person thus categorized may not possess every one of the characteristics attributed to the type as such; his possession of a significant number of the most important characteristics nonetheless enables the researcher to classify him as one type rather than another. Arnold A. Rogow and Harold D. Lasswell (1963, p. 45) discovered in the biographies of thirty "major political bosses who dominated local governments in the late nineteenth and early twentieth centuries . . . two conspicuous types of political boss in the United States." One of these was the game politician. Born of established and well-to-do parents, he had faced in his childhood not severe economic deprivations but insufficient love and emotional security. The gain politician, by way of contrast, stemmed from a poor but closely knit and supportive immigrant family. Because of their early background, the argument goes, these two types of bosses later made different demands upon the environment. For the game politician, politics "functioned as the principal mode of self-expression and self-realization"; he "enjoyed 'the game' for the ego rewards it offered, which were chiefly power, prestige, adulation, and a sense of importance" (p. 47). The gain politician saw politics primarily as a means to rise economically. Both used power and corruption, but to achieve different and yet "specific ends which were generated in the personality system." Similarly, in their study of the American federal executive, based on interviews, W. Lloyd Warner and his associates (1963) delineated the man of reason type, the man after status, and the man who has lost his dedication—without, however going as deeply into the relationship between formative experiences and subsequent behavior as Rogow and Lasswell had.

The systematic study of personality and politics exemplifies the general state of the comparative study of elites. It is highly divergent. Scholars have carved out only a few areas of agreement on such key issues as relevance, focus, and methodology. This, however, is probably a healthy development—as long as a pluralistic attitude of scientific inquiry prevails, one that permits concepts and tools to be judged according to their fruitfulness for the theoretical tasks at hand, one that gives freedom to those wanting to pursue new lines of research. It goes without saying, of course, that much research must be conducted before social scientists will be able to develop a satisfactory empirical theory of the role of elites in society. What is encouraging is the fantastic growth in such research during the last decade and a half (see the bibliography by Beck & McKechnie, 1968). We have now reached the stage in the scientific process at which syntheses of empirical findings can begin to replace analysis of a primarily speculative sort. These in turn can provide a basis for further systematic research. The mysteries of leadership are far from solved, and current steps in this direction are generally more those of ants than of giants. But, at the very least, we are making progress down this particular long road to empirical theory.

REFERENCES

Abrams, Mark. "British Elite Attitudes and the European Common Market," *The Public Opinion Quarterly*. 29:2 (Summer 1965), 236–246.

Adorno, T. W., Else Frenkel-Brunswik, Daniel J. Levinson, and R. Nevitt Sanford. *The Authoritarian Personality*. New York: Harper & Brothers, 1950.

Almond, Gabriel A. *The American People and Foreign Policy*. New York: Harcourt, Brace and Company, 1950; Frederick A. Praeger, 1960.

Almond, Gabriel A. "Wealth and Politics in New York City." Unpublished Ph.D. Dissertation, University of Chicago, 1939.

Aron, Raymond. "Social Structure and the Ruling Class," *The British Journal of Sociology* (jointly published by the London School of Economics and Routledge and Kegan Paul Ltd.). 1:1 (March 1950), 1–16; and 1:2 (June 1950), 126–143.

Atkinson, John W., editor. *Motives in Fantasy, Action, and Society: A Method of Assessment and Study*. Princeton, N.J.: D. Van Nostrand, 1958.

Barber, James David. *The Lawmakers: Recruitment and Adaptation to Legislative Life*. New Haven and London: Yale University Press, 1965.

Barber, James David. *Power in Committees: An Experiment in the Governmental Process*. Chicago: Rand McNally, 1966.

Beck, Carl, and J. Thomas McKechnie. *Political Elites: A Select and Computerized Bibliography*. Cambridge, Mass.: M.I.T. Press, 1968.

Bell, Wendell, editor. *The Democratic Revolution in the West Indies: Studies in Nationalism, Leadership and the Belief in Progress*. Cambridge, Mass.: Schenkman Publishing Company, Inc., 1967.

Bell, Wendell. *Jamaican Leaders: Political Attitudes in a New Nation*. Berkeley and Los Angeles: University of California Press, 1964.

Benda, Harry J. "Non-Western Intelligentsia as Political Elites," *The Australian Journal of Politics and History*. 6:2 (November 1960), 205–218.

Bernd, Joseph L., editor. *Mathematical Applications in Political Science, II*. Dallas, Texas: Southern Methodist University Press, 1966.

Bonjean, Charles M. "Community Leadership: A Case Study and Conceptual Refinement," *The American Journal of Sociology*. 68:6 (May 1963), 672–681.

Bottomore, T. B. *Elites and Society*. London: C. A. Watts, 1964; New York: Basic Books, Inc., Publishers, 1965; and Baltimore, Md.: Penguin Books, 1966.

Clifford-Vaughan, Michalina. "Some French Concepts of Élites," *The British Journal of Sociology*. 11:4 (December 1960), 319–331.

Dahl, Robert A. "The Concept of Power," *Behavioral Science*. 2:3 (July 1957), 201–215.

Dahl, Robert A. "A Critique of the Ruling Elite Model," *The American Political Science Review*. 52:2 (June 1958), 463–469.

Dahl, Robert A. *Who Governs? Democracy and Power in an American City*. New Haven and London: Yale University Press, 1961.

Dahl, Robert A., and Charles E. Lindblom. *Politics, Economics, and Welfare: Planning and Politico-Economic Systems Resolved into Basic Social Processes*. New York: Harper & Row, 1953.

D'Antonio, William V., and Eugene C. Erickson. "The Reputational Technique as a Measure of Community Power: An Evaluation Based on Comparative and

Longitudinal Studies," *The American Sociological Review.* 27:3 (June 1962), 362–376.

Danzger, M. Herbert. "Community Power Structure: Problems and Continuities," *The American Sociological Review.* 29:5 (October 1964), 707–717.

Deutsch, Karl W. *Nationalism and Social Communication: An Inquiry into the Foundations of Nationality* (2d ed.). Cambridge, Mass.: M.I.T. Press, 1966.

Deutsch, Karl W. *The Nerves of Government: Models of Political Communication and Control.* New York: Free Press of Glencoe, 1962.

Deutsch, Karl W., Lewis J. Edinger, Roy C. Macridis, and Richard L. Merritt. *France, Germany and the Western Alliance: A Study of Elite Attitudes on European Integration and World Politics.* New York: Charles Scribner's Sons, 1967.

Dexter, Lewis A. "The Good Will of Important People: More on the Jeopardy of the Interview," *The Public Opinion Quarterly.* 28:4 (Winter 1964), 556–563.

Dick, Harry R. "A Method for Ranking Community Influentials," *The American Sociological Review.* 25:3 (June 1960), 395–399.

Edelman, Murray. *The Symbolic Uses of Politics.* Urbana: University of Illinois Press, 1964.

Edinger, Lewis J. "Continuity and Change in the Background of German Decision-Makers," *The Western Political Quarterly.* 14:1 (March 1961), 17–36.

Edinger, Lewis J. *Kurt Schumacher: A Study in Personality and Political Behavior.* Stanford, Calif.: Stanford University Press, 1965.

Edinger, Lewis J., editor. *Political Leadership in Industrialized Societies: Studies in Comparative Analysis.* New York: John Wiley & Sons, 1967.

Edinger, Lewis J. "Political Science and Political Biography: Reflections on the Study of Leadership," *The Journal of Politics.* 26:2 (May 1964), 423–439; and 26:3 (August 1964), 648–676.

Edinger, Lewis J. "Post-Totalitarian Leadership: Elites in the German Federal Republic," *The American Political Science Review.* 54:1 (March 1960), 58–82.

Edinger, Lewis J., and Donald D. Searing. "Social Background in Elite Analysis: A Methodological Inquiry," *The American Political Science Review.* 61:2 (June 1967), 428–445.

Ehrlich, Howard J., and Mary Lou Bauer. "Newspaper Citation and Reputation for Community Leadership," *The American Sociological Review.* 30:3 (June 1965), 411–415.

Erikson, Erik H. *Childhood and Society* (2d ed.). New York: W. W. Norton, 1963.

Erikson, Erik H. *Young Man Luther: A Study in Psychoanalysis and History.* New York: W. W. Norton, 1958.

Free, Lloyd A. *Six Allies and a Neutral: A Study of the International Outlooks of Political Leaders in the United States, Britain, France, West Germany, Italy, Japan and India.* Glencoe, Ill.: Free Press, 1959.

Freeman, Linton C., Thomas J. Fararo, Warner Bloomberg, Jr., and Morris H. Sunshine. "Locating Leaders in Local Communities: A Comparison of Some Alternative Approaches," *The American Sociological Review.* 28:5 (October 1963), 791–798.

Frey, Frederick W. *The Turkish Political Elite.* Cambridge, Mass.: M.I.T. Press, 1965.

George, Alexander L., and Juliette L. George. *Woodrow Wilson and Colonel House: A Personality Study.* New York: John Day, 1956.

Gorden, Morton, and Daniel Lerner. "The Setting for European Arms Controls: Political and Strategic Choices of European Elites," *The Journal of Conflict Resolution.* 9:4 (December 1965), 419–433.

Greenstein, Fred I. "The Impact of Personality on Politics: An Attempt to Clear Away Underbrush," *The American Political Science Review.* 61:3 (September 1967), 629–641.

Greenstein, Fred I. *Personality and Politics: Problems of Evidence, Inference and Conceptualization.* Chicago, Ill.: Markham Publishing Company, 1969.

Hanhardt, Arthur M., Jr., and William A. Welsh. "The Intellectuals-Politics Nexus: Studies Using a Biographical Technique," *The American Behavioral Scientist.* 7:7 (March 1964), 3–7.

Henkels, Walter. *111 Bonner Köpfe.* Düsseldorf and Wien: Econ Verlag, 1968.

Hunt, William H., Wilder W. Crane, and John C. Wahlke. "Interviewing Political Elites in Cross-Cultural Comparative Research," *The American Journal of Sociology.* 70:1 (July 1964), 59–68.

Hunter, Floyd. *Community Power Structure: A Study of Decision Makers.* Chapel Hill: University of North Carolina Press, 1953.

Kahl, Joseph A. *The American Class Structure.* New York: Holt, Rinehart and Winston, 1961.

Katz, Elihu, and Paul F. Lazarsfeld. *Personal Influence: The Part Played by People in the Flow of Mass Communications.* Glencoe, Ill.: Free Press, 1955.

Keesing, Felix M., and Marie M. Keesing. *Elite Communication in Samoa: A Study of Leadership.* Stanford, Calif.: Stanford University Press, 1956.

Keller, Suzanne. *Beyond the Ruling Class: Strategic Elites in Modern Society.* New York: Random House, 1963.

Kelman, Herbert C., editor. *International Behavior: A Social-Psychological Analysis.* New York: Holt, Rinehart and Winston, 1965.

Kolabinską, Marie. *La circulation des élites en France: Etude historique depuis la fin du XIe siècle jusqu'à la Grande Révolution.* Lausanne: Imprimeries Réunies, 1912.

Lamb, Robert K. Analysis of Eighteenth-Century American Elites. In Deutsch (1966), pp. 32–36.

Lane, Robert E. "Elite Communication and the Governmental Process: Samoa and the United States," *World Politics.* 10:3 (April 1958), 430–437.

Lane, Robert E. *Political Ideology: Why the American Common Man Believes What He Does.* New York: Free Press of Glencoe, 1962.

Lasswell, Harold D. *The Decision Process: Seven Categories of Functional Analysis.* College Park: Bureau of Governmental Research, College of Business and Public Administration, University of Maryland, 1956.

Lasswell, Harold D., and Abraham Kaplan. *Power and Society: A Framework for Political Inquiry.* New Haven: Yale University Press, 1950.

Lasswell, Harold D., and Daniel Lerner, editors. *World Revolutionary Elites: Studies in Coercive Ideological Movements.* Cambridge, Mass.: M.I.T. Press, 1965.

Lasswell, Harold D., Daniel Lerner, and C. Easton Rothwell. *The Comparative Study of Elites.* Stanford, Calif.: Stanford University Press, 1952.

Leites, Nathan. *On the Game of Politics in France.* Stanford, Calif.: Stanford University Press, 1959.

Leites, Nathan. *The Operational Code of the Politburo.* New York: McGraw-Hill, 1951.

Lerner, Daniel. "Interviewing Frenchmen," *The American Journal of Sociology.* 62:2 (September 1956), 187–194.

Lerner, Daniel, with the collaboration of Ithiel de Sola Pool and George K. Schueller. *The Nazi Elite.* Stanford, Calif.: Stanford University Press, 1951. Reprinted in Lasswell & Lerner (1965), pp. 194–318.

Lerner, Daniel, and Morton Gorden. *Euratlantica: The Changing Perspectives of the European Elites.* Cambridge, Mass.: M.I.T. Press, 1969.

Linz, Juan J., and Amando de Miguel. "Within-Nation Differences and Comparisons: The Eight Spains." In Merritt & Rokkan (1966), pp. 267–319.

Maletzke, Gerhard, editor. *Interkulturelle Kommunikation zwischen Industrieländern und Entwicklungsländern: Ein internationales Symposium des Deutschen Instituts für Entwicklungspolitik.* Berlin: Deutsches Institut für Entwicklungspolitik, 1967.

Matthews, Donald R. *The Social Background of Political Decision Makers.* Garden City, N.Y.: Doubleday & Company, 1954.

Matthews, Donald R. *U.S. Senators and Their World.* Chapel Hill: University of North Carolina Press, 1960.

Merritt, Richard L. "Foreign Contacts and Attitude Change: Educational Exchange." In Maletzke (1967), pp. 311–355.

Merritt, Richard L. "The Representational Model in Cross-National Content Analysis." In Bernd (1966), pp. 44–71.

Merritt, Richard L., and Donald J. Puchala, editors. *Western European Perspectives on International Affairs: Public Opinion Studies and Evaluations.* New York: Frederick A. Praeger, 1968.

Merritt, Richard L., and Stein Rokkan, editors. *Comparing Nations: The Use of Quantitative Data in Cross-National Research.* New Haven and London: Yale University Press, 1966.

Mills, C. Wright. *The Power Elite.* New York: Oxford University Press, 1956.

Mosca, Gaetano. *The Ruling Class.* Translator Hannah D. Kahn; editor Arthur Livingston. New York: McGraw-Hill Book Company, 1939.

Moskos, Charles C., Jr. "Attitudes toward Political Independence" [1967a]. In Bell (1967), pp. 49–67.

Moskos, Charles C., Jr. *The Sociology of Political Independence: A Study of Nationalist Attitudes among West Indian Leaders.* Cambridge, Mass.: Schenkman Publishing Company, Inc., 1967b.

Osgood, Charles E., George J. Suci, and Percy H. Tannenbaum. *The Measurement of Meaning.* Urbana: University of Illinois Press, 1957.

Oxaal, Ivar. *Black Intellectuals Come to Power: The Rise of Creole Nationalism in Trinidad and Tobago.* Cambridge, Mass.: Schenkman Publishing Company, Inc., 1968.

Pareto, Vilfredo. *The Mind and Society: A Treatise on General Sociology* (4 volumes). Tranlators Andrew Bongiorno and Arthur Livingston with James Harvey Rogers; editor Arthur Livingston. New York: Harcourt, Brace and Co., 1935.

Parsons, Talcott, and Neil J. Smelser. *Economy and Society: A Study in the Integration of Economic and Social Theory.* Glencoe, Ill.: Free Press, 1956.

Robinson, James A. "Survey Interviewing Among Members of Congress," *The Public Opinion Quarterly.* 24:1 (Spring 1960), 127–138.

Roghmann, Klaus. *Dogmatismus und Autoritarismus: Kritik der theoretischen Ansätze und Ergebnisse dreier westdeutscher Untersuchungen.* Meisenheim am Glan: Verlag Anton Hain, 1966.

Rogow, Arnold A., and Harold D. Lasswell. *Power, Corruption, and Rectitude.* Englewood Cliffs, N.J.: Prentice-Hall, Inc., © 1963.

Rokeach, Milton. *The Open and Closed Mind: Investigations into the Nature of Belief Systems and Personality Systems.* New York: Basic Books, 1960.

Rosenau, James N. *National Leadership and Foreign Policy: A Case Study in the Mobilization of Public Support.* Princeton, N.J.: Princeton University Press, 1963.

Rosenau, James N. "Private Preferences and Political Responsibilities: The Relative Potency of Individual and Role Variables in the Behavior of U.S. Senators." In J. D. Singer (1967).

Schueller, George K. *The Politburo.* Stanford, Calif.: Stanford University Press, 1951. Reprinted in Lasswell & Lerner (1965), pp. 97–178.

Searing, Donald D. "The Comparative Study of Elite Socialization," *Comparative Political Studies.* 1:4 (January 1969), 471–500.

Seligman, Lester G. *Leadership in a New Nation.* New York: Atherton, 1964.

Sereno, Renzo. *The Rulers.* New York: Frederick A. Praeger, 1962.

Singer, J. David, editor. *Quantitative International Politics: Insights and Evidence.* New York: Free Press of Glencoe, 1967.

Singer, Marshall R. *The Emerging Elite: A Study of Political Leadership in Ceylon.* Cambridge, Mass.: M.I.T. Press, 1964.

Snyder, Richard C., H. W. Bruck, and Burton Sapin, editors. *Foreign Policy Decision Making: An Approach to the Study of International Politics.* New York: Free Press of Glencoe, 1962.

Stone, Philip J., Dexter C. Dunphy, Marshall S. Smith, and Daniel M. Ogilvie. *The General Inquirer: A Computer Approach to Content Analysis.* Cambridge, Mass.: M.I.T. Press, 1966.

Thompson, Victor A. *Modern Organization.* New York: Alfred A. Knopf, 1961.

Wahlke, John C., Heinz Eulau, William Buchanan, and LeRoy C. Ferguson. *The Legislative System: Explorations in Legislative Behavior.* New York and London: John Wiley & Sons, 1962.

Walton, John. "Discipline, Method, and Community Power: A Note on the Sociology of Knowledge," *The American Sociological Review.* 31:5 (October 1966a), 684–689.

Walton, John. "Substance and Artifact: The Current Status of Research on Community Power Structure," *The American Journal of Sociology.* 71:4 (January 1966b), 430–438.

Warner, W. Lloyd, Paul P. Van Riper, Norman H. Martin, and Orvis F. Collins. *The American Federal Executive.* New Haven and London: Yale University Press, 1963.

Wilkinson, Rupert. "Political Leadership and the Late Victorian Public School," *The British Journal of Sociology.* 13:4 (December 1962), 320–330.

Wolfenstein, E. Victor. *The Revolutionary Personality: Lenin, Trotsky, Gandhi.* Princeton, N.J.: Princeton University Press, 1967a.

Wolfenstein, E. Victor. "Some Psychological Aspects of Crisis Leaders" [1967b]. In Edinger (1967), pp. 155–181.

Wolfinger, Raymond E. "Reputation and Reality in the Study of 'Community Power,'" *The American Sociological Review.* 25:5 (October 1960), 636–644.

Zapf, Wolfgang. *Wandlungen der deutschen Elite: Ein Zirkulationsmodell deutscher Führungsgruppen, 1919–1961.* München: R. Piper Verlag, 1965.

Zelan, Joseph. "Social Origins and the Recruitment of American Lawyers," *The British Journal of Sociology.* 18:1 (March 1967), 45–54.

5

CROSS-NATIONAL
SURVEY RESEARCH

Social scientists and the general citizenry have grown increasingly sophisticated about public opinion surveying. They have seen poll data flashed in their faces by candidates eager for public office, have heard their leaders citing such data in policy statements, and have learned that different surveying techniques and slightly different questions may well produce apparently contradictory responses. Public opinion surveying has become a fact of our political life, whether we are merely citizens trying to carry out our civic responsibilities or social scientists interested in the analysis of politics. Its very familiarity as a research tool obviates a lengthy discussion here of its methodology (see Stephan & McCarthy, 1958; Backstrom & Hursh, 1963; Glock, 1967; Rosenberg, 1968).

Procedures for Survey Research

The assumptions underlying survey research are simple enough. First, it is important to know what a population's perspectives are (Lane & Sears, 1964). The reasons for wanting to know these vary: The candidate may be interested in finding those issues on which he enjoys considerable support in his constituency so that he can stress them in his campaign; the town official may be interested in the public view as a guide to policy on such diverse issues as urban renewal, school reform, and open housing; the social scientist may be interested in the relationship between a population's perspectives and its behavior. A second assumption is that it is possible to question people about their perspectives and get meaningful responses. This does not mean that the set of responses given by any single individual mirrors accurately and completely his "true" perspectives (see Bogart, 1967). Our concern is rather with the larger groups of which the respondent is a member and for which distributions of responses will be more accurate. Nor does what a person says about how he behaves have an unvarying relationship with his actual behavior (Williams, 1959). Sample surveys have nonetheless proved useful for predicting human behavior in some circumstances (Sheatsley & Hyman, 1953; Pool, Abelson & Popkin, 1965). Third, a well-chosen sample can serve as a substitute for an entire population. To find out how 100 million American voters regard a set of issues, it is not necessary to interview each and every one of them. A carefully designed sample of perhaps 1,500 persons can give us much of the information we need.

Before discussing the peculiarly cross-national aspects of survey research, and the more important cross-national studies (see Rokkan & Verba, 1969), a brief summary of some of the key procedures of survey research may be helpful. These include the formulation of hypotheses, the selection of an appropriate sample of respondents, the preparation of questionnaires, techniques for interviewing respondents, and the analysis of the data produced by the survey.

The Formulation of Hypotheses. At the outset of any research project is the task of defining what it is the researcher wants to know. As I have indicated in previous chapters, he usually proceeds from a set of hypotheses—formulated either as propositions for empirical testing or as hunches that knowledge on a particular point would be relevant for the researcher's interests. Then arises the serious question of whether or not survey research is the most appropriate means to provide answers. The high state of development of this tool has made it attractive for some who might have found better ways to answer their research questions. The expense in research time and money and a plethora of technical problems notwithstanding, survey research appears to be an overused research technique.

Selection of a Sample. Once the researcher has selected the population (college students, registered voters, residents of a particular city) in which he is interested, the next task is to determine means to draw an appropriate sample of them (Deming, 1944; Mosteller, Hyman, McCarthy, Marks & Truman, 1949; Deming, 1950; Hyman, 1955; Scheuch, 1956; Stephan & McCarthy, 1958; Kish, 1965; Scheuch, 1967).

One method is the *simple random* sample. It is particularly useful when the population to be sampled is small or concentrated in a single area. In this case, the researcher selects every *n*th person or uses a table of random numbers to select respondents from a complete listing of the entire population. A directory of students enrolled at a university, a voting list, or a municipal directory might serve this purpose—but not, for instance, a telephone directory, since not everyone is listed in it and since ownership of a telephone may imply something about the socio-economic status of the potential respondent.

If the researcher knows something about the distribution of characteristics within the population, he can use a *stratified random* sample. He can sort college students according to their year in school and take a random sample of each group, making certain that the proportions of each in his sample correspond to the overall distribution of students by school year at the university. Where voters register their party affiliation, the researcher can take separate subsamples for each party. Stratifying a sample is particularly important when the population is large, when it is an entire nation, for example. For any population, however, the success of the stratification rests upon the efficiency of its social bookkeeping. The relatively low reliability of censuses in developing countries imposes severe restraints upon survey researchers operating there (Crespi, 1957; Lerner, 1958a; Girard, 1963; Mitchell, 1965). But even in highly industrialized societies time lags between a census and the revision of a nationwide sample can produce sampling error; or else different agencies may use differing population bases for their sample (Wilson, 1950; Abrams, 1965).

Some agencies use *quota* samples of national populations (see, for example, Noelle, 1963). The sampling procedure first of all determines the distribution of the population in terms of sex, age, race, religion, political affiliation, and other relevant variables. Instructions to the interviewer then specify in some detail the type of respondents he is to search out. Of the twelve respondents that comprise his quota, and whom *he* is to locate, for instance, six must be men; seven Protestant, four Catholic, and one Jewish; four Democratic, three Republican, five independent; and so forth. The advantages of the quota system are great, primarily because it permits the agency to operate rapidly and relatively cheaply (Hochstim & Smith, 1948). The major disadvantage is that it leaves in the hands of interviewers decisions that many (such as Scheuch, 1967) would prefer to see made under more controlled conditions.

Most typically, academic survey researchers use a *cluster* sample, as do many commercial agencies (Perry, 1962). They divide an entire country into types of communities (metropolitan regions, rural towns, and so forth), each area into blocks of dwelling units, and each block into individual households. At each stage, random sampling determines which area, block, or household will be part of the sample. In principle, each household has an equally probable chance of selection; in practice, once the research center has selected its areas (although not its blocks and households), it keeps its interviewers there rather than choosing new areas for each new survey. Some agencies subsequently manipulate the sample slightly—either dropping some respondents or giving a double weight to the response of others, in order to bring the final sample into line with the theoretical distribution of population characteristics according to census data (see, for example, Almond & Verba, 1963, pp. 514–516).

A question frequently asked is, how large must the sample be to reflect accurately the distribution of perspectives within the larger population of which it is a part? There is no inherently valid answer to this question. The size of the sample depends upon several factors. The first of these, of course, is the accuracy both of the sampling procedure and its implementation in the field. The pre-election polls in the 1948 presidential election went awry because of an accumulation of small errors, such as the tendency of interviewers, when asked to interview one resident of an apartment house, to knock on a door on the ground level rather than climbing stairs to the top level (Mosteller, Hyman, McCarthy, Marks & Truman, 1949). Second is the question of the type of data needed. If we are interested solely in the general characteristics of the population at large, then for the United States a sample of 1,500 may be adequate, and for West Germany a sample size of 1,000 may suffice. If, however, we want to make equally reliable breakdowns of the responses according to subgroups within the population (such as to contrast the perspectives of middle-class, Catholic residents of a metropolitan center with those of lower-class, Protestant inhabitants of rural communities), then the size of the sample must be larger. In one imaginative effort to utilize studies with normal-sized samples to get at the perspectives of 480 distinct groups within the American population, Ithiel de Sola Pool, Robert P. Abelson, and Samuel Popkin (1965; see also Roos & Roos, 1967; Rosenthal, 1967) combined more than a hundred separate surveys conducted over the period of several years. Third, and implicit in the above, is the amount of error that the researcher is willing to tolerate (Marks, 1962). If his interests demand results that are accurate to the 99 per cent level of probability (that is, in 100 surveys using the same sampling design, 99 of them would produce results without statistically significant differences), then the size of his sample will have to be considerably larger than if he were satisfied with only a 95 per cent level of accuracy.

Despite the best of sampling designs, there are some cases where the nonresponse rates (that is, the percentage of intended respondents who refuse to be interviewed or whom the interviewer cannot locate) preclude the possibility of an unbiased sample or where, for one reason or another, the researcher deliberately selects a sample not completely representative of the larger population. "It is important in using these biased samples," Edward A. Suchman (1962, p. 110; see also Lowe & McCormick, 1955; Cannell & Fowler, 1963) has warned, "to remember not to generalize to population cross-sections." In these cases, the emphasis must be "upon the phenomenon being studied and not upon its distribution in the general population."

Preparation of a Questionnaire. Drafting a schedule of questions poses several problems (Payne, 1951). First of all, should the questions be closed-ended or open-ended? The former calls for the respondent to select from among a restricted choice of responses. One type of closed-ended question asks for a response of yes or no. Another seeks the respondent's preferred candidate for an electoral office. Still another presents the respondent with a list of topics (or expressions of opinion on a topic) and asks in which of them he is interested or with which he concurs. This type of question has the advantage of facility. The interviewer usually has little difficulty interpreting the response and placing it into the proper response category on the questionnaire, and the resulting data are in such a form that the analyst can process them quickly and easily. By way of contrast, a typical open-ended question might be, What is it that you like about candidate x? The respondent can give any sort of answer that he deems appropriate. If closed-ended questions have facility to commend them, then open-ended questions have the advantage of flexibility. The person who drafts the questionnaire does not have to anticipate in advance all or most conceivable answers to a question. Similarly, the respondent can express subtle qualifications in his comments. But the problems of accuracy both in the interviewer's recording of the response and in the analyst's coding of the recorded response increase commensurately (Wispé & Thayer, 1954). The issues entailed in this latter task are the same as those encountered in the content analysis of written or other communications, discussed in an earlier chapter.

A second concern is the wording of questions. Questions that are only slightly different may lead the same set of respondents (or comparable samples) to give different answers. In the mid 1950s, the United States Information Agency decided to change the response categories to its questions asked in a number of Western European countries, what is your opinion of country x? In surveys from 1954 to 1956, respondents could express a very good or good opinion of the country in question, a bad or very bad opinion, or else a fair opinion. Beginning in 1956 the middle response category available for those reluctant to express either a good or a bad opinion of the country was a neither good nor bad opinion. The USIA then gave both wordings to comparable samples of the populations in four countries to see whether or not significantly different sets of responses emerged. In fact, this was the case only in Great Britain, where, in seven cases with such split samples, four had response differences significant at the .10 level or better. British respondents seemed to view the term "fair" as having a slightly positive connotation. Deprived of it as a response category, they tended to shift toward the "good" category (Merritt, 1968a). Harry W. O'Neill (1967, pp. 96–97) also reports that, in certain circumstances, "people will not respond consistently to the content of an inventory or questionnaire when that content is presented in alternate forms," such as, for example, when the same question is phrased both positively and negatively. The unscrupulous survey researcher, needless to say, can frame his questions in such a way as to increase the probability that he will elicit the desired responses. Or, in a more constructive sense, as Suchman (1962, p. 110) notes, "the deliberate use of biased instruments may be desirable when one wishes greater precision among extreme groups, where only a biased wording results in further discriminations." For all practical purposes, however, imprecision rather than deliberate distortion is the most likely source of error in the surveys we use for political analysis.

Third, since the questionnaire is a framework for getting information, the sequence in which questions are asked can be extremely important (Metzner & Mann, 1953; Becker, 1954). Answers to one question condition the responses to subsequent questions. If a question about arms control precedes a general question about the political issues that the respondent perceives to be important, then we may expect an unusually large number of answers to the latter question to pertain to arms control. Similarly, presented with a list of items from which to choose, the typical respondent tends to opt for those at the top of the list; hence it may be important to prepare a set of questionnaires with different orderings of such lists.

Related is the fact that some types of questions inhibit respondents. Any set of questions may fluster the unsophisticated interviewee, of course, but even people used to public opinion polling may boggle at complexly worded items in an interview. If the first questions on the survey are too difficult to answer, the respondent may become discouraged or apathetic about the remaining questions. Conceivably, embarrassing questions (on the respondent's income or sex life, for example) may arouse his hostility, possibly producing an early end to the interview. So, too, may those questions that would force the respondent, if he gave a truthful answer, to make explicit his unorthodox views. Ray E. Carter, Jr., and F. Gerald Kline (1966), for instance, reported data from matched-group field experiments conducted in Concepción, Chile, and in two neighborhoods in Minnesota supporting "the hypothesis that a secret-ballot interviewing procedure not only would reduce no-answer rates in a pre-election survey, but would also produce larger and more accurate estimates of voting preferences for candidates who had been portrayed as representing political extremes, right or left" (p. 7).

Although many of these issues are technical, care in the framing of questions is extremely important. Empathy with potential respondents may help those drafting the questionnaire, but flexibility is also important—flexibility on the part of interviewers who can note the subtleties of responses, and flexibility on the part of the researcher who processes and analyzes the data.

Field Techniques. The link between the well-designed questionnaire and the carefully drawn sample is the interviewer (Hyman, 1954; Kahn & Cannell, 1957; Hauck & Steinkemp, 1964; Sudman, 1966–1967). A well-trained staff of interviewers can literally make the difference between the successful and the unsuccessful project, particularly when the survey is of a relatively unsophisticated population such as in a developing country (Stycos, 1955; Crespi, 1957; Lerner, 1958a; Frey, 1963; Girard, 1963). Here serveral points are central.

Especially important is the availability of a field staff with trained interviewers (Lewis & Crossley, 1964). Research centers that conduct surveys on a continuing basis find a permanent field staff to be imperative. The scholar who is trying to conduct his own survey, however, may seek to rely upon his colleagues or students as interviewers. This may be a useful educational device for those doing the interviewing, but it is likely to produce considerable discrepancy in the results. The availability of a trained field staff facilitates flexibility in surveys: After a major disaster, such as the assassination of a leading political figure or the occurrence of an international incident, a research center can get its questionnaires into the field very quickly.

Training interviewers is a lengthy and expensive but absolutely necessary task (Cahalan, Tamulonis & Verner, 1947; Anderson, 1952). Some centers have training institutes to which they bring potential interviewers. Others have their field staff train new recruits. In at least one case, however, the research center selects and trains its interviewers by mail, relying on checks built into the practice questionnaires to test the individual interviewer's honesty and reliability. Asking questions, in any event, is an art that must be learned; systematic training procedures are needed to produce interviewers who can carry out field instructions adequately (see Crespi, 1945–1946; Evans, 1961; Olmsted, 1962).

The individual characteristics of the interviewer also make a difference. For one thing, survey research centers in the United States have found that certain types of individuals are more likely than others to become better interviewers. Middle-aged, moderately intelligent housewives seem to be best suited for interviewing, in the sense of both presenting a nonthreatening image to the respondent and filling out the questionnaires properly; college students are more likely to phrase questions or to give other clues that bias the respondent's answers.

Second, the personal appearance of the interviewer can contribute to imprecision in the responses. Aaron M. Bindman (1965; see also Axelrod, Matthews & Prothro, 1962; and Dohrenwend, Colombotos, & Dohrenwend, 1968) found that in some instances black respondents in a small midwestern town gave varying responses to black and white interviewers. He concluded that neither set of responses represented the truth as far as the sample was concerned, but rather two versions of it: "The respondents were far from absolutely sure of their own attitudes as they examined the different perceptions of their 'social responsibility,' and the alternate possible choice of answers, in the presence of the Negro and white interviewers" (p. 288). One can also imagine that the well-dressed, college-educated interviewer might not get the same responses from slum dwellers as would someone closer to their own social class.

Finally, the interviewer's own perspectives may get in the way of accuracy. Herbert H. Hyman and his associates (Hyman, 1954, pp. 196–197, 255–256) found that interviewers tended to distort in the direction of their own policy preferences the statements of respondents on such topics as conscription and the Henry Wallace campaign of 1948, with differences between opinions recorded by two independent groups of interviewers ranging up to 18 per cent. Again, in all these cases, adequate training may help to mitigate the level of error stemming from the personal characteristics of the interviewers.

A word should be added about mail questionnaires. Sometimes the researcher may opt to send questionnaires to his prospective respondents, asking them to fill out the questionnaires and return them (Wallace, 1954). One study (Magid, Fotion & Gold, 1962) used mail questionnaires as an adjunct to their interview survey—to check upon the reliability of interviewers and interviewees alike, and to ask questions that might have been embarrassing enough to destroy rapport in a face-to-face interview (see also McDonagh & Rosenblum, 1965). William A. Glaser (1966) sent mail questionnaires to members of an international nongovernmental organization, since interviewing them individually would have been far too time consuming and expensive. Response rates are frequently quite low. Many studies report 40 to 50 per cent returns, and others still lower, although some researchers (Levine & Gordon, 1958–1959, for example) have reported how care in the preparation of cover letters, questionnaires, and follow-ups enhanced their own response rates. Incidentally, differences between respondents and nonrespondents seem most likely to occur when the questions deal with perspectives rather than with such relatively uncomplicated things as consumer preferences (Robin, 1965).

Data Analysis. The techniques that the researcher uses to analyze his data will, of course, vary. The simplest is the presentation of the frequency distribution of responses—what percentages responded yes, no, and don't know to a particular question. Bivariate analysis may look at the response distributions of different groups within the sample. How do men, as opposed to women, respond to a given question? Or young people as opposed to their elders? Alternatively, it may cross-tabulate the responses to two different questions. What percentage of those responding yes to question x also responded yes to question y? Multivariate techniques are diverse. It is possible to look at the relationship between two variables while holding constant a third variable. That is, if we look at men and women separately (holding the sex variable constant), then what difference does the age of a respondent make with respect to his view on a particular topic? Of growing importance has been the use of scales that combine responses to several questions into a single index. And, more recently, scholars have submitted survey data to factor analysis.

The researcher can make his analytic task considerably easier if he prepares his questionnaire with the analysis routines in mind. At the lowest level this may mean nothing more than the careful enumeration of questions so that the coder can punch IBM cards directly from the questionnaires. At a more sophisticated level it may mean that the researcher deliberately designs the questionnaire with the possibilities for scaling in mind. Thus he might include questions that he would otherwise ignore, in the hope that they would usefully supplement other questions in a scale. And yet, equally clearly, the investigator should not structure his interview or questionnaire in such a rigid fashion that he has no flexibility when he turns to analysis. Some questions included solely for the purpose of scaling may be helpful, but too many will surely make the research results somewhat trivial. As in other technical aspects of survey research, the scholar must seek a balance.

Functional Equivalence

Although the issue of functional equivalence arises in every form of comparative research, it is particularly striking in survey research (Duijker, 1955; Girard, 1963; Mitchell, 1965). As Laszlo Radvanyi (1947, p. 32) pointed out, "international opinion surveying can have validity only if the results obtained in different countries are commensurable." The issue of equivalence manifests itself in every stage of a project.

Conceptualization. Functional equivalence is critical at the stage of hypothesis formulation. With Robert O. Blood, Jr., and Yuzuru John Takeshita (1964) we can distinguish among three types of nonequivalence at this conceptual level. First, there is *pragmatic* nonequivalence. Some countries simply do not have phenomena common in others. It would be just as senseless to ask villagers of northern India about their television-viewing habits as it would be to ask a cross-section of American children whether they found coal or a gift in their shoes on the morning of December sixth, celebrated in some European countries as St. Nicholas' Day.

Second is nonequivalent *variability.* On the one hand, variations in a pattern among one population may be irrelevant for another population. Such is the case with patterns of companionship, important in the study of American family life but not germane for analyzing family life in Japan (Blood & Takeshita, 1964, p. 338). Similarly, except for Quakers and other groups that sometimes distinguish between "you" and "thou," the *"Sie-Du"* variation that confounds American students learning German does not exist in modern English. On the other hand, cross-national variability around concepts that appear to be equivalent in two societies can sometimes be misleading. The American patriot, asked his favorite colors, might respond red, white, and blue. We might expect that the functionally equivalent response for a German patriot would be black, red, and gold, the colors on the flags of both the Federal Republic in the west and the German Democratic Republic in the east. But certain types of nationalists (and perhaps some unreconstructed Nazis) might respond red, white, and black, the colors of the house of Hohenzollern. The possible variability in the German response, evident to the respondent regardless of which answer he chooses, points to an underlying ambivalence about recent German history that simply does not exist among most Americans when they review the course of their country's history. Similarly, bullfighting is as much the national sport of

Mexico as baseball is that of the United States. A close examination of their importance for individuals even reveals that "both national sports provide a socially acceptable channel for the expression of hostility toward authority" (Zurcher & Meadow, 1967, p. 117). There are nonetheless subtle yet important differences. Bullfighting in Mexico reflects "the cultural centrality of death, dominance, 'personal' relationships, respect for and fear and hatred of authority, and the defense systems of the passive-aggressive character structure." Baseball in America, by way of contrast, reflects "the cultural importance of equality, impersonality, and the defense mechanism of intellectualization." In short, what is different, but appears to serve the same function, may upon closer investigation prove to be serving fundamentally different functions (see Osgood, 1967).

Finally, *normative* nonequivalence may exist either when an activity that is legal in one country is prohibited in another or when an activity legal in both countries is not a proper topic of conversation in one of them. Blood and Takeshita (1964, p. 337) give an interesting example of the former:

> The legalization of induced abortion in Japan enabled Takeshita to ask about it directly. However, its illegal status in the United States prevented Takeshita's predecessors from obtaining equally direct information here. Even if Americans were asked about induced abortion, information about deviant behavior is difficult to secure from respondents. Hence the presumed cross-national gap in frequency of induced abortion made possible by differential legality of the behavior is likely to be widened by differential willingness to report the behavior.

In other situations researchers have been unwilling to jeopardize their entire project by asking tabu questions. Laurence Wylie (1957, p. 115), in his interviews with French villagers in the Vaucluse, found that "it is considered bad taste for a person to discuss his own sex life with anyone else, just as it is in bad taste for anyone to inquire into another person's sexual experiences." Only after long acquaintanceship did he feel free to broach the subject with those of the villagers who understood the scholarly nature of his project. "Even these people, however, firmly changed the subject," Wylie recalled, "whenever my questions took too intimate a turn."

Sampling. Since almost all cross-national surveys are conducted by national surveying agencies working independently in each country, sampling procedures are also a matter of concern. We might expect that sampling procedures appropriate to one country would produce comparable results in another, particularly if the countries are at roughly the same stage of development. Scattered research findings, however, indicate that this is not the case (Mitchell, 1965). Clodwig Kapferer (1964) reported the conclusion reached by the Organization for Economic Cooperation and Development that the procedures for quota sampling used in various European countries were basically noncomparable. Philip Abrams (1965, pp. 17–18), reporting on the production of survey data in Great Britain alone, wrote:

> The research procedures of the agencies conducting surveys are so disparate that any attempt to generalise about the data currently available (unless based on the most scrupulous and searching analysis) is likely to border on the meaningless. To take the two most obvious examples: the majority of commercial research organisations claim to include information on "socio-economic class" as a regular background factor in most of their surveys . . . , and all types of organisation undertake surveys involving "national" samples—but closer study suggests that there is little agreement as to the criteria of socio-economic status between organisations or even as to the proper base for a national sample; thus the same people, especially if they are on the critical manual-nonmanual borderline, may appear in different classes in different surveys; and the two main political opinion polls by drawing their samples differently achieve consistently divergent electoral predictions. . . .

Variations in samples shown by Marten Brouwer's survey (1965) of Western European institutes, 78 of which reported having conducted a total of 2,772 sample surveys in 1963 alone, gives us additional pause for thought on the comparability of sampling procedures.

In a cross-national survey, explicit instructions from the project director may find varying interpretations among the individual surveying agencies. Each usually has a set sampling procedure which it feels is most appropriate to the country in which it operates. An outsider seeking to revise the procedure for a particular project—to interview eighteen-year-olds when the normal sample comprises those aged twenty-one or older, for instance, or to change the basis for clustering—may well encounter staunch resistance. The UNESCO study of international images in nine countries (Buchanan & Cantril, 1953, p. 121) specified that the sample should comprise 1,000 persons—the "usual political cross section, adult men and women." In fact, the actual sample sizes ranged from 942 in the Netherlands to 3,371 in Germany; the German sample comprised residents of the British Zone of Occupation and West Berlin only, the Mexican sample residents of towns with 10,000 or more inhabitants; the French sample excluded Corsica, the Norwegian sample Finmark; and, although most national agencies interviewed persons aged twenty-one or older, the French and Mexican samples included twenty-year-olds as well. Similar variations in samples appear in the study of political attitudes and democracy in five nations by Gabriel A. Almond and Sidney Verba (1963), the USIA's surveys in Western Europe (Merritt & Puchala, 1968), and others.

Variations in the groups sampled can also make a difference. How reasonable is it to equate the perspectives of an American farmer with those of Italian or French peasants? Is the American university professor truly comparable to a German university professor? In such cases, the researcher must take into account differences in the roles played or functions performed by groups that, on the surface anyway, may seem to be the same (Barthes, 1957). Similarly, societal conditions may make other distinctions misleading. Is "married" the same in a Catholic and a non-Catholic country, or in those Moslem countries that permit polygamy? Can age categories be the same in countries where life expectancy differs, where ages of the majority are not the same, where attitudes toward youth and old age differ? In these cases the analyst must be familiar with cultural variations that may not be at all obvious to the casual observer.

Questionnaires. The preparation of questionnaires for cross-national surveys poses several levels of problems. The simplest level is literal equivalence (Ervin & Bower, 1952–1953): Is the question translated accurately? A common way of checking this is to have, let us say, a native French-speaker translate the questionnaire from English into French, and then have a native English-speaker retranslate it into English. If both translations are correct, then the final version should jibe quite closely with the original version. To this point, however, must be added Charles E. Osgood's observation (1967, p. 19) that "back-translation" proves to be "ambiguous with single words," that is, words out of context. For his own project using the semantic differential, "words which were difficult to translate or yielded variable translations in any language were dropped for all."

More complicated is the level of semantics. Does the question as translated tap the same underlying concepts in both sets of respondents? For one thing, a single word or phrase may conjure up a variety of connotations among respondents in different countries. Again Osgood's semantic differential (1967, p. 34) provides a relevant example: "The American politician who uses the concept *future* with his own *good, strong, active* connotations might fail to communicate accurately when he talks to an audience in Finland, where *future* is *good* and *strong,* but *passive.*" Similarly, as noted earlier, directors of the USIA surveys found that their British respondents attached a positive meaning to the term "fair opinion" that Frenchmen, Germans, and Italians did not to *"opinion moyenne," "mittelmässige Meinung,"* and *"opinione discreta,"* respectively.

The other side of this particular coin is that modes of viewing things vary. "Evaluation," wrote Osgood (1967, p. 34), "is defined, in part, by American English-speakers as *sweet-sour* [that is, along a 7-point scale ranging from "very sweet" to "very sour"], by Lebanese Arabic-speakers as *merciful-cruel,* by Finnish as *light-gloomy,* by Indian Hindi-speakers as *nectarful-poisonous,* by Japanese as *comfortable-uncomfortable,* by Mexican-Spanish speakers as *sympathetic-antipathetic,* and so on." He concluded that "the *metaphors* of 'good-bad' vary with the cultures under consideration."

Another semantic issue arises when a term referring in one culture to a specific concept does not have a precise equivalent in another culture. But, as Joshua A. Fishman (1960, p. 326) has pointed out, "the fact that there is no handy English equivalent for the German *Gemütlichkeit* is rarely explained as an indication that Germans *are* more *gemütlich."* The English-speaker must merely express the concept circumlocutiously, describing it perhaps as a sociable, good-natured, comfortable, and cozy or snug atmosphere.

At a still higher level of complexity, the very structure of language seems to be one determinant (among others) of perceptions and behavior. This hypothesis, advanced first by Edward Sapir, but in its most complete form by Benjamin Lee Whorf, has found some empirical verification in recent years (see Fishman, 1960). Its full implications for the social scientist engaged in cross-national research are, however, not completely clear. If it is true, for instance, that the position of adjectives in sentences tends to make French thinking patterns more deductive and those of English-speakers more inductive, then even the most functionally equivalent questionnaires prepared in the two languages may produce results that are fundamentally noncomparable.

Field Technique. The possibility that nonequivalencies arise in the conduct of the interviews themselves is great. Some stem from the characteristics of the interviewers. Differences in the selection and training of interviewers from one country to the next may cause variations in responses. Or the caste, class status, or ethnicity of the interviewers may create biases (Jones, 1963; Hanna & Hanna, 1966): How successful would a black interviewer be in getting responses from members of Alabama's White Citizens Council? Would a member of an Unscheduled Caste (an Untouchable) be any more successful in interviewing respondents from other Indian castes? In the United States, middle-aged housewives seem to be the most satisfactory interviewers, but what would be the response of Arabs or Latin Americans to the appearance in their doorways of a woman asking questions?

Some groups seem to be relatively inaccessible in even the most carefully designed surveys. For this reason, and also because men were more socially mobilized than women, the Bureau of Applied Social Research consciously oversampled men in its Middle Eastern surveys (Lerner, 1958b). Similarly, the relative inaccessibility of Indians in the Mexican hinterlands (some of whom proved to be quite inhospitable toward interviewers) led the agency conducting interviews for Almond and Verba's five-nation study (1963) to concentrate upon residents of towns with more than 10,000 inhabitants. United States Information Agency efforts to conduct systematic research under wartime conditions in South Vietnam are another example of the problems of accessibility. "It is unlikely," wrote Robert L. Sullivan (1967, p. 447; see also Ramond, 1967), "that researchers anywhere have been faced with such requirements as transporting interviewers around the countryside by helicopter, or carrying out cover interviews in rural villages in order to protect the really selected respondents from Vietcong reprisals."

The interview situation also produces variations in responses. One key aspect is the respondent's attitude toward the interview itself (Hyman, 1947; Sjoberg, 1954–1955; Landsberger & Saavedra, 1967). Daniel Lerner (1958b, pp. 147–148), in contrasting different levels of sophistication among American and Turkish respondents, wrote:

> It is axiomatic among American communication specialists that most Americans are not at all intimidated by opinion surveys which demand their views on great men and great matters well outside their actual experience. . . .
> The contrast with the social psychology of the interview situation among Turks is striking. How little they perceive the essential impersonality of the situation is clear from the excessive preoccupation of Turkish interviewees with what the interviewers might think of them. With extraordinary frequency, for example, interviewers were thanked profusely for their personal interest. Said one 47-year-old illiterate villager after a three-hour interrogation: "You are the nicest *effendi* [roughly, gentleman] I have ever known. No other *effendi* has ever cared to know my thoughts on so many things."

In other places individual and group values lead to an unwillingness to discuss perspectives with interviewers; fear of political reprisal may inhibit respondents; or a "courtesy bias" (Jones, 1963, p. 70) may lead respondents to "express only views which they think the interviewer or investigator wants to hear."

Reactions to the interviewer or his sponsor may also vary. Just as black and white interviewers secure slightly different responses from black residents of a small town in the American midwest (Bindman, 1965), so too the skin color of the interviewer seems to make a difference to the Bantu in the Union of South Africa (Langeschmidt, 1958), Laotians (Fink, 1963), and others. Some sponsorship bias emerged in studies that the American Military Government conducted in postwar Germany (Crespi, 1950). Responses given to interviewers reporting their American sponsorship varied in 1948 by an average of 6.6 per cent (on 38 questions explicitly designed to maximize sponsorship bias) from those given to interviewers who said that they worked for an "independent" German agency. But, with respect to both types of bias, we must again ask which set of responses represented the "truth"—a question that rests upon the fundamental query "Do respondents tell the truth anyway?"

Finally, the timing of a cross-national survey can produce noncomparability. On the one hand, surveys conducted in different countries at different times run into the problem of intervening events. Imagine a survey on international communism that went into the field in France in early October 1956, but not until late November in West Germany. In the intervening weeks both the Suez and the Hungarian crises had occurred, washing out any comparability between the French and the West German results. On the other hand, surveys conducted in different countries simultaneously may encounter vastly different circumstances. In one country the next major election may be just around the corner, and in the other none will take place for another two to three years. We would not be too surprised to find political interest higher in the former case—but it also seems probable that this finding would merely be an artifact of the temporal situation.

Analysis. Problems of functional equivalence at the analytic stage are basically the same as at the conceptualization stage. Two points nonetheless merit further comment. One is that the analyst must exert considerable empathy in interpreting results from a culture other than his own. H. L. Ansbacher (1950, p. 126) provided a striking example of how the analyst's own perspectives can get in his way:

> On the basis of responses given by French, Italian, and Russian workers in wartime Germany, the U.S. Strategic Bombing Survey concluded that the Russians were most anti-German. The same data may be interpreted, however, to mean that the Russian workers were actually more favorable to the Germans than were the other groups. This reinterpretation also appears to fit certain facts now available regarding foreign workers in Germany better than does the interpretation put forward by the Bombing Survey. A possible explanation for the original interpretation is afforded by the theory that new data (including survey data) tend to be incorporated in an existing

cognitive structure. The complexity of international attitudes also contributes to the difficulty of interpreting statements of individuals as to what they think about other national groups.

Second, the analyst should pay attention to within-national differences. That national samples hold similar views may cover up the fact that comparable subsamples (for example, young males) do not (Przeworski & Teune, 1966–1967). If in one democracy the bulk of the anticonstitutional extremists are husky young men and in another they are nice old ladies in white tennis shoes, but the overall level of anticonstitutional extremism is uniformly high in both countries, then we would hardly want to attribute to both the same potential for stability. It is precisely this possibility to study within-nation variations that gives cross-national survey research much of its value (Linz & de Miguel, 1966).

Overall Reliability. Any one of these various types of nonequivalence —conceptual, sampling, questionnaire, field technique, or analytic—can lead the unwary researcher into a trap. It is highly unlikely that any cross-national survey can produce completely equivalent results in all the countries included. But, then, the same problem holds, although in a less severe form, for surveys conducted within a single nation. Concepts may mean different things to different citizens of any country, interviewer effects constitute an important source of bias, and a multitude of other minor or major discrepancies calls into question the reliability of any single survey. Since we know a great deal about the magnitude of error in a domestic survey, however, we are able to evaluate its findings properly.

Cross-national surveys confront a double problem of reliability. Not only is there a question about the reliability of each national survey relative to the population sampled, but there is also the reliability of the procedure from one country to the next. In the case of a national survey conducted by an experienced agency, many small errors may cancel each other out. The types of specifically cross-national problems suggested in the previous paragarphs seem to be cumulative (although, it must be added, relevant research is scattered and far from complete).

Such cross-national nonequivalencies, however, need not be crippling. If the researcher is alert to the ever-present possibility of functional noncomparability, knowledgeable in depth about the countries in which he is conducting his surveys, and ingenious in devising research designs that can get at underlying variables covered up by apparent noncomparability, then his research may well prove fruitful. It may even be the case that his design deviates considerably from nominal equivalence in an effort to secure functional equivalence. Ragnar Rommetveit and

Joachim Israel (1954, p. 68), in their discussion of small group research, even argued that

> conceptually identical experimental conditions, in some cases, can best be established by deliberate and systematic deviations from traditional standardization procedures, e.g., by "objectively" different experimental manipulations designed to rule out the effects of specific, culturally determined situational factors intervening between a set of stimuli and a genotypically defined independent variable.

Ideally, of course, the researcher should strive to ascertain a margin of error for each country included in his survey, together with one for the survey as a whole; such information would greatly facilitate the reader in his task of evaluating the research.

However problematic the issue of functional equivalence has been, scholars interested in aspects of political behavior have clearly demonstrated the usefulness of cross-national surveys. They have used four kinds of research strategy: the initiation of an original survey, with national agencies conducting the surveying under the general direction of the researcher; secondary analyses of such coordinated surveys; replication in a second country of a survey already conducted in one country; and secondary analysis of a variety of uncoordinated surveys. Since these four strategies entail separate problems, the remainder of this chapter will examine each in turn.

Original Analyses

Perhaps most scholars interested in testing their theoretical propositions by means of cross-national attitudinal data would prefer to initiate their own surveys. To do this maximizes the investigator's flexibility in one sense. He can select his own consultants at every stage of the project, specify the countries and populations in which he is interested, try to operationalize the concepts that he considers important and to formulate them in such a way that survey data can test them, determine what questions will comprise the questionnaire, and select and carry through the modes of analysis. And yet, in another sense, the conduct of such a survey imposes severe limitations upon the researcher. Extensive cross-national projects seem to require about four or more years to complete, dozens of collaborators at various stages, financial support amounting to tens if not hundreds of thousands of dollars, and, above all, immense organizational skill. Once the survey instrument has gone into the field, the researcher cannot modify or improve it, except at the cost of initiating a new follow-up survey. On top of this, as the initiators of Project

Camelot learned to their distress, even the most carefully designed research project may encounter political blocks in foreign countries (Horowitz, 1967).

Such problems notwithstanding, a number of significant cross-national surveys mark the recent history of the social sciences. Some of these were commercial ventures, initiated by one of the worldwide networks of polling agencies (Crossley, 1953; Wilson, 1957; Crespi, 1958). In 1946 and again in 1948, for instance, Elmo Roper surveyed several European populations for the American news magazine *Time* (Wallace, Woodward, Stern, Barioux & Ylvisaker, 1948–1949; Stern, 1953). The latter of these (*Time,* 1948) focused on the views of six Western European countries toward several international issues: evaluation of American vs. Soviet strength, hopes for the United Nations, willingness to join a Western European Union, and views on the Marshall Plan. Since the earliest postwar years, the international affiliates of Gallup Polls asked the same questions simultaneously in several countries (see, for example, Adamec, 1947; Gallup International, 1963; Wuelker, 1963; Gallup International, 1967). The *Reader's Digest* (1963) also conducted a politically relevant survey in Great Britain and the countries of the European Economic Community. It dealt with the ownership of specific commodities (automobiles, washing machines) as well as with the future development of the Common Market.

Other original cross-national surveys sprang from the desire of social scientists to know more about people's perspectives and behavior. It is these that comprise the focus of this section.

The UNESCO Tensions Project, 1948. The earliest of the extensive original analyses stemmed from a meeting in 1947 in Mexico City of the UNESCO General Assembly. In a directive to the agency's director-general, the meeting called for systematic studies of "national cultures, ideals, and legal systems," as well as "the ideas which the people of one nation hold concerning their own and other nations." Hadley Cantril, charged with the task of organizing such a cross-national survey project, subsequently designed a questionnaire comprising five types of questions (Buchanan & Cantril, 1953, p. 5):

1. The individual's estimate of his own position in the class structure of his country, and its relation to his view of other people at home and abroad.
2. His feeling of personal security in matters unrelated to international affairs, and his satisfaction with life in his own country.
3. The peoples toward whom he feels friendly or unfriendly.
4. The stereotypes he carries in his head of his own and certain foreign peoples.

SYSTEMATIC APPROACHES TO COMPARATIVE POLITICS

5. His ideas about human nature, peace, world government, and national character.

Other questions asked about the demographic characteristics of the respondent (sex, socioeconomic status, age, education, and occupation) and his general political views. National surveying agencies administered the questionnaires during the last half of 1948 to nationwide samples in nine countries: Australia, France, West Germany (British Zone of Occupation and West Berlin), Great Britain, Italy, the Netherlands, Norway, Mexico, and the United States. And, as indicated earlier, the sample sizes ranged from 942 in the Netherlands to 3,371 in the British Zone of occupied Germany. The project also included a follow-up survey among West Berliners in October 1949.

The design of the UNESCO project was to explore the cognitive maps of the respondents rather than to test specific propositions. Indeed the authors stressed (p. 11, in italics) that theirs was "a pilot study," disclaiming any intent to be more than "descriptive and suggestive." Their analysis consisted of an examination of marginal frequency distributions of responses for the nine countries, cross-tabulations according to demographic characteristics or attitudes, and a few simple scales. An example of the latter is their security index (pp. 26–27). Four questions about the respondents' initial postwar expectations, job security, security sufficient to be able to plan ahead, and general satisfaction formed the basis of the index:

$$SI = \frac{\underset{\text{Expectations}}{\underset{\text{Postwar}}{(\text{worse}-\text{better})}} + \underset{\text{Security}}{\underset{\text{Job}}{(\text{more}-\text{less})}} + \underset{\text{Ahead}}{\underset{\text{Plan}}{(\text{yes}-\text{no})}} + \underset{\text{Satisfaction}}{\underset{\text{General}}{(\text{very}-\text{dissatisfied})}}}{10} + 40.$$

Scores on the security index ranged from 42 for Australia (with Mexico, Norway, and the United States tying for second place at 39) to 20 for France, well below eighth-place Germany, which scored 26.

However modest the intent of the UNESCO survey, and some shortcomings notwithstanding, it made an important contribution to the systematic study of international political communication. First of all, it demonstrated that the respondents in all nine countries had narrow horizons. They usually found salient only those issues affecting them directly, were rather materialistic in their own values, and tended to view international relations through the bottleneck of personal interests. Socioeconomic position and feelings of security strongly conditioned their images of the world. Second, the respondent's friendliness or hostility toward other countries seemed "to be influenced by the proximity of the latter, their language, and the policies of their government which are discernible in the history of their neutrality or military and ideological alliances" (p. 93). The stereotypes used to characterize other nations were rather consistent among all the populations surveyed, and each population viewed its own nation in positive terms. Finally (p. 94),

> Certain ideas about human nature, national characteristics, peace, and world government, with national politics also involved, combine to form a rationale within which the individual views international affairs. Ideas on these topics run in certain patterns so that, knowing an individual's views on one or two of them, one might predict the others with better than chance results, regardless of the individual's nationality. However, these ideas are not consistently related to sex, age, status, and education. They apparently have been influenced by the subject matter of the formal educational system in certain countries.

In this regard two clear patterns emerged in all nine countries. First, "the respondents who 'believe human nature can be changed' are more likely than others to believe that 'it will be possible for all countries to live together in peace with each other' "; and second, "those respondents who believe that such a peace is possible are more likely than others to agree that 'there should be a world government able to control the laws made by each country.' "

A follow-up study in 1956–1957 by Erich Reigrotski and Nels Anderson (1959–1960, p. 528; see also Anderson, 1957; Brouwer, 1965) lent support to the "idea that stereotypes tend to be modified through education and through foreign contact and acquaintance." Reigrotski and Anderson also suggested that there may be a reciprocity between self-images and the stereotypes of others: "The French self-image may be in part an assimilation of the national stereotype of the French held by the Germans, and vice versa."

The OCSR Teachers Survey, 1953. In the first four months of 1953 the Organization for Comparative Social Research interviewed primary and secondary school teachers in seven countries of Western Europe: Belgium, England and Wales, France, the Netherlands, Norway, Sweden, and West Germany (Duijker & Rokkan, 1954). Unlike the UNESCO survey, under centralized direction and relying upon existing commercial agencies to conduct the polling and prepare reports, the OCSR project had three major aims. One was to develop a framework of cooperation among social scientists in Western Europe (Rokkan, 1955a). The project began as a series of seminars sponsored in 1951 by the Institute for Social Research in Oslo, Norway. Within a year the seminars had developed into the OCSR, comprising more than thirty European social scientists and six American professors in Europe on Fulbright grants, as well as an international directorate. The project that emerged was truly an experiment in international cooperation.

SYSTEMATIC APPROACHES TO COMPARATIVE POLITICS

A second aim was to create a set of institutions and procedures that would permit these social scientists to carry out significant cross-national research. Only two of the seven national teams had at their disposal structures already engaged in public opinion surveying. For the rest, according to Eugene Jacobson (1954, p. 40), the OCSR decided,

to use a set of pre-tests or model studies that would permit the national teams to test the equivalence of operations that would be appropriate for the ultimate data gathering and processing in each of the countries, and, at the same time, develop more nearly similar research facilities. It was intended that at the end of the series of pre-tests the teams would be staffed and equipped in comparable fashion and that the questionnaire and content analysis procedures, though perhaps modified to meet situational country demands, would be producing equivalent data.

This procedure produced some difficulties as far as comparability of data was concerned, particularly since each team included country-specific items in its questionnaire. Extensive coordination nonetheless minimized the resulting nonequivalencies.

Third, and not least important, the OCSR project sought to discover something about the political attitudes of Western European teachers. In all the survey included 2,758 teachers, with the sizes of the national samples ranging from 350 in France to 443 in Sweden. Approximately three-quarters of them taught in primary schools, the remainder in secondary schools. Regarding sampling procedure (Jacobson, 1954, p. 44):

The ultimate selection of respondents was the task of the research director, not the interviewers, in all of the countries. Interviewers were furnished either the names of the teachers or the characteristics of classrooms designated unambiguously, and had no opportunity to influence the choice of respondent. The research directors made their selections randomly from lists of teachers or classrooms both for the original sample and for the replacements of sample loss. In replacement, selection was made from strata representing the loss.

Arbitrary limitations on the geographic basis of some of the samples, however, together with large numbers of teachers refusing interviews in France and West Germany, produced a sample not entirely representative of the teachers in the seven countries.

Unfortunately, the OCSR never published its complete set of findings. Some preliminary reviews were nonetheless suggestive. For instance, Vilhelm Aubert, Burton R. Fisher, and Stein Rokkan (1954, p. 32) reported that, in each of the seven countries, teachers

who *could* conceive of circumstances under which a world war would be the "lesser of two evils" [a majority in all countries except France and West

Germany] were more likely to put the blame exclusively on the Soviet bloc, while those who *could not* conceive of any such circumstances were less likely to blame the Soviet bloc and more likely to stress the general features of the bipolar power struggle or, more rarely, the responsibility of the Western powers.

Rokkan (1955b, p. 589) subsequently reported that "in all the countries without exception there is a higher proportion of teachers expressing fear of the Soviet Union as a primary source of danger among the Christian or Conservative party identifiers than among the 'left' identifiers." Other demographic variables did not correlate highly with the respondents' position on the Cold War. The OCSR also found some confirmation for its central hypothesis that persons who perceive an external threat to their nation's security are also those most likely to frown upon dissent in that nation's domestic politics (Rokkan, 1955b, p. 594).

The USIA Surveys. One of the more interesting phenomena in the postwar conduct of American foreign policy has been the emphasis on survey research as a tool for planning policy. This is true not only of the public perspectives of Americans but of those of foreign populations as well. Only hours after American soldiers, in their race to the Elbe, had overrun German cities and villages, social psychologists under Army auspices began interviewing their inhabitants. Of immediate importance were attitudes toward Nazism and, more generally, the potential for resistance to the occupying forces. Later surveys tried to evaluate the effectiveness of American information programs, the acceptability of rationing and other controls, images of American troops (and, in particular, black soldiers), and related issues important for the day-to-day operation of the occupation, the formulation of long-range strategy in the emerging Cold War, and the theoretical concerns of individual researchers (Merritt & Merritt, 1970). Over the next half dozen years the United States Army and the United States Department of State (1951; Brouwer, 1965) greatly expanded their interest in public opinion surveying. They conducted or commissioned literally hundreds of surveys, not only in Germany but throughout Western Europe and the rest of the world.

In September 1952, the USIA, charged with gathering some types of data abroad as well as disseminating information about America and its policies, initiated its first major cross-national survey. It commissioned commercial polling agencies to administer standardized questionnaires in France, West Germany, Italy, the Netherlands, and Great Britain. The focus of this survey was diverse. It included questions on

European integration and the Schuman Plan; attitudes toward the United States and the Soviet Union, toward domestic and international communism; reactions to current proposals for a European Defense Community; the role of Germany in any program for the defense of Europe; and the willingness to trust individual NATO allies in the event of war. What made the survey cohesive was its concern with key foreign policy issues facing the United States.

Twenty-one times since then the USIA has initiated similar polls in Western Europe. The USIA itself, in hearings before a congressional committee in August 1965, outlined the broad scope of its research program, pointing out that such studies sought to determine:

> The basic beliefs and attitudes of the foreign audiences we wish to address;
>
> The current preoccupations and opinions of these peoples in a rapidly changing world;
>
> The attitudes in depth of special foreign audiences we wish especially to persuade;
>
> The communications channels and methods by which we can reach these foreign audiences most effectively; and
>
> The impact of specific USIA programs and products designed to reach, inform, and persuade foreign audiences (cited in Merritt, 1968a, p. 4).

The basic format of the surveys remained quite stable. In each case the survey included at least four countries: France, West Germany, Italy, and Great Britain. This basic pattern was supplemented upon occasion either by the inclusion of another country or two (such as Belgium, the Netherlands, Norway, Denmark, or Austria), or by additional single-country surveys on foreign policy problems particularly relevant to those countries, or by spot checks on reactions to specific events, such as the construction in August 1961 of the Berlin Wall. In each case the USIA's Research and Reference Service staff designed the survey and formulated the questions. This was done in consultation with other departments and agencies of the United States government. Many of the specific questions changed over time, reflecting changes in the problems facing American policy planners. But, whenever it seemed feasible or desirable, the designers of the surveys repeated questions asked in previous surveys, thereby providing a basis for estimating changes over time in Western European perspectives. In each case commercial polling agencies in the individual countries translated the questionnaire (if necessary), drew carefully designed samples of the population, tested the questionnaire in the field, administered it to the samples, and analyzed in a preliminary fashion the results of the survey, leaving more detailed analysis to the Research and Reference Service staff in Washington (Merritt & Puchala, 1968).

Only a few of the USIA reports analyzing these data have found their way into print. The remainder are harbored in files both in Washington and at several major universities. Those that have been published, however, show the immense potentiality that the USIA data hold for cross-national research. One of these is Ralph K. White's analysis (1966) of the semantics of capitalism and socialism. His review of data from several countries in Western Europe revealed that the United States is hurting itself abroad by stressing its supposedly capitalist economic system. For one thing, the Western European image of socialism more adequately approximates the realities of the American system than does their image of capitalism; for another, the term capitalism bears negative connotations in the imagery of Western Europeans whereas the term socialism is positively evaluated. White urged that, in its information programs for audiences abroad, the United States should emphasize the social welfare aspects of its economy. The next section of this chapter will discuss other uses of the USIA data.

The Civic Culture, 1959–1960. The most extensive academic project seeking to build empirical political theory on the basis of an original cross-national survey is the study by Gabriel A. Almond and Sidney Verba (1963) of political attitudes and democracy in five nations. Commercial polling agencies, national affiliates of the International Research Associates, conducted interviews in West Germany, Great Britain, Italy, and Mexico, and the National Opinion Research Center of the University of Chicago interviewed an American sample. The size of the samples ranged from 937 in the United Kingdom to 1,008 in Mexico. As indicated earlier, the Mexican sample poses a special problem of equivalence. Unlike the other samples, it excludes eighteen- to twenty-year-olds, and includes only residents of cities with more than 10,000 inhabitants. Moreover, the polling agency deliberately undersampled Mexico City by one half "in order to allow for greater interior city coverage" and, in the final tabulation, upweighted the Mexico City interviews "by a factor of 2.5 in order to bring them once again to their true proportion within the sample as a whole" (p. 514). (Weighting also raised the British sample from 937 to 963.) The analytic techniques used by Almond and Verba consisted in the presentation of marginal frequency distributions, cross-tabulations, and Guttman scales.

Underlying this study was the concept of political culture, defined as "specifically political orientations—attitudes toward the political system and its various parts, and attitudes toward the role of the self in the system" (p. 13). The term orientation (p. 15)

> refers to the internalized aspects of objects and relationships. It includes (1) "cognitive orientation," that is, knowledge of and belief about the political system, its roles and the incumbents of these roles, its inputs, and its outputs; (2) "affective orientation," or feelings about the political system, its roles, personnel, and performance; and (3) "evaluational orientation," the judgments and opinions about political objects that typically involve the combination of value standards and criteria with information and feelings.

Political culture, for Almond and Verba (p. 33), is "the connecting link between micro- and macropolitics," between "the attitudes and motivations of the discrete individuals who make up political systems and the character and performance of political systems." Their typology contained parochial, subject, participant, and mixed political cultures.

The survey sought to ascertain the respondents' cognitive, affective, and evaluational orientations toward matters political: patterns of political cognition, feelings toward government and politics, patterns of

---

TABLE 5.1
Levels of Subjective Civic Competence, by Nation
(in per cent)

Percent who report	U.S.	U.K.	Germany	Italy	Mexico
National and local competence	67	57	33	25	33
National competence only	8	5	4	2	5
Local competence only	10	21	29	26	19
Neither national nor local competence	15	19	34	47	43
Total per cent	100	100	100	100	100
Total number of cases	970	963	955	995	1,007

Source: Almond & Verba (1963), p. 186.

---

partisanship, sense of obligation to participate in civic life, sense of civic competence, as well as patterns of organizational membership and socialization. The questions on civic competence, for instance, aimed at "the perceptions that individuals have about the amount of influence they can exercise over governmental decisions" at the local and national levels (p. 183). But high levels of civic competence in some countries (Table 5.1) do not mean that individuals actually try to influence such decisions, no more than does a felt obligation to participate in civic life mean that these people actually seek to play a role. Indeed, these two disparities between orientations and behavior, according to Almond and Verba (p. 481) contribute to a democracy's stability:

> The inactivity of the ordinary man and his inability to influence decisions help provide the power that governmental elites need if they are to make decisions. But this maximizes only one of the contradictory goals of a democratic system. The power of the elites must be kept in check. The citizen's opposite role, as an active and influential enforcer of the responsiveness of elites, is maintained by his strong commitments to the norm of active citizenship, as well as by his perception that he can be an influential citizen.

(Erwin K. Scheuch [1965], by way of contrast, suggested that most voters, rather than being apathetic about the fulfillment of norms of participation, are unwilling to let their political beliefs endanger the stability of their family and other primary relationships that are continuing and diffuse. So long as the existence of the political community is not threatened, there is no controversy about what the nature of the political system should be, the distribution of power remains fairly stable, and the purpose of politics is seen to be improvement of rather than struggle against the current structure of government, then, said Scheuch, the voters will view government as a form of administration of the community in which active participation can be reduced to a minimum.)

Almond and Verba found that the five democracies have substantially different political cultures. "The picture of Italian political culture" that emerged from their data, they wrote (p. 402), "is one of relatively unrelieved political alienation and of social isolation and distrust." Alienation together with democratic aspiration characterized the Mexican political culture. Among Germans, they noted (p. 429), "awareness of politics and political activity, though substantial, tend to be passive and formal." "Germans tend to be satisfied with the performance of their government, but to lack a more general attachment to the system on the symbolic level"—a situation that could prove problematic should the government, for whatever reason, be unable to produce a satisfactory performance. The United States, they observed, has a participant civic culture. That is, "the role of the participant is highly developed and widespread," Americans "tend to be affectively involved in the political system," and "their attachment to the political system includes both generalized system affect as well as satisfaction with specific governmental performance" (p. 440). Indeed, the United States comes closest of the five democracies to being the mixed and incorporative culture identified by Almond and Verba as the civic culture, in which, as the previous paragraph suggested, "the participant role is highly developed, but the more passive roles of subject and parochial persist, and are fused with the political system." Great Britain has more of a deferential civic culture (p. 455): "Despite the spread of political competence and participant orientations, the British have maintained a strong deference to the independent authority of government."

Other Original Surveys. In studying the "politics of despair" in postwar France and Italy, Hadley Cantril (1958) commissioned two national sample surveys in each country—one in November 1955, and the second in the late winter of 1956–1957, shortly after the ruthless Soviet suppression of the Hungarian uprising. The latter survey oversampled Communists, to permit a more refined analysis of their perspectives. Among other things, the project demonstrated the stability of images in the face of countervailing information. Although news of the Soviet action, widely reported in the Western European news media, staggered some Communist party members and sympathizers, the bulk belonged to relatively stable human networks, both formal and informal, that resisted the negative information conveyed about the Soviet Union and encouraged the restoration of a favorable image of that country. Even among those who defected from the party as a consequence of the Soviet action, the overwhelming majority, according to Cantril (p. 196), "still regard themselves as Marxists and will probably still vote for the Communist Party." He concluded (p. 187):

> These survey data reveal that the Hungarian revolt unquestionably was something quite different for different people. What people believed the Hungarian uprising to be apparently depended upon the particular significances they saw. And these significances were determined by the assumptions they brought to the series of happenings that constituted the uprising for them.

And, of course, for students of cross-national political behavior, a particularly interesting finding is that differences in party identification were more significant than national differences among the respondents.

Cantril subsequently undertook an ingenious cross-national survey (1965) aimed at uncovering people's hopes and fears, aspirations and sense of accomplishment for both themselves and their countries. In all, national research teams in 14 countries interviewed 18,663 individuals (adjusted upward to 33,337 to account for undersampling in rural regions and other problems). In addition to asking a battery of questions about background, hopes, and fears, interviewers presented respondents with a visual scale, drawn to resemble a ladder with ten rungs. Respondents were asked to imagine at the top of the ladder the best possible life they could have. The worst possible life, then, would be at the bottom. Respondents then rated themselves on this self-anchoring ladder according to where they saw themselves standing at the time of the interview, where they had been five years earlier, and where they expected to be in the future. They also rated their countries on this ladder over the same ten-year time span. The ratings were, of course, subjective (p. 25): "All ratings are anchored within an individual's own reality world." In this sense they are not directly comparable in terms of any objective scale of income, social status, or achievement. What is more relevant in this survey is the possibility to compare how people think they are doing in terms of their own aspirations and accomplishments, their outlooks on life, and the degree to which they are satisfied with themselves and the world in which they live.

Upon occasion, as indicated earlier, the worldwide affiliates of the Gallup Polls coordinate their efforts to get an estimate of cross-national opinion on particular topics. One of the more extensive of these international surveys stemmed from the request of the Press and Information Services of the European Communities (Gallup International, 1963). In February and March, 1962, Gallup affiliates surveyed national samples in the Europe of the Six—Belgium, France, West Germany, Italy, Luxembourg, and the Netherlands—to get their views on European unification. Three points are of particular interest. First, although there was widespread support for the idea of a united Europe, it seemed to enjoy little salience among the respondents. Second, there was considerable divergence in their expectations about what unification would bring. The French stressed a third bloc to balance the United States and the Soviet Union; the Germans, strengthening of the West vis-à-vis the communist bloc; the Dutch, national prosperity; the Italians, improved individual standards of living. Only a minority in each country emphasized intellectual, spiritual, and humanistic (as opposed to materialistic) progress. Finally, a breakdown of attitudes according to the demographic characteristics of the respondents revealed less disagreement than a glance at national averages might have suggested (Table 5.2). Indeed, widespread consensus existed among those population groups perhaps most instrumental in encouraging or discouraging further steps toward European unity: Education and socioeconomic status correlate highly with positive views toward European unity. Women were both less interested and less knowledgeable than men. Contrary to some expectations young people were not more enthusiastic than their elders. And, in all five countries, those who had travelled abroad during the previous ten years held a distinctly more "European" perspective. This finding led the investigators to support the idea that increased intra-European travel among citizens of the Six would enhance their predispositions toward European unification.

TABLE 5.2
Attitudes Toward European Unity Among Some Population Groups
Percentage "strongly in favor" of European Unity

	Belgium	France	Germany	Italy	Netherlands
The highly educated	64	57	73	69	70
The high income groups	45	44	61	63	69
The industrialists and the professional classes	50	47	58	65	78
Average of "elite" groups	53	49	64	66	72
National average	31	28	50	36	62
Difference ("elites" average minus national average)	+22	+21	+14	+30	+10

Source: Adapted from Gallup International (1963), pp. 116–117; Luxembourg data were omitted, since the size of the sample was too small for detailed analysis.

The significance of Nils H. Halle's study (1966) of social position and foreign policy attitudes is twofold. For one thing, it was the first major cross-national study to report politically relevant survey data from both sides of the late Iron Curtain. Its basis comprised national samples from France, Norway, and Poland. The Institut Français d'Opinion Publique in Paris, the International Peace Research Institute in Oslo, and the Public Opinion Research Center at the Polish Radio and Television conducted the field work in the winter of 1964–1965 under the general direction of the European Social Science Center in Vienna. Its focus was perspectives on foreign affairs, especially disarmament. Second, it made a serious attempt to relate cross-national survey data to theoretically oriented propositions about attitude formation and change. Halle's basic instrument was a center-periphery index, combining additively eight background variables (age, education, income, occupational sector, occupational position, and so forth) into a single scale showing the respondent's overall social position. He found that, for all three countries, those at the periphery of society held foreign policy attitudes that were more extreme than the "gradualist" views held by persons at the center. In other respects the countries differed: "The degree of knowledge of foreign affairs," for instance (p. 67), "varies more with social position in France than in Poland." Similarly, France and Poland were closer together "with regard to relative impact, within each country, of social position on the questions used" than were either France and Norway or Norway and Poland (p. 74).

A cross-national study including still more countries in East and West is the Multinational Comparative Time Budget Research Project, under the guidance of Alexander Szalai of the Hungarian Academy of Sciences. Its purpose is "to study the time budgets of adult populations subjected in varying degrees to the influences of industrialization and urbanization" (Szalai, 1966b, p. 8). Preliminary studies in the Soviet Union and Hungary had already demonstrated their usefulness for long-term planning. They showed, for instance, marked differences in the patterns of time use between men and women in the industrial labor force, and documented the heavy costs to the national economy and to leisure-time culture of time-consuming household obligations such as standing in line at markets (Szalai, 1966a). The current project has completed interviews in 15 sites in Belgium, Bulgaria, Czechoslovakia, the Federal Republic of Germany, the German Democratic Republic, France, Hungary, Peru, Poland, the Soviet Union, the United States, and Yugoslavia. Although in some cases it included national samples, usually the surveys were of one or several towns in each country—towns such as Kazanlik and its eleven adjoining villages in Bulgaria, Osnabrück in West Germany, Pskov and its suburbs in the Soviet Union, or Jackson and ten neighboring communities in Michigan—each with 30,000 to 280,000 inhabitants, a distinct urban center, and a diversity of industry. Regarding the information they sought, Szalai (1966b, p. 11) wrote:

For each individual within the sample, . . . it was intended to establish a time-budget of a "complete day". . . .

The record of a day was the enumeration, for the 24-hour period from midnight to midnight, of all the successive activities of these 24 hours, in chronological order, with their respective durations. . . .

The enumerated activities could be of any duration; the hours and minutes of starting and finishing were recorded, and the duration obtained by simple subtraction. The sum of the durations of all activities had to be 1,440 minutes, or 24 hours, each and every utilization of time, including doing nothing at all, being considered as an activity. . . .

The method of collecting information combined the techniques of self-recording (on the part of the subject) and of the retrospective interview. . . .

Although the complete set of findings has not yet appeared, the foretaste was promising. The project documented cross-nationally, for instance, the exploited state of womankind—"the working women because they are overburdened with work, the non-working women because their labors are underestimated and their existence is much more drab than that of the men" (p. 22). The analysts found "a remarkable homogeneity in the general proportions of the time-budgets" despite varying levels of industrial development and urban growth among the different countries (p. 25). Other data reported differences in working and non-working time to be small from one country to the next, the "compressibility" of time on weekdays as compared to Sundays, and the fact that most of the time spent listening to the radio (an average of 87 per cent for the studies cited) was secondary activity while doing something else whereas television-viewing was generally (81 per cent) a primary activity.

Until very recently the only public opinion data that researchers in the West could get about Eastern Europe comprised surveys of refugees and of visitors to the West. In the former case, most of the scholarly studies have been of single countries (for example, Schröter, 1958; Inkeles & Bauer, 1959; Gleitman & Greenbaum, 1960), although an occasional study would concentrate upon cross-national considerations (such as Radio Free Europe's publication of September 1963, "Flight Motivations of Refugees from Four Soviet Bloc Countries"). Possibilities for interviewing visitors from the East have grown as East-West travel barriers have weakened (see, for example, Radio Free Europe, 1965–1968; Free Europe, Inc., 1966). Both types of studies are fraught with methodological problems. The most important of these is the lack of representativeness of the respondents. Refugees and visitors by their very nature will not comprise a random cross-section of the population from which they come; and, if they happen to be fairly representative in terms of their demographic characteristics, then it is still no more likely that their views will mirror those of their fellow citizens who remained at home. Then, too, one may wonder about the accuracy of their responses. Refugees may be apt to overstate their previous miseries as justification for their flight, and visitors who expect to return to their homeland may well be reluctant to give information that could leak back to their own government. What enhances the credibility of such studies is the fact that their results show considerable variation in response patterns. Not all refugees condemn unstintingly the regime from which they fled. And significant differences appear in the attitudes of different nationalities toward such issues as the Vietnam war or the Arab-Israeli conflict. Despite the absence of scholarly studies utilizing these reports, it would seem that they contain considerable information that could be of value if properly handled.

Secondary Analysis of Original Cross-National Surveys

Perspectives and behavior reported in interviews are multifaceted. It is therefore no wonder that the researcher who initiates a cross-national study does not exhaust its possibilities for analysis. Sometimes the development of new techniques makes secondary analysis of the original set of data tempting. Usually, however, such secondary analyses stem from other researchers who see in the data possibilities that either did not interest the original investigator—perhaps because of pressure on him to produce a report covering the main findings or those of particular interest to the sponsor of the project—or failed to catch his attention.

Secondary analyses are possible only when the original investigator has made available to other scholars his data, codebooks, sample specifications, and other information. To facilitate this, social scientists have begun to create data archives, and have set up a Council on Social Science Data Archives to coordinate their efforts. Working with someone else's data, of course, imposes limitations on the researcher. He can only accept and do the best he can with the decisions made and data generated by the original investigator. Even so, imaginative scholars have demonstrated that secondary analyses can make solid and occasionally insightful contributions to our knowledge of political perspectives and behavior.

The Passing of Traditional Society in the Middle East, 1950–1951. The most impressive secondary analysis of a cross-national survey to date is that from the pen of Daniel Lerner, with the collaboration of Lucille Pevsner (1958b). In the fall of 1950 Charles Y. Glock, then of the Bureau for Applied Social Research at Columbia University, initiated surveys in the Middle Eastern countries of Egypt, Jordan, Iran, Lebanon, Syria, and Turkey. (The Bureau also interviewed Greek respondents as a pretest; Lerner did not report these Greek data.) The size of each national sample was roughly 300 persons. The questions focused on the respondents' "habits and preferences with regard to the mass media of communication, their attitudes toward foreigners and foreign countries, their general outlook on life, as well as certain features of their daily lives" (p. vii). Researchers at the Bureau (including Lerner) analyzed the data and wrote reports on their findings in the individual countries. Aspects of the project appeared in print in some instances (Ringer & Sills, 1952–1953; Kendall, 1956). Subsequently, in 1953, the Bureau invited Lerner to reanalyze the entire set of data. Visits in 1954 and 1958 to the countries surveyed supplemented the survey material from 1950–1951 to provide the basis for Lerner's highly interesting account of modernization in the Middle East.

The basic model of modernization outlined by Lerner centered on the development of a participant society. This takes place in three stages

(p. 60; see also McCrone & Cnudde, 1967):

> Urbanization comes first, for cities alone have developed the complex of skills and resources which characterize the modern industrial economy. Within this urban matrix develop both of the attributes which distinguish the next two phases—literacy and media growth. There is a close reciprocal relationship between these, for the literate develop the media which in turn spread literacy. But, historically, literacy performs the key function in the second phase. The capacity to read, at first acquired by relatively few people, equips them to perform the varied tasks required in the modernizing society. Not until the third phase, when the elaborate technology of industrial development is fairly well advanced, does a society begin to produce newspapers, radio networks, and motion pictures on a massive scale. This, in turn, accelerates the spread of literacy. Out of this interaction develop those institutions of participation (e.g., voting) which we find in all advanced modern societies. . . .

Lerner found that a common psychological mechanism underlay these three phases—empathy, which is a combination of projection and introjection that produces "the capacity to see oneself in the other fellow's situation" (p. 50). The mass media in turn act as a multiplier upon the psychic mobility of the empathic. "It is the more empathic individuals who respond, in the first place, to the lure of cities, schools, media," wrote Lerner (p. 60); "Urban residence, schooling, media exposure then train and reinforce the empathic predisposition that was already present."

The key to modernization, in Lerner's view, is the emergence of what he called "Transitionals." Several questions asked the Middle Eastern respondent to "imagine himself in a situation other than his real one" (p. 70). These role-playing questions, requiring "some capacity to empathize," were then correlated with others designed to discover the extent of the individual's modernity, as indicated by "a broad range of opinions on public questions" (p. 71). Traditionals scored low on both sets of questions, Moderns high. But in the middle was a large group of Transitionals. For Lerner (p. 72),

> the true Transitional is defined, dynamically, by what he wants to become. What differentiates him from his Traditional peers is a different *latent structure* of aptitudes and attitudes. The aptitude is *empathy*—he "sees" things the others do not see, "lives" in a world populated by imaginings alien to the constrictive world of the others. The attitude is *desire*—he wants *really* to see the things he has hitherto "seen" only in his mind's eye, *really* to live in the world he has "lived" in only vicariously. These are the sources of his deviant ways. When many individuals show deviation in this direction, then a transition is under way in their society.

In the remainder of his study, Lerner showed "empirically how this transition is at work in every Middle Eastern country, with results that spell the passing of traditional society from that area of the world."

The USIA Surveys. The availability to scholars of the USIA's survey data on Western European (and other) countries has spawned several secondary analyses. In one of these Gabriel A. Almond (1960) focused upon the impact of space technology from 1957 to 1960 on Western European public opinion. He found that people were unusually well informed about and interested in these developments. The view, formed in the light of the early Soviet spectaculars in outer space, that the Soviet Union was ahead of the United States in the space race seemed to spill over into other areas of competition as well. This was particularly true with regard to long-run military capabilities—a fact that had a doubly negative effect upon Western European attitudes toward the Atlantic Alliance (pp. 569–570):

> First, it has shaken confidence in American technological and military strength and hence sharpened doubts as to the wisdom of alliance with the United States. Second, by demonstrating the delivery capabilities of modern warfare it has brought even further into question the utility of conventional security arrangements, weapons systems, and military deployments on the part of powers who do not possess these capabilities.

Indeed, there seemed to be growing pressure among Western Europeans both for a *détente* between East and West and for greater reliance upon the peacekeeping potentiality of the United Nations.

Richard L. Merritt (1968b) developed two-dimensional vector paths to describe visually changes over time in the predispositions of four Western European populations toward each other as well as the United States and the Soviet Union. His findings were both theoretical and substantive. On the one hand, a high degree of association between consensus on the direction of a predisposition and the salience of the predisposition itself appeared. Change from positive to negative predispositions (or vice versa) was accompanied by decreased salience, not unlike one effect of psychological cross-pressures. Attitude change in the middle of the range between "very good opinion" and "very bad opinion" of the country in question was more dramatic in extent than that at either end of the range. On the other hand, it turned out that the overall climate of Western European predispositions warmed up during the decade from October 1954 to February 1964. This was most markedly so with regard to French predispositions toward other countries and in the case of other populations' views of Italy. Although the United States was the country most likely to be viewed intensely and positively, the image of the Soviet Union improved sharply, possibly intimating a desire on the part of the Western European publics (other than the West Germans) for a greater measure of East-West *détente*. Predispositions toward one another increased most strikingly between France and West Germany, accompanying a sharply growing antipathy on the popular level between France and Great Britain. This finding, together with the increasing warmth between Italy and Great Britain, suggests in turn a need for closer examination of their official relationships, particularly on the question of British ties to the European Economic Community.

Donald J. Puchala (1968) applied factor analysis to USIA data on French and West German attitudes in October 1954, shortly after the French parliamentary defeat of the European Defense Community and while negotiations were under way to permit West Germany to join the North Atlantic Treaty Organization. Generally speaking, he found that both populations were paying attention to the same aspects of international relations but that their views on them differed considerably. Frenchmen, for instance, "were stimulated both to reject West German rearmament on the basis of general negative feelings for 'things German' and to accept West German rearmament in the interest of European unity" (p. 165). By way of contrast, "the average West German faced no perceptual dilemma in thinking about West German rearmament in 1954":

> Though recalled images of European unity, style in international politics and generalized internationalism entered German thinking on the rearmament issue to some extent, German positions were by and large determined by the recalled "image of the West." That is, for the average West German rearmament was a question of strengthening the West against the East, and since the affect associated with the German "image of the West" was highly positive, one would expect to find West Germans largely in favor of rearmament.

Similarly, the issues of greater sovereignty for Germany evoked the negative "image of Germany" held by the French, whereas West Germans viewed it in the light of their threatening "image of Russia" as well as an "image of threats to international peace." The French tended to associate the United States with a threat to world peace, in sharp contrast to West Germans, for whom the United States conjured up a highly positive "image of the West." These divergences, based on surveys conducted in 1954, continue to plague West German-French amity to the present day.

Marten Brouwer's secondary analysis (1959) of an earlier cross-national survey conducted for the American government deserves mention here. In March 1951, a "morale" survey sought to determine the preparedness of the Austrian, British, French, Dutch, Italian, and West German populations "to build up, jointly with the United States, a defense organization against a possible Russian aggression" (p. 252). The original investigators used two different questionnaires in each country, giving them to two separate samples of roughly 1,500 respondents each. The reason for the split-ballot was twofold. First, this procedure enabled the investigators to ask more questions while at the same time keeping the ballot relatively short for each group of respondents. Second, and more important, it permitted them to ask one group within each country its views on Western defense arrangements, making no mention of any American role, and to ask a second group similar questions that explicitly provided for American participation. Brouwer's two main findings in this regard were (p. 263): "(1) Explicit mention of the United States in questions about the defense of Western Europe against Russian aggression clearly strengthened the tendency of interviewees to reply that in that case Russia might be defeated or, at any rate, held; (2) This explicit mention of the U.S.A., generally speaking, lessened the tendency to react with a neutral reply."

Replications of Original Studies

Still another fruitful procedure for students of cross-national political behavior is to replicate in one country a study performed somewhere else, or to replicate the study at a later date in the same country to see whether or not its findings hold over time. The USIA surveys (Merritt & Puchala, 1968) and Reigrotski and Anderson's replication (1959–1960) of the UNESCO tensions project are excellent examples of the latter type of study. In the former instance, the researcher performing the replication can follow as exactly as possible the research design used in the original project, adapting it where necessary to local conditions in the country or countries he is studying. This procedure enables him not only to say something about his own results but also to discuss the cross-national validity of his own and the original findings. Among the usual drawbacks of functional equivalence encountered in any cross-national project, the issue of timing is particularly important. The researcher must be sure that no significant events have intervened between the conduct of the original survey and his own field work that would distort the comparability of the two sets of data. This may be of little importance in studies concentrating upon aspects of the electoral process. It may be of immense significance, however, in surveys aimed at ascertaining the international perspectives of different populations.

The importance of the electoral studies conducted in the United States by the Survey Research Center of the University of Michigan has led scholars in other countries to adapt SRC questions to their own surveys. Frequently this is done in collaboration with SRC researchers who would like to test the cross-national validity of their findings on American political behavior. In 1957, for instance, the Institute for Social Research in Oslo and the Chr. Michelsen Institute in Bergen, under the direction of Stein Rokkan, included some SRC questions both in their nationwide study of the Norwegian parliamentary election and in a regional sample in Rogaland (Valen & Katz, 1964). Comparisons with the SRC's 1956 election survey in the United States (Campbell, Converse, Miller & Stokes, 1960) revealed many similarities between Norwegian and American recruitment and voting patterns. In general, however, identification of persons with the Norwegian parties was "associated with greater demographic and political distinctiveness"—in terms of socioeconomic differences, perceptions of policy differences between the parties, stands on issues, and practices of voting according to party identification—than was the case for identification by Americans with political parties (Campbell & Valen, 1961, p. 523). A similar differentiation existed with respect to party recruitment. Comparing not Norway and the United States but types of political parties in the two countries, Angus Campbell and Stein Rokkan (1960, p. 93) found that the degree to which lower-stratum economic organizations dominate a party varies inversely with "the importance of formal education and occupational position in the recruitment of active participants among its voters."

In the fall of 1958, the Institut Français d'Opinion Publique used some SRC questions in its survey of the French electorate (Dupeux, Girard & Stoetzel, 1960). The results enabled some interesting comparisons with the 1952 and 1956 election studies in the United States. Philip E. Converse and Georges Dupeux (1962, p. 23), for instance, found

no striking reason to believe that the French citizen, either through the vagaries of national character, institutions, or history, is predisposed to form political opinions which are more sharply crystallized or which embrace a more comprehensive range of political issues than do comparable Americans. On both sides, opinion formation declines as objects and arrangements become more remote from the observer; and much of politics, for both French and Americans, is remote. Hence the proliferation of choices offered by the multiparty system is itself a mixed blessing: it is capitalized upon only by the more politically interested segments of the electorate, and appears to represent "too much" choice to be managed comfortably by citizens whose political involvement is average or less.

The major difference they found was that the French public was much less inclined than were Americans to identify themselves strongly with a political party. This fact, which seems to stem from differences in processes of socialization, in turn contributed to the fluidity, not to say turbulence, of French party politics.

Their analysis of public images in France of President Charles de Gaulle and in the United States of President Dwight D. Eisenhower led Converse and Dupeux (1966) to assert that, despite obvious differences between the two generals in politics, their immense appeal for the masses was largely similar. It was their personal image rather than their politics that gave them the warm approval of all segments of the public. Although the effects of party identification altered the level of this approval, even here the differences were "between enthusiastic approval and tempered approval rather than between approval and disapproval" (p. 344). The generals protected their personal prestige by "avoiding or minimizing party commitment." But, even where such a strategy was impossible, Converse and Dupeux concluded (pp. 344–345), "the victorious general alone among political aspirants appears to have the potential of maximizing the electoral strength of his own party to its very limit while achieving some inroads among parties unequivocally opposed to him and large inroads among parties who hesitate." Party elites, if they would prevent the ascendance in politics of a popular military figure, must act to discourage his movement into a political role rather than waiting until he has assumed it to try to control him.

Cross-National Comparisons of National Surveys

The general lack of truly cross-national surveys has led a number of researchers to undertake cross-national comparisons of data from a set of national surveys. Sometimes this entails little more than juxtaposing and analyzing the results of several such surveys containing questions relevant to the researcher's theoretic interests (see, for example, Brouwer & Mokken, 1958; or, for a more complex and theoretic-oriented study see Schubert, 1968). In other cases he searches out and reprocesses the data on punchcards from surveys that are as directly comparable as possible in terms of the questions asked, timing, sampling procedure, and so forth. As data banks containing large numbers of national surveys picked for their basic comparability multiply (see Pool, Abelson & Popkin, 1965; Roos & Roos, 1967; Rosenthal, 1967), analyses of this latter type will become increasingly feasible.

The methodological problems encountered in the secondary analysis of national surveys, although not overwhelming, are mammoth. They generally are magnifications of all the issues discussed in this chapter. Are the questions nominally or functionally equivalent, for instance, that is, are they likely to tap the same underlying attitudes in each set of respondents? How differently are the questionnaires structured, and what effect are these differences likely to have upon the respondents' reactions? Do the sampling procedures produce comparable groups of respondents? How sure can we be that variation in field techniques did not introduce biases into the findings? Were the societal circumstances of the countries roughly similar at the time of interviewing? In the time between the field work in one country and interviewing in others, did any significant events intervene to complicate the comparability of the findings?

And yet the bold researcher has ample justification for piecing together as best he can a coherent mosaic from disparate pieces of data. It is, quite simply, that the absence of wholly satisfactory sets of cross-national data should not prevent theorizing on the basis of partially comparable data, *provided* that the researcher fully alerts the reader about possible sources of error and noncomparability. If he can discover significant relationships, then perhaps his findings will spur the efforts of those who are able and willing to conduct cross-national surveys, and to encourage them to seek the data that will test his propositions more adequately. As it has turned out, some scholars have brought considerable insight to bear upon such diverse data. They have discovered relationships sufficiently striking in their strength and direction that variations in the surveys alone could not begin to account for them.

In one such type of study, political sociologists have used survey data from various countries to examine cross-national patterns of social mobility. Seymour Martin Lipset and Hans L. Zetterberg (1959), for instance, in their study of social mobility in industrial societies, relied upon independent surveys from Finland, West Germany, Sweden, and the United States. S. M. Miller (1960; see also Fox & Miller, 1965) subsequently analyzed social mobility in 18 countries, using both survey data—ranging from nationwide samples of as many as 4,760 Finnish men to as few as 121 males in Melbourne, Australia—and census data (of 4.4 million adult Hungarians, for example). Among the findings stemming from Miller's work, one of the more interesting is that, contrary to the thesis originally set forth by Lipset and Zetterberg, advanced industrial nations have different basic patterns of mobility (Fox & Miller, 1966). This suggests the importance of cultural variations both for the definitions of occupational strata and for the degree to which the channels of recruitment are open or closed. It also points to a need to pay attention to the culturally determined distances between statistical strata and the corresponding strains on family cohesion brought about through father-son mobility.

Seymour Martin Lipset (1960) used survey data from 20 countries to develop and support his idea of working-class authoritarianism. Like the social mobility studies, this analysis juxtaposes relevant findings from the various countries—usually broken into cross-tabulations showing the effect of occupation or social status, level of education, or income upon attitudes toward such topics as democracy, civil liberties, and party preference. Lipset found (p. 97) that "extremist and intolerant movements in modern society are more likely to be based on the lower classes than on the middle and upper classes." He continued (p. 100):

> The social situation of the lower strata, particularly in the poorer countries with low levels of education, predisposes them to view politics as black and white, good and evil. Consequently, other things being equal, they should be more likely than other strata to prefer extremist movements which suggest easy and quick solutions to social problems and have a rigid outlook.

Membership in organizations fostering liberal causes may mitigate the authoritarian tendency of the society's lower strata, he added, particularly when such organizations, including trade unions, have as their main aim improvement of the economic position of these strata.

Morris Davis and Sidney Verba (1960) examined reports based on surveys conducted between 1947 and 1956 in France and Great Britain. Their goal was to link (dichotomized) opinion on international affairs to party affiliation. Their use of reports rather than unit-record data (that is, the IBM punchcards for the individual respondents) added a severe constraint to those already imposed by the use of national data for cross-national analysis. They wrote (p. 595):

> Because our basic unit is not (as is almost always the case in scholarly analyses of public opinion data) the individual respondent but rather a cell in a table of printed results, we have been unable to perform any individual correlations either between party affiliation and any other sorts of ecological data or between one attitude and another.

With this and other limitations well in mind, they pointed to a positive relationship between international opinion and party affiliation. Generally speaking, conservative parties in both France and Great Britain were more pro-American in their foreign policy orientation; and the further to the left the respondents were, the less likely they were to favor American foreign policy objectives. Unless the French communists are excepted, there was greater congruence among the British than among the French. Excluding the French communists from consideration left the French with a more congruent set of opinions on international affairs, since the greatest divergence seemed to stem from attitudes vis-à-vis the Soviet Union.

Robert R. Alford (1963) has performed the most extensive cross-national secondary analysis of disparate national surveys. In his study of the relationship between social class and voting in the Anglo-American democracies, he used 53 surveys comprising nationwide samples from Australia, Canada, Great Britain, and the United States. Some of these surveys had produced usable data in tabular form. For three-quarters of them, however, he had to retabulate their IBM punchcards. The criteria for selection for the surveys were two: first, they had to contain comparable information on the respondents' occupation and party preference (and preferably other background characteristics such as religion and region of residence); second, Alford gave priority to those surveys conducted within the three months preceding a major national election. The surveys covered the period from 1936 to 1962.

To examine the effects of social class upon voting patterns, Alford designed an index of class voting, which subtracts "the percentage of persons in non-manual occupations voting for Left parties from the percentage of persons in manual occupations voting for Left parties" (pp. 79–80). Using this index, he found considerable variation among the four countries: Great Britain, with a mean index score of 40 during the decade 1952–1962, had the purest form of class voting, followed by Australia (33), the United States (16), and Canada (8) trailing far behind. This relationship held for all age categories, for highly urbanized areas (cities with 100,000 or more residents), and for several alternative definitions of social class; but class voting was "consistently higher among Protestants than among Catholics," and a considerable difference appeared "between the regions with the highest and the lowest average levels of class voting" (p. 104).

In summarizing his findings, Alford pointed out (p. 292) first of all, that,

> where class factors are paramount in determining national political cleavages, religious and regional loyalties do not significantly affect political behavior. Where social classes do not support the national parties in sharply different degrees, regional and religious loyalties are strong.

He also uncovered no evidence to indicate that "class voting is decreasing substantially in any of the four countries" (p. 292). Finally, he discovered "clear differences in the consequences and correlates of class polarization" (p. 302):

> The more class-polarized systems are more likely to have strongly organized and disciplined parties extending their influence even to the city level. Where workers have a party clearly appealing to their interests, their partici-

pation and sense of political efficacy is as great as middle-class persons. Where class polarization is greater, politics tends to be more universalistic, in the sense that political corruption is less evident and candidates are not as likely to be rejected on the grounds of personal characteristics. Political shifts may take place more readily in the more class-polarized systems, which are also more homogeneous and have fewer regional one-party bastions. Overt class conflict in the form of strikes is less evident in the class-polarized systems—which possess labor parties with greater control over collective bargaining, and have a higher level of trade union organization.

Among the conclusions Alford drew from his findings, one of the more interesting pertained to the danger that societal cleavages pose for the maintenance of existing political institutions. "Under conditions of highly developed industrialism," he pointed out (p. 339), "class cleavages may actually be the cleavages which are most easily compromised and the ones most likely to retain national unity and political consensus." By way of contrast, regional and religious loyalties, which rest upon differences in values rather than interests, are less subject to compromise, and hence may be both more disintegrative as well as less flexible than class cleavages.

The limitations of secondary analysis of national and cross-national surveys notwithstanding—access to them, problems of using data for purposes other than those foreseen by their originators, the overriding issue of functional equivalence—they hold great promise for future scholarship. Few researchers are going to want or be able to muster the organizational and financial resources required to conduct original surveys. Besides, in some regards it may not even be necessary. If students of cross-national politics could organize and comprehend the survey data currently at their disposal they could make great strides in their research.

One hopeful sign is that social scientists are now working actively to make both national and cross-national survey data readily available. For one thing, commercial agencies and academicians are publishing at least their rough findings more regularly than heretofore. In the immediate postwar period, both the *Public Opinion Quarterly* and the *International Journal of Opinion and Attitude Research* printed some marginal frequency tabulations of data; and, under the editorial direction of Hadley Cantril (1951), Mildred Strunk prepared a monumental compilation of such findings for the dozen years from 1935 to 1946. Nowadays, the *Public Opinion Quarterly* concentrates upon data from American surveys; a new international journal, *Polls,* published by the International Opinion Research Documents division of the Steinmetz Stichting in Amsterdam, includes national results from a wide variety of countries as well as cross-national findings from such survey centers as the Peace Research Laboratory in St. Louis, Missouri, and the European Coordination Center in Vienna, no less than from such commercial agencies as Gallup International; and at least a dozen of the commercial agencies in several countries publish their results at periodic intervals. For another thing, data repositories are springing up. Among the more prominent of these are the Inter-University Consortium for Political Research at the University of Michigan, the Survey Research Center of the University of California, the International Survey Library Association at the Roper Public Opinion Center in Williamstown, Massachusetts, and, in Europe, both the Zentralarchiv für empirische Sozialforschung at the University of Cologne and the Steinmetz Stichting in Amsterdam. In the United States, the Council on Social Science Data Archives is seeking to coordinate these efforts; in Europe it is the European Federation of Social Science Data Archives.

Another encouraging sign is the development of newer and more powerful techniques for analyzing data. One of the more prominent of these, but by no means the only one, is factor analysis (see Puchala, 1968). It seems quite possible that secondary analysis of some of the earlier surveys using such techniques could bring to light new dimensions of the old data. Since an increasing number of students in the social sciences are learning techniques for computer analysis, the prospects for such secondary analyses are bright.

Some tasks will still remain for original research, however, even after we have exhausted the analytic possibilities of the cross-national data currently available. One set of these has to do with the basics of survey research—improving research methodology, eliminating areas of noncomparability, distinguishing between meaningful and meaningless expressions of opinion (Converse, 1964). And another set deals with relating mass opinion to the larger political processes (Galtung, 1967). Of what importance actually is public opinion in a democracy? What is its relationship to elite perspectives? What is the process that shapes public perspectives, and how does it vary cross-nationally? These tasks, as important for theory as they are intrinsically interesting, will occupy scholars' attention for some time to come.

REFERENCES

Abrams, Philip. "The Production of Survey Data in Britain," *Social Sciences Information*. 4:3 (September 1965), 17–25.

Adamec, Cenek. "Experiences with an International Question," *International Journal of Opinion and Attitude Research*. 1:4 (December 1947), 40–44.

Alford, Robert R. *Party and Society: The Anglo-American Democracies*. Chicago: Rand McNally, 1963.

Almond, Gabriel A. "Public Opinion and the Development of Space Technology," *The Public Opinion Quarterly*. 24:4 (Winter 1960), 553–572. Reprinted in Merritt & Puchala (1968), pp. 86–110.

Almond, Gabriel A., and Sidney Verba. *The Civic Culture: Political Attitudes and Democracy in Five Nations*. Princeton, N.J.: published for the Center of International Studies by Princeton University Press, 1963.

Anderson, Dale. "Roper's Field Interviewing Organization," *The Public Opinion Quarterly*. 16:2 (Summer 1952), 263–272.

Anderson, Nels. "Opinion on Europe," *Annuaire Européen/European Yearbook*. 5 (1957), 143–160.

Ansbacher, H. L. "The Problem of Interpreting Attitude Survey Data: A Case Study of the Attitude of Russian Workers in Wartime Germany," *The Public Opinion Quarterly*. 14:1 (Spring 1950), 126–138.

Association Française de Science Politique, editor. *L'établissement de la Cinquième République: Le Référendum de Septembre et les Élections de Novembre 1958*. Paris: Librairie Armand Colin, 1960.

Aubert, Vilhelm, Burton R. Fisher, and Stein Rokkan. "A Comparative Study of Teachers' Attitudes to International Problems and Policies: Preliminary Review of Relationships in Interview Data from Seven Western European Countries," *The Journal of Social Issues*. 10:4 (1954), 25–39.

Axelrod, Morris, Donald R. Matthews, and James W. Prothro. "Recruitment for Survey Research on Race Problems in the South," *The Public Opinion Quarterly*. 26:2 (Summer 1962), 254–262.

Backstrom, Charles H., and Gerald D. Hursh. *Survey Research*. Evanston, Ill.: Northwestern University Press, 1963.

Barthes, Roland. *Mythologies*. Paris: Éditions du seuil, 1957.

Becker, Sam L. "Why an Order Effect," *The Public Opinion Quarterly*. 18:3 (Fall 1954), 271–278.

Bindman, Aaron M. "Interviewing in the Search for 'Truth,'" *The Sociological Quarterly*. 6:3 (Summer 1965), 281–288.

Blood, Robert O., Jr., and Yuzuru John Takeshita. "Development of Cross-Cultural Equivalence of Measure of Marital Interaction for U.S.A. and Japan." In International Sociological Association (1964), pp. 333–344.

Bogart, Leo. "No Opinion, Don't Know, and Maybe No Answer," *The Public Opinion Quarterly*. 31:3 (Fall 1967), 331–345.

Brouwer, Marten. "International Contacts and Integration-Mindedness: A Secondary Analysis of a Study in Western Europe," *Polls*. 1:2 (Summer 1965), 1–11.

Brouwer, Marten. "The 1963 Production of Sample Surveys in Continental Europe: Report on a Census," *Social Sciences Information*. 4:3 (September 1965), 26–64.

Brouwer, Marten. "Some Data from a Six-Country Split Ballot Survey on European Military Co-operation Anno 1951," *Gazette.* 5:2 (1959), 249–264.

Brouwer, Marten, and R. J. Mokken. "Public Opinion and the Nuclear Bomb," *Gazette.* 4:1 (1958), 113–116.

Buchanan, William, and Hadley Cantril, with the assistance of Virginia Van S. Zerega, Henry Durant, and James R. White. *How Nations See Each Other: A Study in Public Opinion.* Urbana: University of Illinois Press, 1953.

Cahalan, Don, Valerie Tamulonis, and Helen W. Verner. "Interviewer Bias Involved in Certain Types of Opinion Survey Questions," *International Journal of Opinion and Attitude Research.* 1:1 (March 1947), 63–77.

Campbell, Angus, Philip E. Converse, Warren E. Miller, and Donald E. Stokes. *The American Voter.* New York: John Wiley & Sons, Inc., 1960.

Campbell, Angus, Philip E. Converse, Warren E. Miller, and Donald E. Stokes. *Elections and the Political Order.* New York: John Wiley & Sons, Inc., 1966.

Campbell, Angus, and Stein Rokkan. "Citizen Participation in Political Life: Norway and the United States," *International Social Science Journal.* 12:1 (1960), 69–99.

Campbell, Angus, and Henry Valen. "Party Identification in Norway and the United States," *The Public Opinion Quarterly.* 25:4 (Winter 1961), 505–525. Reprinted in Campbell, Converse, Miller & Stokes (1966), pp. 245–268.

Cannell, Charles F., and Floyd J. Fowler. "Comparison of a Self-Enumerative Procedure and a Personal Interview: A Validity Study," *The Public Opinion Quarterly.* 27:2 (Summer 1963), 250–264.

Cantril, Hadley. *The Pattern of Human Concerns.* New Brunswick, N.J.: Rutgers University Press, 1965.

Cantril, Hadley. *The Politics of Despair.* New York: Basic Books, Inc., Publishers, 1958.

Cantril, Hadley, editorial director, prepared by Mildred Strunk. *Public Opinion, 1935–1946.* Princeton, N.J.: Princeton University Press, 1951.

Carter, Roy E., Jr., and F. Gerald Kline. "Secret Ballots and Extreme Candidates," *Polls.* 1:4 (Summer 1966), 1–7.

Converse, Philip E. "New Dimensions of Meaning for Cross-Section Sample Surveys in Politics," *International Social Science Journal.* 16:1 (1964), 19–34.

Converse, Philip E., and Georges Dupeux. "De Gaulle and Eisenhower: The Public Image of the Victorious General." In Campbell, Converse, Miller & Stokes (1966), pp. 292–345.

Converse, Philip E., and Georges Dupeux. "Politicization of the Electorate in France and the United States," *The Public Opinion Quarterly.* 26:1 (Spring 1962), 1–23. Reprinted in Campbell, Converse, Miller & Stokes (1966), pp. 269–291.

Crespi, Leo P. "The Cheater Problem in Polling," *The Public Opinion Quarterly.* 9:4 (Winter 1945–1946), 431–445.

Crespi, Leo P. "The Influence of Military Government Sponsorship in German Opinion Polling," *International Journal of Opinion and Attitude Research.* 4:2 (Summer 1950), 151–178.

Crespi, Leo P., chairman. "International Survey Research in Developed and Underdeveloped Areas: Papers Presented at the 12th Annual Conference of the American Association for Public Opinion Research, Washington, D.C., 11 May 1957," *The Public Opinion Quarterly.* 21:3 (Fall 1957), 413–418.

Crespi, Leo P., chairman. "Some Recent Major Advances in International Public Opinion Polling: Papers Presented at the 13th Annual Conference of the American Association for Public Opinion Research, Chicago, Ill., 8-11 May 1958," *The Public Opinion Quarterly.* 22:2 (Summer 1958), 181–186.

Crossley, Archibald M., chairman. "Problems of International Polls: Papers Presented at the 4th Annual Conference of the World Associatian for Public Opinion Research, Tunbridge Wells, England, September 1951," *International Social Science Bulletin.* 5:3 (1953), 534–536.

Davis, Morris, and Sidney Verba. "Party Affiliation and International Opinions in Britain and France, 1947–1956," *The Public Opinion Quarterly.* 24:4 (Winter 1960), 590–604.

Deming, W. Edwards. "On Errors in Surveys," *American Sociological Review.* 9:4 (August 1944), 359–369.

Deming, William Edwards. *Some Theory of Sampling.* New York: John Wiley & Sons, Inc., 1950.

Dohrenwend, Barbara Snell, John Colombotos, and Bruce P. Dohrenwend. "Social Distance and Interviewer Effects," *The Public Opinion Quarterly.* 32:3 (Fall 1968), 410–422.

Duijker, H. C. J. "Comparative Research in Social Science with Special Reference to Attitude Research," *International Social Science Bulletin.* 7:4 (1955), 555–566.

Duijker, H. C. J., and Stein Rokkan. "Organizational Aspects of Cross-National Social Research," *The Journal of Social Issues.* 10:4 (1954), 8–24.

Dupeux, Georges, Alain Girard, and Jean Stoetzel. "Une enquête par sondage auprès des électeurs." In Association Française de Science Politique (1960), pp. 119–193.

Ervin, Susan, and Robert T. Bower. "Translation Problems in International Surveys," *The Public Opinion Quarterly.* 16:4 (Winter 1952–1953), 595–604.

Evans, Franklin B. "On Interviewer Cheating," *The Public Opinion Quarterly.* 25:1 (Spring 1961), 126–127.

Fink, Raymond. "Interviewer Training and Supervision in a Survey of Laos," *International Social Science Journal.* 15:1 (1963), 21–34.

Fishman, Joshua A. "A Systematization of the Whorfian Hypothesis," *Behavioral Science.* 5:4 (October 1960), 323–339.

Fox, Thomas G., and S. M. Miller. "Economic, Political and Social Determinants of Mobility: An International Cross-Sectional Analysis," *Acta Sociologica.* 9:1–2 (1965), 76–93.

Fox, Thomas, and S. M. Miller. "Occupational Stratification and Mobility." In Merritt & Rokkan (1966), pp. 217–237.

Free Europe, Inc. "What Do East Europeans Think?" *East Europe.* 15:3 (March 1966), 26–28.

Frey, Frederick W. "Surveying Peasant Attitudes in Turkey," *The Public Opinion Quarterly.* 27:3 (Fall 1963), 335–355.

Gallup International. *Gallup Opinion Index.* Report No. 29 (November 1967).

Gallup International. "Public Opinion and the European Community," *Journal of Common Market Studies.* 2:2 (November 1963), 101–126.

Galtung, Johan. "Some Aspects of Comparative Research," *Polls.* 2:3 (Spring 1967), 1–19.

Girard, Alain, editor. "Opinion Surveys in Developing Countries: Special Issue," *International Social Science Journal.* 15:1 (1963), 7–110.

Glaser, William A. "International Mail Surveys of Informants," *Human Organization.* 25:1 (Spring 1966), 78–86.

Gleitman, Henry, and Joseph J. Greenbaum. "Hungarian Socio-Political Attitudes and Revolutionary Action," *The Public Opinion Quarterly*. 24:1 (Spring 1960), 62–76.

Glock, Charles Y., editor. *Survey Research in the Social Sciences*. New York: Russell Sage Foundation, 1967.

Halle, Nils H. "Social Position and Foreign Policy Attitudes: A Comparative Study of France, Norway and Poland," *Journal of Peace Research*. 3:1 (1966), 46–74.

Hanna, William John, and Judith Lynne Hanna. "The Problem of Ethnicity and Fractionalism in African Survey Research," *The Public Opinion Quarterly*. 30:2 (Summer 1966), 290–294.

Hauck, Mathew, and Stanley Steinkemp. *Survey Reliability and Interviewer Competence*. Urbana: University of Illinois, Bureau of Economic and Business Research, 1964.

Hochstim, Joseph R., and Dilman M. K. Smith. "Area Sampling or Quota Control? — Three Sampling Experiments," *The Public Opinion Quarterly*. 12:1 (Spring 1948), 73–80.

Horowitz, Irving Louis, editor. *The Rise and Fall of Project Camelot: Studies in the Relationship between Social Science and Practical Politics*. Cambridge, Mass.: M.I.T. Press, 1967.

Hyman, Herbert. *Survey Design and Analysis: Principles, Cases and Procedures*. Glencoe, Ill.: The Free Press, Publishers, 1955.

Hyman, Herbert H. "World Surveys—The Japanese Angle," *International Journal of Opinion and Attitude Research*. 1:2 (June 1947), 18–29.

Hyman, Herbert H., with William J. Cobb, Jacob J. Feldman, Clyde W. Hart, and Charles Herbert Stember. *Interviewing in Social Research*. Chicago, Ill.: University of Chicago Press, 1954.

Inkeles, Alex, and Raymond A. Bauer, with the assistance of David Gleicher and Irving Rosow. *The Soviet Citizen: Daily Life in a Totalitarian Society*. Cambridge, Mass.: Harvard University Press, 1959.

International Sociological Association. *Transactions of the Fifth World Congress of Sociology, Washington, D.C., 2–8 September 1962*. Volume IV: *Nature and Problems of Sociological Theory, Sociology of Knowledge, the Research Committees: Abstracts of Papers and Discussions*. Louvain, Belgium: International Sociological Association, 1964.

Jacobson, Eugene. "Methods Used for Producing Comparable Data in the OCSR Seven-Nation Attitude Study," *The Journal of Social Issues*. 10:4 (1954), 40–51.

Jones, Emily L. "The Courtesy Bias in South-East Asian Surveys," *International Social Science Journal*. 15:1 (1963), 70–76.

Kahn, Robert L., and Charles F. Cannell. *The Dynamics of Interviewing: Theory, Technique and Cases*. New York: John Wiley & Sons, Inc., 1957.

Kapferer, Clodwig. "The Use of Sample Surveys by OECD," *International Social Science Journal*. 16:1 (1964), 63–69.

Kendall, Patricia L. "The Ambivalent Character of Nationalism among Egyptian Professionals," *The Public Opinion Quarterly*. 20:1 (Spring 1956), 277–289.

Kish, Leslie. *Survey Sampling*. New York: John Wiley & Sons, Inc., 1965.

König, René, editor. *Handbuch der Empirischen Sozialforschung*. Rev. ed. Two volumes. Stuttgart: Ferdinand Enke Verlag, 1967.

Landsberger, Henry A., and Antonio Saavedra. "Response Set in Developing Countries," *The Public Opinion Quarterly*. 31:2 (Summer 1967), 214–229.

Lane, Robert E., and David O. Sears. *Public Opinion*. Englewood Cliffs, N.J.: Prentice-Hall, Inc., 1964.

Langeschmidt, Waldo. "Studies of the South African Bantu: Paper Presented at the 13th Annual Conference of the American Association for Public Opinion Research, Chicago, Ill., 8–11 May 1958," *The Public Opinion Quarterly.* 22:2 (Summer 1958), 194–195.

Lerner, Daniel, editor. "Attitude Research in Modernizing Areas: Special Issue," *The Public Opinion Quarterly.* 22:3 (Summer 1958a), 217–420.

Lerner, Daniel, with the collaboration of Lucille W. Pevsner. *The Passing of Traditional Society: Modernizing the Middle East.* Glencoe, Ill.: The Free Press, 1958b.

Levine, Sol, and Gerald Gordon. "Maximizing Returns on Mail Questionnaires," *The Public Opinion Quarterly.* 22:4 (Winter 1958–1959), 568–575.

Lewis, Ralph, and Helen M. Crossley. "Opinion Surveying in Korea," *The Public Opinion Quarterly.* 28:2 (Summer 1964), 257–272.

Linz, Juan J., and Amando de Miguel. "Within-Nation Differences and Comparisons: The Eight Spains." In Merritt & Rokkan (1966), pp. 267–319.

Lipset, Seymour Martin. *Political Man: The Social Bases of Politics.* Garden City, N.Y.: Doubleday & Company, Inc., 1960; copyright © 1960 by Seymour Martin Lipset; reprinted by permission of Doubleday & Company, Inc.

Lipset, Seymour Martin, and Reinhard Bendix. *Social Mobility in Industrial Society.* Berkeley and Los Angeles: University of California Press, 1959.

Lipset, Seymour Martin, and Hans L. Zetterberg. "Social Mobility in Industrial Societies." In Lipset & Bendix (1959), pp. 11–75.

Lowe, Francis E., and Thomas C. McCormick. "Some Survey Sampling Biases," *The Public Opinion Quarterly.* 19:3 (Fall 1955), 303–315.

Magid, Frank N., Nicholas G. Fotion, and David Gold. "A Mail-Questionnaire Adjunct to the Interview," *The Public Opinion Quarterly.* 26:1 (Spring 1962), 111–114.

Marks, Eli S. "The Fetish of Sample Size," *The Public Opinion Quarterly.* 26:1 (Spring 1962), 92–97.

McCrone, Donald J., and Charles F. Cnudde. "Toward a Communications Theory of Democratic Political Development: A Causal Model," *The American Political Science Review.* 61:1 (March 1967), 72–79.

McDonagh, Edward C., and A. Leon Rosenblum. "A Comparison of Mailed Questionnaires and Subsequent Structured Interviews," *The Public Opinion Quarterly.* 29:1 (Spring 1965), 131–136.

Merritt, Anna J., and Richard L. Merritt, editors. *Public Opinion in Occupied Germany: The OMGUS Surveys, 1945–1949.* Urbana: University of Illinois Press, 1970.

Merritt, Richard L. "The USIA Surveys: Tools for Policy and Analysis" [1968a]. In Merritt & Puchala (1968), pp. 3–30.

Merritt, Richard L. "Visual Representation of Mutual Friendliness" [1968b]. In Merritt & Puchala (1968), pp. 111–141.

Merritt, Richard L., and Donald J. Puchala, editors. *Western European Perspectives on International Affairs: Public Opinion Studies and Evaluations.* New York: Frederick A. Praeger, Publishers, 1968.

Merritt, Richard L., and Stein Rokkan, editors. *Comparing Nations: The Use of Quantitative Data in Cross-National Research.* New Haven and London: Yale University Press, 1966.

Metzner, Helen, and Floyd Mann. "Effects of Grouping Related Questions in Questionnaires," *The Public Opinion Quarterly.* 17:1 (Spring 1953), 136–141.

Miller, S. M. "Comparative Social Mobility: A Trend Report and Bibliography," *Current Sociology.* 9:1 (1960), 1–89.

Mitchell, Robert Edward. "Survey Materials Collected in the Developing Countries: Sampling, Measurement, and Interviewing Obstacles to Intra- and International Comparisons," *International Social Science Journal.* 17:4 (1965), 665–685.

Mosteller, Frederick, Herbert Hyman, Philip J. McCarthy, Eli S. Marks, David B. Truman, with the collaboration of Leonard W. Doob, Duncan MacRae, Jr., Frederick F. Stephan, Samuel A. Stouffer, and S. S. Wilks. *The Pre-Election Polls of 1948: Report to the Committee on Analysis of Pre-Election Polls and Forecasts.* New York: Social Science Research Council, 1949.

Noelle, Elisabeth. *Umfragen in der Massengesellschaft: Einführung in die Methoden der Demoskopie.* Reinbek bei Hamburg: Rowohlt Taschenbuch Verlag GmbH, 1963.

Olmsted, Donald W. "The Accuracy of the Impressions of Survey Interviewers," *The Public Opinion Quarterly.* 26:4 (Winter 1962), 635–647.

O'Neill, Harry W. "Response Style Influence in Public Opinion Surveys," *The Public Opinion Quarterly.* 31:1 (Spring 1967), 95–102.

Osgood, Charles E. "On the Strategy of Cross-National Research into Subjective Culture," *Social Sciences Information.* 6:1 (February 1967), 5–37.

Payne, Stanley L. *The Art of Asking Questions.* Princeton, N.J.: Princeton University Press, 1951.

Perry, Paul. "Gallup Poll Election Survey Experience, 1950 to 1960," *The Public Opinion Quarterly.* 26:2 (Summer 1962), 272–279.

Pool, Ithiel de Sola, Robert P. Abelson, and Samuel Popkin. *Candidates, Issues & Strategies: A Computer Simulation of the 1960 and 1964 Presidential Elections.* Cambridge, Mass.: M.I.T. Press, 1965.

Przeworski, Adam, and Henry Teune. "Equivalence in Cross-National Research," *The Public Opinion Quarterly.* 30:4 (Winter 1966–1967), 551–568.

Puchala, Donald J. "Factor Analysis in International Survey Research." In Merritt & Puchala (1968), pp. 142–172.

Radio Free Europe, Audience Research. *Flight Motivations of Refugees from Four Soviet Block Countries.* Munich: Radio Free Europe, September 1963; mimeographed.

Radio Free Europe, Audience Research. Reports on Eastern European visitors to the West: *America or Russia: 3200 East European Respondents Select the "Most Influential Country in the World"* (June 1965). *East European Respondents Assess Future East-West Relations* (September 1965). *The Image of National Economic Independence: An Attitude Survey of 3,000 East Europeans* (December 1965). *The Attitudes of Czechoslovak, Hungarian and Polish Respondents toward Cooperation with the Government* (January 1966). *The Arab-Israeli Conflict and Public Opinion in Eastern Europe* (July 1967). *East European Attitudes to the Vietnam Conflict: A Study in Radio Effectiveness* (July 1967). *Identification with North or South Vietnam in Eastern Europe* (April 1968). Munich: Radio Free Europe, 1965–1968; mimeographed.

Radvanyi, Laszlo. "Problems of International Opinion Surveys," *International Journal of Opinion and Attitude Research.* 1:2 (June 1947), 20–51.

Ramond, Charles, chairman. "Public Opinion in South Vietnam: Papers Presented at the 22nd Annual Conference of the American Association for Public Opinion Research, Lake George, N.Y., 18–21 May 1967," *The Public Opinion Quarterly.* 31:3 (Fall 1967), 446–448.

Reader's Digest. *The European Common Market and Britain.* New York: The Reader's Digest Association, Inc., 1963.

Reigrotski, Erich, and Nels Anderson. "National Stereotypes and Foreign Contacts," *The Public Opinion Quarterly.* 23:4 (Winter 1959–1960), 515–528.

Ringer, Benjamin B., and David L. Sills. "Political Extremists in Iran: A Secondary Analysis of Communications Data," *The Public Opinion Quarterly.* 16:4 (Winter 1952–1953), 689–701.

Robin, Stanley S. "A Procedure for Securing Returns to Mail Questionnaires," *Sociology and Social Research.* 50:1 (October 1965), 24–35.

Rokkan, Stein. "An Experiment in Cross-National Research Co-operation: The Organization for Comparative Social Research," *International Social Science Bulletin.* 7:4 (1955a), 645–652.

Rokkan, Stein. "Party Preferences and Opinion Patterns in Western Europe: A Comparative Analysis," *International Social Science Bulletin.* 7:4 (1955b), 575–596.

Rokkan, Stein, and Sidney Verba. *Comparative Survey Analysis.* Paris and The Hague: Mouton & Co., 1969.

Rommetveit, Ragnar, and Joachim Israel. "Notes on the Standardization of Experimental Manipulations and Measurements in Cross-National Research," *The Journal of Social Issues.* 10:4 (1954), 61–68.

Roos, Leslie L., Jr., and Noralou P. Roos. "Secondary Analysis in the Developing Areas," *The Public Opinion Quarterly.* 31:2 (Summer 1967), 272–278.

Rosenberg, Morris. *The Logic of Survey Analysis.* New York: Basic Books, Inc., Publishers, 1968.

Rosenthal, Howard. "The Popularity of Charles de Gaulle: Findings from Archive-Based Research," *The Public Opinion Quarterly.* 31:3 (Fall 1967), 381–398.

Scheuch, Erwin K. *Die Anwendung von Auswahlverfahren bei Repräsentativ-Befragungen, Unter besonderer Berücksichtigung der Sozialforschung durch akademische Institute.* Inaugural-Dissertation zur Erlangung des Doktorgrades der Wirtschafts- und Sozialwissenschaftlichen Fakultät der Universität zu Köln, 1956.

Scheuch, Erwin K. "Auswahlverfahren in der Sozialforschung." In König (1967), pp. 309–347.

Scheuch, Erwin K. "Die Sichtbarkeit politischer Einstellungen im alltäglichen Verhalten." In Scheuch & Wildenmann (1965), pp. 169–214.

Scheuch, Erwin K., and Rudolf Wildenmann, editors. *Zur Soziologie der Wahl.* Köln and Opladen: Westdeutscher Verlag, 1965.

Schröter, Gerhard. *Jugendliche Flüchtlinge aus der SBZ.* München: infratest-Verlag-G.m.b.H., 1958.

Schubert, Glendon. "Ideological Distance: A Smallest Space Analysis Across Three Cultures," *Comparative Political Studies.* 1:3 (October 1968), 319–349.

Sheatsley, Paul B., and Herbert H. Hyman. "The Use of Surveys to Predict Behavior," *International Social Science Bulletin.* 5:3 (1953), 467–519.

Sjoberg, Gideon. "A Questionnaire on Questionnaires," *The Public Opinion Quarterly.* 18:4 (Winter 1954–1955), 423–427.

Stephan, Frederick F., and Philip J. McCarthy. *Sampling Opinions: An Analysis of Survey Procedures.* New York: John Wiley & Sons, Inc., 1958.

Stern, Eric. "Comparing Results from Different Countries: Paper Presented at the 4th Annual Conference of the World Association for Public Opinion Research, Tunbridge Wells, England, September 1951," *International Social Science Bulletin.* 5:3 (1953), 534–535.

Stycos, J. Mayone. "Further Observations on the Recruitment and Training of Interviewers in Other Cultures," *The Public Opinion Quarterly.* 19:1 (Spring 1955), 68–78.

Suchman, Edward A. "An Analysis of 'Bias' in Survey Research," *The Public Opinion Quarterly*. 26:1 (Spring 1962), 102–111.

Sudman, Seymour. "Quantifying Interviewer Quality," *The Public Opinion Quarterly*. 30:4 (Winter 1966–1967), 664–667.

Sullivan, Robert L. "Problems of Public Opinion Measurement in Vietnam: Paper Presented at the 22nd Annual Conference of the American Association for Public Opinion Research, Lake George, N.Y., 18–21 May 1967," *The Public Opinion Quarterly*. 31:3 (Fall 1967), 447.

Szalai, Alexander. "Differential Evaluation of Time Budgets for Comparative Purposes" [1966a]. In Merritt & Rokkan (1966), pp. 239–258.

Szalai, Alexander, with Suzanne Ferge, Claude Goguel, Vallili D. Patrouchev, Henri Raymond, Erwin K. Scheuch, and Annerose Schneider. "The Multinational Comparative Time Budget Research Project: A Venture in International Research Cooperation," *American Behavioral Scientist*. 10:4 (December 1966[b]), 1–31. (Sage Publications, Inc., Beverly Hills, Calif.)

Time. "Plain People: Europe in the Spring," *Time*. 51:15 (12 April 1948), 28–32.

United States Department of State, Office of Intelligence Research, External Research Staff. *European Attitudes Relating to the East-West Conflict: A Summary of Individual Reports on Public Opinion Surveys Conducted in France, Great Britain, Italy, Sweden and Western Germany during 1950*. Series 3, No. 52. Washington, D.C.: Department of State, Office of Intelligence Research, External Research Staff, 1 May 1951.

Valen, Henry, and Daniel Katz. *Political Parties in Norway: A Community Study*. Oslo: Universitetsforlaget; and London: Tavistock Publications, 1964.

Wallace, David. "A Case For—and Against—Mail Questionnaires," *The Public Opinion Quarterly*. 18:1 (Spring 1954), 40–52.

Wallace, David, Julian L. Woodward, Eric Stern, Max Barioux, and Hedvig Ylvisaker. "Experience in the *Time* International Survey: A Symposium," *The Public Opinion Quarterly*. 12:4 (Winter 1948–1949), 709–721.

White, Ralph K. "The Semantics of 'Socialism' and 'Capitalism,'" *Foreign Affairs*. 44:2 (January 1966), 216–228. Reprinted in Merritt & Puchala (1968), pp. 38–53.

Williams, Thomas Rhys. "A Critique of Some Assumptions of Social Survey Research," *The Public Opinion Quarterly*. 23:1 (Spring 1959), 55–62.

Wilson, Elmo C. "Adapting Probability Sampling to Western Europe," *The Public Opinion Quarterly*. 14:2 (Summer 1950), 215–223.

Wilson, Elmo C. "World-Wide Development of Opinion Research," *The Public Opinion Quarterly*. 21:1 (Spring 1957), 174–178.

Wispé, Lauren G., and Paul W. Thayer. "Some Methodological Problems in the Analysis of the Unstructured Interview," *The Public Opinion Quarterly*. 18:2 (Summer 1954), 223–227.

Wuelker, Gabriele. "Questionnaires in Asia," *International Social Science Journal*. 15:1 (1963), 35–47.

Wylie, Laurence. *Village in the Vaucluse*. Cambridge, Mass.: Harvard University Press, 1957.

Zurcher, Louis A., Jr., and Arnold Meadow. "On Bullfights and Baseball: An Example of Interaction of Social Institutions," *International Journal of Comparative Sociology*. 8:1 (March 1967), 99–117.

6

RELATED CONTRIBUTIONS
FROM THE BEHAVIORAL SCIENCES

Although the most frequently used, the research methodologies discussed in the previous four chapters are by no means the only ones germane to the systematic cross-national study of politics. Still others stem from the fields of social psychology, anthropology, and psychology. The purpose of this chapter is to describe some of these related approaches and, through examples from recent research, to suggest their use to the student of comparative politics. But first, two caveats.

Only rarely are the approaches to be described in this chapter directly applicable to comparisons of the attributes of nation-states. The student who wants to compare, let us say, the politics of Germany and France will find these approaches only partly useful. In the case of surveys with special samples, there is the critical problem of representativeness: How confident can we be that the views of 100 schoolchildren in Boston or Los Angeles will reflect accurately the perspectives of all American youngsters (not to speak of the adult population as well)? Political anthropology usually deals with groups that are only more or less well integrated subcultures of a national society: To what extent can we extrapolate findings from a small Indian village in southern Mexico to all of that country's political culture? And, of course, the various types of cross-cultural studies of personality raise much the same kind of question, as well as others about the basic validity of the research instruments used in such studies. Only in a few cases are the units of analysis used in all these approaches directly or even indirectly isomorphic with national populations.

The usefulness of these various approaches lies rather in their relevance to more general theories of politics. In this sense they parallel and complement direct cross-national studies. Both aim at providing data for testing universal propositions about politics. The very fact that their units of analysis vary is their strength. Cross-national and cross-cultural data provide the researcher with a double-edged sword to use in replacing parochial with general postulates about political institutions and processes. And, if nothing else, propositions with cross-cultural validity across perhaps a hundred tribal societies throughout the world should give the student of cross-national politics interesting hypotheses that he can test using his own brand of data.

The second caveat is that each of the approaches discussed in this chapter carries with it a heavy burden of methodological problems. Some of these—the representativeness of samples, the validity of indicators, the reliability of data, and so forth—crop up in each of the other types of research reviewed in this volume. Others are unique to the particular approach. This chapter will not go into such methodological issues. Its purpose is solely to make the reader aware of approaches supplemental to those customary in cross-national research; to discuss methodological issues in great detail would, besides doubling or tripling the length of the chapter, take us far afield from this central concern.

Surveys with Limited Samples

One type of approach is similar in most respects to the sample surveys outlined in Chapter 5. It asks a restricted number of individuals to respond to oral or written questionnaires containing a variety of questions and other testing instruments. The difference lies in the sample. Those surveys discussed earlier aimed almost exclusively at the selection of randomized national samples. It is also possible, however, to restrict the sample to a small subgroup within the national population. The advantage of such a strategy is flexibility. (Sometimes at least, given the high cost of nationwide sample surveys, such restricted samples may also lighten the researcher's economic burdens.) If the researcher uses as his sample the students in his introductory psychology course or children in the local elementary school, then it is more likely that he can personally supervise the field research, he can ask more detailed questions or search for responses that require the interviewees to perform some intellectual labor, and he can afford more easily to revise his research instruments and even, if necessary, repeat the entire survey.

Broadening the project to include comparable samples elsewhere may require the recruitment of personnel to carry it through in the new areas. Provided that the instruments are functionally equivalent, the samples are truly comparable, and the field work is conducted with equal care, it is possible to make comparisons of the various samples' responses. But—and this is a crucial point—the fact that samples of high school students in Nashville and Nancy give comparable responses in a survey does not necessarily mean that the finding are valid for all American and French high school students or for the American and French populations as a whole. To find that out the researcher would have to conduct surveys with national samples of the high school or adult populations of the two countries. If the researcher bears this limitation in mind, however, he will still be able to make limited generalizations with cross-national validity on the basis of his data from high school students in Nashville and Nancy.

The research reported here consists exclusively of projects conducted in several countries among schoolchildren and college students. There are, of course, many similar projects dealing with other special groups, such as trade unionists (Wipper, 1964) or teachers (Rokkan, 1955; see also the OCSR survey reported in Chapter 5). And still others compare groups within only two or three countries (Lentz, 1965; Seeman, 1966).

Youth's Outlook on the Future. One of the earliest of these was an analysis of college students' attitudes, undertaken in 1949–1951 by James M. Gillespie and Gordon W. Allport (1955). In all, they interviewed 1,819 students in ten countries: Egypt, France, West Germany, Israel, Italy, Japan, Mexico, New Zealand, the Union of South Africa, and the United States. In the case of the last two countries, subsamples aimed at various segments of the college population: Harvard and Radcliffe students as contrasted with those from Miami University in Ohio for the United States; and, in South Africa, samples of Afrikaans-speakers, English-speakers. Bantu, and Indians. The hope to secure 100 male and female students in each country was not fulfilled. Indeed, the sample size ranged from 31 in West Germany to 783 in the United States, from 11 women in Israel and West Germany to 119 in Japan and 189 in America, and from 20 men in West Germany to 112 in Mexico and 594 in the United States.

The main concern of the study was youth's outlook on the future. To get at this, the investigators used two instruments. The first was an autobiography written by each respondent, telling what his vision of and hopes for the future (until the year 2000 A.D.) were. These future-oriented autobiographical statements were content analyzed in a search for key concepts. Second, each respondent filled out a schedule containing 50 open- and closed-ended questions. Besides some items to delineate his social background characteristics, the student discussed his marriage and travel plans, his view of nationalism and internationalism, the probability of a major war, racial equality, democracy, and related topics.

Regarding the students' expectations for themselves, Gillespie and Allport found a great deal of cross-national congruence. All ten sets of students viewed and planned their futures within a framework of familism: There was relatively little diversity on "attitudes toward the family of orientation and aspirations respecting the family of procreation," philosophies of childrearing, and the importance of basic moral values and ethical codes of conduct (p. 37). The Anglo-Saxon students emphasized privatism, a relatively high status for women, and an optimistic outlook for the future. Women were more family-oriented than men, and also stressed the desire for more freedom and autonomy (p. 39):

> Yet in certain countries women face special handicaps, judging from our samples. They are particularly disadvantaged in Egypt, Mexico, Japan, and Italy. But here, as in all cases where countries form clusters, there is a local flavor to each national situation. What worries women in Egypt (the vote) is not what troubles them most in the United States (careers along with marriage). The solution commonly sought among the Bantu (a kind of partnership in social service) is not the solution of many Mexican women (a brief independent career prior to marriage).

But perhaps it bears stressing at this point that the women in the sample were university students and, hence, certainly not representative of all women in their respective cultures.

Regarding international affairs, most of the respondents saw war to be both needless and preventable, however pessimistic they were regarding the prospects for the maintenance of peace. "Their predictions regarding the rise of nationalism, regionalism, and a future world government do not differ greatly from nation to nation," wrote Gillespie and Allport (p. 37). "Realism seems to dominate their outlook on international affairs; wishful thinking is negligible." They found four groups to be more nationalistic than the rest, but the forms of nationalism varied. The Bantu in South Africa emphasized ethnic nationalism, an ambition "for personal achievement and for family development, but always in a manner that shows marked devotion to the welfare of their people" (p. 38), in contrast to the more political nationalism of the Afrikaans; the Egyptians expressed their nationalism both in the form of hostility toward Great Britain and in a concern for the progress of their country; Mexicans combined an optimistic nationalism with "aspirations and plans for individual achievement."

Of the clusters of nations that stood out in the analysis, the most significant comprised the European samples (France, West Germany, and Italy). The investigators discovered "strong similarities in values (for example, the desire to build a consistent personal character) and a generally pessimistic outlook" with respect to politics (p. 38).

Children's Reactions to Conflict. From 1952 to 1957 research teams under the direction of Harold H. and Gladys L. Anderson asked more than 9,000 fourth- and seventh-grade schoolchildren in eight countries to write endings to a series of 11 uncompleted stories. The surveying took place in England, Finland, West Germany, Mexico, Norway, Puerto Rico, Sweden, and the United States. One of these stories was entitled "The Lost Composition" (Anderson, Anderson, Cohen & Nutt, 1959, p. 47):

> Betty often handed in her homework composition late to the teacher. This time it was an especially important composition and she had, moreover, finished it. On the way to school she lost her composition book and could not find it anywhere.
> What does Betty say to her teacher?
> What does the teacher say?

Samples of American, English, German, and Mexican children were asked to think about these questions and finish the story with a few sentences. The researchers were especially interested in determining "(a) Who initiated the contact, the child or the teacher? (b) Whether the child told the truth or a lie? (c) Whether the teacher believed or disbelieved the child? (d) Whether the teacher punished the child in any way?" (p. 54).

The hypotheses tested were that children in a more dominating or authoritarian culture (Germany and Mexico) would respond differently from those in a more integrative or democratic culture (England and the United States). The researchers predicted that, in the former pair of countries, the children would be more likely to see the teacher initiating contact, the child lying, and the teacher disbelieving and punishing the child. By way of summary, they reported (p. 54):

> In all locations there were more child-initiated contacts than teacher-initiated contacts, and more truths than lies told. The hypothesis regarding teacher-initiated contacts and lies told were supported with but minor exceptions. In the more dominative or authoritarian locations, without exception the children wrote stories in which the teacher more frequently did not believe the child; conversely, in the more integrative or democratic samplings without exception the children wrote stories in which the teacher more frequently did believe the child. The hypotheses regarding punishment were supported with some exceptions: e.g., Birmingham [England], which was higher than expected, and Karlsruhe [West Germany], which was lower than expected.

The authors concluded that "children reared in allegedly more authoritarian and dominating cultures hold images of the teacher that are significantly different from those held by children in less dominating, that is, more integrative or democratic cultures" (pp. 54–55).

The reactions of American, English, Finnish, German, and Mexican children to a similar story, in which a child loses the meat that he bought at the store for his mother, were rather similar, confirming the hypotheses correlating authoritarian cultures and a high propensity to lie (Anderson & Anderson, 1956).

Children's Views of Foreign Peoples. In the first half of 1959, a team of researchers under the direction of Wallace E. Lambert and Otto Klineberg (1967) interviewed 3,300 children between the ages of six and fourteen in ten countries on their images of themselves, their own nationalities, and foreign peoples. To get an idea of developmental patterns of stereotyping, they concentrated upon three specific age groups: Each national sample comprised 100 children aged six or seven, another 100 aged ten, and 100 aged fourteen. The countries sampled were Brazil, Canada (with separate samples of French- and English-speaking children), France, West Germany, Israel, Japan, Lebanon, Turkey, the Union of South Africa (Bantu only), and the United States. In each country the structured interviews used open-ended questions: "It was planned in advance that the child would be free to spontaneously mention various foreign groups before being asked about a number of standard reference peoples, and that in either case he should be allowed to describe and evaluate these peoples in his own terms and indicate from where he thought he got his information about them" (p. 12).

The results of the survey focused upon both the children's differential views of themselves and other groups as well as age differences in the types of views held. An instance of the former is "the cross-national tendency to view Western nations as similar" (p. 206). This, according to Lambert and Klineberg,

> suggests that children from different parts of the world may try to identify with American, British, and French people, possibly using them as models for appropriate behavior, just as the Eastern and African peoples may be used as bad models or negative reference groups.

But these views were far from identical (pp. 208–209):

> Although there was a good deal of overlap in the children's conceptions of similar peoples and desirable nationalities on the one hand, and dissimilar peoples and undesirable nationalities on the other, still important distinctions were made. For example, the Bantu children mentioned most frequently that the Whites and the British were different from them and yet they would most like to be White or British if they were not Zulu or Sesotho. However, it is very often the case that the countries children think of as

desirable places to live are populated by people who are "like us," even though the similarity, from the children's perspectives, could be even greater if, for example, their own nation were wealthier or more peaceful. It is of interest that more children from Japan, Lebanon, France, and Brazil see the American way of life as desirable than see the American people as similar. In contrast, greater proportions of children see the Russian nationality as undesirable than see the Russian people as dissimilar. These findings suggest that at least certain groups of children, in deciding about the desirability of foreign nations, place somewhat more importance on the way of life and the opportunities available than on the characteristics of the people who live there.

"The main point," the authors concluded, "is that the children's concepts of desirability and similarity as used in this context overlap to a great extent although important distinctions were made between attractive or unattractive places to live and the similarity or dissimilarity of the inhabitants."

A study of age differences revealed that the older the child, the more likely he was to make evaluative statements (although there were some exceptions). The diversity of the descriptive content of the children's remarks, however, increased from the youngest to the middle groups, but did not change much thereafter. The overall findings of Lambert and Klineberg indicated that children learn stereotyping at a very early age. They described the process by which children develop their views of foreign peoples as one in which

> parents and other signficant people in the child's environment transfer their own emotionally-toned views of other peoples to the child by assigning specific attributes to members of particular groups during that very period of a cognitive development when he has not fully differentiated one group from another or his own group from others. By incorporating these views, he learns to distinguish his own group from those others who are said to be hateworthy, untrustworthy, and so forth.

Lambert and Klineberg concluded, "When the assignments are finally mastered, the child will be able to rationalize the generalizations that are commonly made either about minority groups at home or peoples in foreign lands, and will be able to use them autonomously (pp. 227–228; see Greenstein, 1965; Hess & Torney, 1967).

The Semantic Differential and Subjective Culture. Finally, Charles E. Osgood's imaginative efforts to extend the use of the semantic differential to cross-cultural studies should be noted, despite the fact that the work is still in progress and few substantive results have been published. One of his goals has been to test the hypothesis that, "regardless of language or culture, human beings utilize the same qualifying (descriptive) framework in allocating the meanings of concepts" (Osgood, 1967, p. 8). The verification of this hypothesis, he expected, would permit the development of "efficient and comparable linguistic instruments . . . in each language-culture community for measuring concept meanings, or, at least, their affective meanings."

By 1967, Osgood had expanded his sampling areas to 22 language-culture communities, including American English, Japanese (its own language family), Chinese in Hong Kong (Sino-Tibetan), Kannada in Mysore, India (Dravidian), Farsi in Iran (Indo-European), Arabic in Lebanon (Semitic), and Finnish in Finland (Finno-Ugric). In each such community he sampled male high school students aged thirteen to sixteen—old enough to use their own language with facility and yet young enough to have avoided heavy contamination with foreign cultures and languages. In each community he selected his sample from average high schools in urban settings.

Although the semantic differential is a rather elaborate technique, its main procedures can be stated fairly briefly (Osgood, 1964; see also Osgood, Suci & Tannenbaum, 1957; Maclay & Ware, 1961). The first step was to construct a list of 100 substantives or nouns, such as house, girl, anger, mother, that would be common to the cultures under study. Each member of a sample of 100 adolescent boys in each community went over the list and provided for each substantive the first qualifier that crossed his mind: "The house is hot," "the girl is beautiful," and so forth. Computer routines ordered the resulting list of 10,000 qualifiers according to the three criteria of "overall frequency of usage, diversity of usage across the 100 nouns, and independence of usage across the nouns (to avoid redundant dimensions)" (Osgood, 1967, p. 24). This produced a list of about 60 qualifiers, which was then returned to the language-culture community so that the members of the sample could specify opposites for each item on it. After eliminating those for which the sample could not agree upon an opposite, the end result was a list of 50 bipolar qualifiers, such as good-bad, sweet-sour, light-dark, light-heavy. This list, it must be stressed, was specific to the language-culture community that produced it; it is conceivable, although it did not work out that way in practice, that a second community could have produced an entirely different list of 50 bipolar qualifiers. To complete the first phase of the procedure, each of these bipolar qualifiers was transformed into a seven-point continuum, ranging, for example, from "extremely good" ($= +3$) through "equally good and bad or neither" ($= \pm 0$) to "extremely bad" ($= -3$).

The second phase asked a second but equivalent sample in each language-culture community to rate each of the original 100 substantives according to the 50 bipolar qualifier scales. The results were then factor analyzed. Among the more significant findings of this portion of the analysis was that, in each case, the first three factors extracted were the same: an evaluative factor (such as good-bad, pleasant-unpleasant), a potency factor (such as strong-weak, big-little), and an activity factor (such as fast-slow, active-passive). Thus, according to Osgood (1964, p. 185), "the major hypothesis of this research—that human beings share a common framework for differentiating the affective meanings of signs—is clearly borne out in the data." The final step was to assemble "the scales most purely and highly representative of each factor in each language (three or four for each) . . . as a measuring instrument—a semantic differential which can be shown to be comparable with others despite differences in language."

Work is currently under way to develop an Atlas of Affective Meaning for some 500 concepts. Very few of these concepts, it may be added, have direct relevance for the study of politics. Some, such as wealth, trust, freedom, future, and policeman, nonetheless touch upon values crucial in the political process. We read among Osgood's findings (1964, p. 195) that

> only for Americans is policeman *good-strong-active,* being *bad-strong-passive* for the Flemish and *bad-strong-active* for the Japanese (unassigned for Finns); . . . the concept of power is *good-strong-active* for both Americans and Flemish speakers; but it becomes *passive* for Finns and turns both *bad* and *weak* (but still *active*) for Japanese. . . .

These results cry out for interpretation in terms of that political process. This task is clearly on the agenda for Osgood and his associates at the Institute of Communications Research of the University of Illinois.

Political Anthropology

Properly speaking, as David Easton (1959), Carl J. Friedrich (1968), and others have pointed out, there is no completely developed sub-discipline of political anthropology. Research into the comparative behavior of tribal societies—the task of which, according to Kenneth S. Carlston (1968, p. 89), is "to perceive regularities and similarities and differences in behavior, institutions, and systems of behavior, and to develop therefrom correlations and principles of behavior"—is, of course, not a new phenomenon. And political institutions and processes have been studied since scholars first became interested in tribal society. Early reports described the role of headmen and other leaders, value structures, the processes for making key decisions, modes of declaring war and making peace, and procedures for distributing values within many such groups. The political interest, however, was usually ancillary to broader societal and cultural concerns. Not until the publication in 1940 of the collection of articles on African political systems, edited by Meyer Fortes and E. E. Evans-Pritchard, did "political" anthropology become of major importance. Since then there has been "a trend—at first almost imperceptible, then gaining momentum in the late 1950's and early 1960's—away from the earlier preoccupation with the taxonomy, structure, and function of political systems to a growing concern with the study of political processes" (Swartz, Turner & Tuden, 1966, p. 1). And, by now, the field is flowering.

Paradoxically, it is the customary method of the anthropologist, who studies in great depth individual societies, that is at once a boon to and the bane of the further development of political anthropology. Anthropological research requires an immense personal commitment on the part of the scholar. He must study carefully the general principles of anthropology and related disciplines, and he must obtain a thorough grounding in the societies in which he will perform research, both through the study of material already published and through linguistic training. His field research may require many years of intimate living with the peoples he is observing, watching their behavior in wide varieties of circumstances, and asking questions of those in the society who are both knowledgeable and willing to discuss with strangers the ways of their people. It is no small wonder that the profession has produced many competent and conscientious scholars who have made serious contributions to our knowledge of tribal and other societies.

By the same token, because of the intensity of his training, the anthropologist frequently does not have the time to become basically well versed in contemporary political science. The consequence is that his own ideas of what politics is all about tend to be simplistic, outmoded in terms of contemporary research, or else strongly derivative of the one or two political theoreticians whose writings he has encountered. Thus Easton (1959, pp. 213–214) has complained that too many anthropologists see the chief function of politics to be merely the maintenance of order, and stress unduly the existence of administrative structures as the criterion for distinguishing politically organized from politically unorganized societies. Friedrich (1968, p. 536) noted an "obvious confusion of power and authority" in anthropological writings, scoring them for an "undue preoccupation with the formalistic aspects of power" that leads to "insufficient appreciation of the informal aspects of social coercion which are among the dominant means of social control in primitive societies." A case in point of anthropologists' lack of concern with modern political thinking is a recent collection (otherwise excellent) entitled *Political Anthropology* (Swartz, Turner & Tuden, 1966b). The volume's 18 articles, all written by anthropologists, contain 270 references (including duplicates). Of these, only 7 are works by political scientists (1 each by Robert A. Dahl and Carl J. Friedrich; and 4 by David Easton, one of them cited in two articles), and 5 of these 7 are cited in the editor's introduction (1966a); another 27 items were written by such social scientists as Durkheim, Mannheim, Pareto, Parsons, and Weber; and the remaining 236 were by anthropologists or early travellers. The political scientist who reads anthropological studies touching on politics constantly wants to ask questions that evidently did not occur to the researcher, and which the latter might not even be able to answer satisfactorily because they are outside his own conceptual framework.

In addition to this special concern of insufficient background in the scientific study of politics, of course, lurks a much broader set of problems dealing with cross-cultural methodology in anthropology (see Whiting, 1954; Moore, 1961; Naroll, 1962; van Nieuwenhuijze, 1963; Carter, 1966; and Ford, 1966). Perhaps Kenneth S. Carlston (1968, p. 88) has most succinctly summarized the more important of these:

> First, the data about any one people is always a product of a particular observer. Its validity is subject to his limitations in training and personality, system of perception and cognition, values, biases, prejudices, and cultural background. Second, the data about any one people, in most cases, and about a number of peoples, in all cases, will be the product of the writing of a number of observers, thereby multiplying the distortion noted above. Third, the literature about a people which eventuates is spotty, episodic, and of uneven quality and depth. There is no standarized reporting system, as it were. Fourth, communication by informants to the observer is subject to . . . semantic difficulties . . . as well as the personal biases and limitations of the informant.

Even more basic is the legitimate question about how useful it is in the first place to compare aspects of societies that only make sense in the totality of the societal contexts. Researchers have usually proceeded on the twin assumptions that aspects of societal systems are indeed comparable (with limitations), and that the writings of past ethnographers, unless proved otherwise, can be viewed as relatively accurate. Such concerns have nonetheless slowed progress toward the development of the field of political anthropology.

With increased emphasis upon interdisciplinary research in the behavioral sciences, however, this state of affairs is showing prospects for improvement. Scholars whose primary interests are anthropological are now beginning to turn to what Swartz, Turner, and Tuden (1966a, p. 39) termed a general framework of political dynamics, with such subordinate processes as "decision-making, the judicial process, the agitation and settlement of policy issues, the application of sanctions, the resolution of disputes, etc." And, in turn, political scientists are coming to the recognition articulated by Carl J. Friedrich (1964, p. 138) that

> until political theory utilizes to the full the findings of anthropological researchers (and stimulates researchers to extend them in accordance with the questions political theory asks), we can hardly expect political theory to be "general" in any justifiable sense of a systematic set of generalizations concerning established matters of political experience.

It is this aspect of enlarging our array of relevant studies and data, permitting greater comparative experimentation (as discussed in Chapter 1), that makes many anthropological studies similar to cross-national research in their implications for developing political theory.

Case Studies of Politics in Tribal Societies. Perhaps no area of the behavioral sciences has produced so many case studies as has anthropology. Indeed, as the French scholar Marcel Mauss (cited by Gluckman, 1965, p. xxi) said, somewhat derisively, "In that mighty ocean anyone can catch a fish." Here is clearly not the place to set forth an annotated bibliography of such works. Their rich variety nonetheless bears noting. And in them—whether they be general examinations of such societies as the Cheyenne (Llewellyn & Hoebel, 1941, for example) or specific treatises on such topics as the "politics of pestilence" as practiced by the priests of Kinga in the Livingstone Mountains (Park, 1966), whether they be devoted to a single preliterate society such as the Nuer of the southern Sudan (Evans-Pritchard, 1940a; Evans-Pritchard, 1940b) or to a group of societies separated by space or time, such as the Muslims on both sides of the Sahara (Cohen, 1966)—the political scientist can find much of value for his own work.

The main uses of such case studies are two. First, and most frequently, the political scientist can utilize the information contained in them to broaden his own perspectives, to cast a light upon problems currently germane to political theory-building. Of recent efforts to do this, three stand out. The first is Roger D. Masters' comparison (1964) of tribal systems with world politics. He discovered four common elements (p. 597; see also Naroll, 1966):

> First, the absence of a formal government with power to judge and punish violations of law; second, the use of violence and "self-help" by the members of the system to achieve their objectives and enforce obligations; third, the derivation of law and moral obligations either from custom or from explicit, particular bargaining relationships (i.e., the absence of a formal legislative body operating on the basis of—and making—general

rules); and fourth, a predominant organizational principle which establishes political units serving many functions in the overall social system.

Obvious differences include the greater measure of cultural homogeneity within tribal societies and the greater propensity for change in the international arena. Among other things, Masters' comparison led him to question "the sufficiency of the theory of politics established by Hobbes and elaborated by Locke, Rousseau, and Kant" that would ascribe to international politics the "state of nature" supposedly characteristic of preliterate societies.

Carl J. Friedrich (1968), as noted earlier, objected generally to anthropologists' misuse of such concepts as power and authority, and particularly to their overemphasis upon formal procedures in the settlement of conflict. In fact, he pointed out on the basis of information culled from the Human Relations Area Files, all societies have three modes of settling disputes (p. 542): "If there are no rules at all, we may speak of expedient settling of disputes, if only broad general rules, of discretionary settling, if detailed rules, of judicial settling." But these procedures need not be formal to be effective. The fact that preliterate societies lack "a determinate legal sovereign" or "a formal judicial authority that has explicit powers to enforce its decision" may make it difficult to identify modes of judicial conflict resolution, as does the fact that "the specific and detailed customary rules for settling disputes" remain unarticulated. But neither justifies an assumption that judicial settlement is absent in a given society. Three propositions derived by Friedrich from the information in the Human Relations Area Files are of special interest to students of political development (pp. 544–545):

. . . Where a centralized governmental system exists, one can expect a fairly well defined system of law. . . .

As the centralized governmental institutions become more powerful, there is some tendency for a society to regard a greater number of misdeeds offenses against the body politic as distinguished from mere private offenses against persons or things. . . .

. . . When a society becomes more interdependent and heterogeneous it inclines to treat an ever greater number of offenses as affecting the body politic.

Thus, as Friedrich pointed out, "the extent to which offenses are considered public . . . provides an important measure of the complexity of a society."

The most elaborate attempt to use materials from case studies to develop politically relevant theory comes from the pen of Kenneth S. Carlston (1968). His primary object was a theory of the organization of action. After outlining the basic elements of such a theory, he investigated social processes in 20 tribal societies in seven African states, with reference to their geography, social organization, religion, war, conflict and its control, and law. The 20 societies, of which 13 were described in considerable detail, were chosen to be broadly representative of ecological, linguistic, and cultural factors in Africa. His inductive cross-cultural findings consisted of 274 interrelated statements expressing principles or propositions. Illustrative of these are three dealing with constitutive conflict, control, and law (pp. 404–405, 406, 408):

4.2.1. Constitutive conflict will tend to appear in a group and disintegration will tend to take place therein when its members find that identification with and participation in the group fails to provide adequate value realization and goal attainment in comparison with constituting a new group or the availability of other groups for the desired purposes.

5.1.1. The absence in a society of adequate processes of control of a temporal character conduces to the appearance of tension and hostility among its members and supernatural or symbolic processes of control, such as rituals of rebellion, witchcraft, and supernatural sanctioning processes.

6.2.5. The jurisdiction of a third-party decision-making body over subject matter is influenced by the structural distance of its members from the persons subject to its jurisdiction. The greater the structural distance the more likely its jurisdiction will be confined to important offenses and appeals from third-party decision-making bodies which are closer in structural relationship to the persons subject to their jurisdiction.

In discussing the modern implications of such findings, Carlston found many parallels between the development of principles of human dignity and law in tribal societies and current needs in the international society. Drawing upon his summary of data, for instance, which showed that "where there is a minimal development of a sanctioning process to support legal norms, a mediation process may appear and develop to great refinement," he argued (p. 423) that "the possibilities of the mediation process in the settlement of international disputes . . . be vigorously pursued."

Conversely, it is also possible to use materials stemming from case studies to impose intellectual order upon diverse forms of tribal politics. Thus many anthropologists have developed taxonomies of political systems. Fortes and Evans-Pritchard (1940b, p. 5), for instance, divided societies into those with and those without "centralized authority, administrative machinery, and judicial institutions—in short, a government—and in which cleavages of wealth, privilege, and status correspond to the distribution of power and authority"; and Max Gluckman (1965, p. 83) ranged tribal political systems along a scale of morphological development, beginning with the small hunting-band, all of whose members are related to one another by blood or marriage and who accept the leadership of one or more of their senior members. There are larger bands composed of more people. Then we find fairly large tribes organized in an elaborate framework of "kinship" groups, or sets of age-mates, before we come to chiefdoms with some instituted authority and governmental organization, and finally to quite large-scale kingdoms.

Gluckman's scale necessitated the assumption that "governmental apparatus with authority" makes a difference in types of political systems but, unlike Fortes and Evans-Pritchard, he denied that types of political systems were necessarily associated with the degree to which social organization was complicated. More recently Lucy Mair (1962) published an analysis of "primitive government" that went far in removing the institutional bias of earlier studies. Her concern was not so much the identification of governmental structures (such as a code of laws, a judiciary, a police force) as it was determining how preliterate societies in East Africa perform such vital functions of government as rule-making, adjudication, and enforcement. Her organization of traditional material in a new—and, from the viewpoint of contemporary political science, sounder and more relevant—conceptual framework has in turn contributed to political theorists' trying to improve upon such frameworks.

Cross-Cultural Studies: Systematic Secondary Analyses. The sheer mass of travellers' and ethnographers' reports has led some scholars to seek ways of systematizing the information contained in them. In 1937 George Peter Murdock and a group of social scientists at Yale University's Institute of Human Relations initiated what came to be called the Human Relations Area Files (HRAF). It was to be a systematic collection and organization of data on all aspects of human behavior and social life in primitive cultures throughout the world as well as such historical cultures as imperial Rome and such modern cultures as twentieth-century Japan and Connecticut (Murdock, 1940; Murdock, Ford, Hudson, Kennedy, Simmons & Whiting, 1965). The present system of files, according to the June 1968 listing, includes 286 different societies and cultures. "The file on each society consists of pages from both published and unpublished sources which are photographed, reduced to a standard size, coded for topical content by trained analysts, printed in multiple copies, and cross-filed under topical categories" (HRAF, n.d., p. 4). These files, available in printed form at close to two dozen American and foreign universities and in microfilm form at as many again, may well serve the political scientist interested in cross-cultural patterns of authority, socialization of the young, adjudication of disputes, social stratification, governmental activity, political behavior, warfare, and still other topics (see Friedrich, 1964, 1968).

To date, the potential for systematic studies with political relevance based upon HRAF data has not been fulfilled. Of the more important cross-cultural studies using these data, the earliest focused upon social structure (Murdock, 1949) and the next on the effects of childrearing practices on personality (Whiting & Child, 1953). Murdock's revamping of the cross-cultural files in the late 1950s enhanced considerably their usefulness for politically oriented research. In the years since then have come studies on the organization of productive processes among primitive peoples (Udy, 1959), the origin of primitive religious beliefs (Swanson, 1960), and two broader projects correlating large numbers of variables (Sawyer & LeVine, 1966; Textor, 1968). None of these studies bears primarily on the political process. Their importance for the present purpose is twofold: One is the light they shed upon ways in which imaginative researchers can use such data; the other is the fact that, as political scientists concern themselves to an ever growing extent with aspects of political culture (see, for example, Pye & Verba, 1965) and socialization processes (see Greenstein, 1968), cross-cultural studies provide a useful basis from which to proceed.

George Peter Murdock himself was the first scholar to use the HRAF data in an extensive, systematic manner. His study *Social Structure* (1949) examined sociocultural variables for 250 societies: residence, kinship, marriage, incest, nomenclature, and the like. It concentrated almost solely, however, on "a single aspect of the social life of man— his family and kinship organization and their relation to the regulation of sex and marriage" (p. vii). Hence political structures and functions as such played little role in the study. In Murdock's view, which he characterized as the "cross-cultural perspective," government served a double function (p. 84): "channelizing collective action and social control," and offering "to those in authority an opportunity to use their power for selfish aggrandizement." But the only variable for which he offered data was the relative dependence or independence of the societies. "Among the factors favoring wider political organization, settled life appears to be peculiarly important," he wrote (p. 85) on the basis of data for 212 societies; "the bands of migratory tribes are usually politically independent, whereas the villages and settlements of sedentary populations are more commonly organized into larger aggregates." In subsequent publications, Murdock was to become more interested in political processes.

John W. M. Whiting and Irvin L. Child (1953) had coders evaluate HRAF and supplementary material on 75 different cultures in terms of five systems of behavior—oral, anal, sexual, dependence, and aggression —relevant to child-training practices. A basic assumption was that "infants in every society would initially develop habits" in each system and, further, that each process of development was subject to control and discipline on the part of parents and others (p. 46). Thus,

> it appears that in every society children must be weaned from breast to bottle and taught to eat food in an appropriate manner; that in every society children must be taught to defecate at the proper time and the proper place; that in every society children must be taught the rules of sexual propriety; that in every society children must be taught to be self-reliant and responsible; and that in every society children must be taught to curb their aggressive impulses and express them only when it is considered appropriate or tolerable by the rules of the society.

Whiting and Child were interested not only in "the age at the onset of socialization for each of the five systems" in each of the 75 cultures, but also in "the relative importance of various agents of socialization, e.g., parents, relatives, nonrelatives, and specialists, and the frequency and intensity of various techniques of socialization such as physical punishment, threats, ostracism, denial of love, and ridicule" (pp. 47–48). More important was their concern with initial satisfaction potential —the development of satisfactions during "an initial period when certain habits motivated by each of these five drives are learned"—and with socialization anxiety potential—the amount of anxiety in a later period of socialization during which the "initial habits are replaced, generally under pressure from parents, by habits appropriate to older children and adults" (p. 47).

The findings discovered by Whiting and Child related primarily to the integration of culture and personality development. With respect to the former, they found "ample, though not uniform, verification" of a special version of the "hypothesis that personality variables function to integrate culture"—namely, "that customs relating to childhood are integrated with customs in the projective systems of a culture through personality variables" (p. 309). Regarding personality development, their data clearly confirmed the hypothesis that "extreme frustration . . . of a particular form of behavior in childhood may produce a continuing fixation of interest on that particular form of behavior," and tentatively confirmed a similar hypothesis about the effect of extreme indulgence of the particular form of behavior in childhood (p. 315). They also demonstrated that guilt is less a consequence of the degree of socialization anxiety than of problems of identification (p. 317). Accordingly, the child rewards himself

> by imitation of the parents' evaluative responses, showing that the tendency

for the child to do so is especially strong if the parents' direct expression of approval is partially withdrawn at a time when the child is strongly driven to obtain that approval.

Finally, they showed that "fear of others is primarily associated with anxiety about aggression"—the result either of the mechanism of projection or that of displacement (p. 318). In a world that seems to be witnessing an increase in violence, this finding is one that deserves more careful attention in empirical political research.

In 1957 George Peter Murdock published his proposal for a world ethnographic sample to provide a basis for systematic cross-cultural research. He divided the world into six large regions and each of these into ten smaller areas. Within each area he sought to select ten cultures meeting certain criteria of importance, description in the ethnographic literature, and representativeness in terms of the various types of economies, descent rules, and linguistic stocks in the individual subregions. The list published in 1957 comprised 565 separate cultures. By 1967 he had increased it to 862 societies classified into 412 clusters: 85 in Africa; 55 in Circum-Mediterranean (which includes Europe, Caucasia, the Near East, and northern and northeastern Africa); 66 in East Eruasia; 70 in the Insular Pacific; 69 in North America; and 67 in South America. For each, he then proposed to gather cultural data on a variety of factors. On the degree of political integration in a culture, for instance, he hoped to code each of the cultures in his sample into one of seven discrete categories (p. 674):

A. Autonomous local communities, i.e., politically independent local groups which do not exceed 1500 in average population.
D. Dependent societies lacking any political organization of their own, e.g., those forming an integral part of some larger political system and those governed exclusively and directly by agents of another and politically dominant society. Colonial governments operating through indirect rule are ignored.
L. Little states, i.e., political integration in independent units averaging between 10,000 and 100,000 in population.
M. Minimal states, i.e., political integration in independent units averaging between 1,500 and 10,000 in population.
O. Absence of any political integration even at the local level, e.g., where family heads acknowledge no higher political authority.
P. Peace groups transcending the local community where the basis of unity is other than political, e.g., derived from reciprocal trade relations, defensive military agreements, or a common cult or age-grade organization.
S. States, i.e., political integration in large independent units averaging at least 100,000 in population.

Beginning in 1962 the quarterly journal *Ethnology* published lists of data for Murdock's ethnographic atlas, and by 1967 a small handbook had appeared, containing the coded data that had been published up until that time (see Murdock, 1966, 1967).

Subsequent to Murdock's major revision, Stanley H. Udy, Jr., (1959) investigated production processes among 150 nonindustrial peoples, using in part these data from the ethnographic survey. A search of the literature turned up 426 "clearly reported production organizations," which Udy then classified along 25 variables: stratification, political structure, division of labor, type of reward system, and so forth. His conclusions were grouped around two working hypotheses (pp. 126–133):

> The structure of any production organization is determined partly by the characteristics of the technological process which it is carrying on, and partly by the social setting within which it exists.
>   The structure of any reward system is determined partly by the characteristics of the production organization involved, and partly by the social setting, within limits imposed by features of the technological process.

The specific conclusions comprised 58 verified propositions. Societies with centralized governments, for instance, are more likely than those without them "to possess complex hierarchies of general social stratification" and "to practice settled agriculture"; in such societies, "production organizations are characterized by managerial or separated, rather than corporate, proprietorship" (p. 131).

Guy E. Swanson (1960) investigated the origins of religious beliefs in 50 primitive and ancient peoples. Drawing upon Murdock's list of 556 societies (a list that predated the publication of the world ethnographic sample [1957]), grouped into 50 broad regions of the world, and after checking for the availablity of material, Swanson selected at random one society from each region. He coded each on 39 variables, ranging from the societies' means of sustenance, to their kinship structure and political organization, to their belief in supernature. In some cases the coding was dichotomous—the presence or absence of cannibalism, headhunting, or exuvial magic (that using the excreta, spittle, or some other part or organic product of a person's body to control him or his soul). Other cases provided multiple possibilities, such as the "nature of the ultimately sovereign organization—territorial," which permitted gradations all the way from the household, hamlet, scattered rural neighborhood, or small nomadic band to the kingdom or intertribal league. Correlational techniques permitted the statistical analysis of the scores for the 50 societies.

The findings, among other things, enabled Swanson to reject four alternative explanations of supernature (pp. 177–178): "Beliefs in

supernature are fantasies which arise to compensate for deprivations";
"Conceptions of many types of spirits, especially of superior gods, spring
from man's acquaintance with such great natural forces as the winds or
sun or sea"; "Gods, especially monotheistic gods, are projections from
men's experiences with their fathers"; and "Spirits represent the element
of chance in human experience—they symbolize and rationalize the un-
known, irrational, and mysterious." Instead, he found support in his
data for the idea that "the belief in a particular kind of spirit springs
from experiences with a type of persisting sovereign group whose area
of jurisdiction corresponds to that attributed to the spirit" (p. 175). This
relationship between a type of political organization and supernatural
belief is again one that deserves further exploration, particularly with
respect to its causal aspects.

Using the rather sophisticated statistical model of factor analysis,
Jack Sawyer and Robert A. LeVine (1966) analyzed Murdock's original
data (1957) on 30 cultural characteristics of 565 cultures. They found nine
factors which, taken together, accounted for 69.4 per cent of the total
variance in the 30 variables. Sociopolitical stratification (accounting for
6.4 per cent of the total variance), for instance, had high individual
correlations with Murdock's variables of social stratification, political
integration, slavery, and hereditary political succession. Repeating the
analysis for each of Murdock's six large regions showed that these
variables were "related at least partly because of functional necessity
rather than solely because of historical diffusion from a common source"
(p. 708). One of their specific findings, for instance, pointed to "the
relation between social stratification and political integration, which
suggests both that stratification permits amalgamation and that larger
size demands more levels" (p. 729).

By far the most elaborate attempt to analyze statistically such data is
Robert B. Textor's *Cross-Cultural Summary* (1968). Both in technique
and format it follows the pattern of Banks and Textor's *Cross-Polity
Survey* (1963), discussed in Chapter 2. Textor either coded information or used existing coded data from Murdock, Udy, Swanson, and
others on 42 main categories of variables for 400 societies listed in
Murdock's *Ethnographic Atlas* (1967). One such variable (or raw
characteristic) is "Level of Political Integration," as defined by Murdock
(1957, p. 674) and discussed above. Each culture was coded into one
of seven discrete categories (or raw attributes) describing levels of
political integration (p. 82):

S. States (42 cultures)
L. Little states (28 cultures)
M. Minimal states (78 cultures)

A. Autonomous local communities (133 cultures)
O. Absence of any political integration even at the local level (23 cultures)
D. Dependent societies (24 cultures)
P. Peace groups (9 cultures)

(The level of political integration of the remaining 63 cultures could not be ascertained.) The raw characteristics were then dichotomized in various ways to produce "finished characteristics". One of these (FC 84), for instance, separated those 42 cultures with higher levels of political integration (Code S) from the 262 with lower levels (Code L, M, A, or O), with the level of the remainder either irrelevant (Code D or P = 33) or unascertained (63); another (FC 86) had 148 cultures at higher levels (Code S, L, or M) and 156 at lower levels of political integration (Code A or O), with the level of integration in the remaining cultures irrelevant (Code D or P = 33) or unascertained (63). Finally, the Pattern Search and Table Translation Technique cross-tabulated each finished characteristic with every other one to produce a large matrix of two-by-two contingency tables (which it then reduced by winnowing out those with a degree of association under a certain level of statistical significance); and "translated" each remaining table into "a proposition or 'statement' (a pair of contrasting English sentences) which states the manifest content of the table" (p. 7).

As in the case of the *Cross-Polity Survey,* the findings of the *Cross-Cultural Summary* comprise almost 2,500 pages of computer printout, listing the most significant contingency tables. Illustrative of these is the finding that, if we use the less restrictive definition (FC 86), then the more highly integrated cultures lean toward ($p < .01$) being those where codified laws are present (FC 147) and the less highly integrated cultures lean toward being those where codified laws are unimportant or absent. The more highly integrated cultures lean toward being those where societal complexity is high (FC 91), tend ($p < .001$) to be those where class stratification is present (FC 102), and tend to be those where class stratification, if present, is based on a hereditary aristocracy (FC 108). They also tend to be those where a high god is present (FC 426) and lean toward being those where a high god, if present and active, supports human morality, rather than not supporting it (FC 428). These findings, together with those discussed by Sawyer and LeVine (1966), suggest that anthropologists and political scientists will discover much of interest in such cross-cultural summaries of anthropological data.

Research in a Cross-Cultural Framework. An outgrowth of anthropologists' concern with cross-cultural studies has been the initiation of original field research conceived and implemented within a cross-cultural framework. Such projects are far from simple. If the cultures are varied or the project extensive, it almost always necessitates the organization of research teams, careful attention to the construction of a research instrument that will have cross-cultural validity, and efforts to maintain satisfactory levels of communication among the research teams scattered across the globe. These requirements in turn mean that the amount of time and financial resources needed for such projects can be immense.

One such project, carried through in 1951–1952 under the direction of Florence Rockwood Kluckhohn and Fred L. Strodtbeck (1961), examined variations in value orientations among the residents of five culturally diverse villages in a common ecological area of the American Southwest. "Value orientations," they wrote (p. 4),

> are complex but definitely patterned (rank-ordered) principles, resulting from the transactional interplay of three analytically distinguishable elements of the evaluative process—the cognitive, the affective, and the directive elements—which give order and direction to the ever-flowing stream of human acts and thoughts as these relate to the solution of "common human" problems.

They singled out five groups of value orientations as crucial to all human groups: the character of innate human nature, the relation of man to nature (and supernature), the temporal focus of human life, the modality of human activity, and the modality of man's relationship to other men. Each of these orientations has a range: past, present, and future for the time orientation; subjugation to nature, harmony with nature, and mastery over nature for the man-nature orientation; and so forth. And within each orientation different individuals or societies may rank the range of orientations differently.

Of the five communities studied, two were Indian (Zuni and Navaho), one Spanish-American, and the other two English-speaking (one a Mormon village and the other a relatively new farming community of homesteaders from Texas and Oklahoma). The researchers aimed at samples of ten men and ten women in each community; in all they interviewed 106 persons. The instrument used in the interviews was a schedule of 22 items, each of which described a real-life situation and asked the respondent to continue the story or provide a solution. Item A3, for instance, entitled "Ways of Living," focused on the respondents' activity orientation (pp. 87–88):

> There were two people talking about how they liked to live. They had different ideas.
> A   One said: What I care about most is accomplishing things—getting
> (Doing) things done just as well or better than other people do them.

```
                I like to see results and think they are worth working for.
    B           The other said: What I care most about is to be left alone to
(Being)         think and act in the ways that best suit the way I really am.
                If I don't always get much done but can enjoy life as I go
                along, that is the best way.
```
Which of these two persons do you think has the better way of thinking?
Which of the two do you think you are more like?
Which do you think most other _____ would say had the better way of
living?

On the basis of responses to such questions it was possible to rank-order
individual value preferences and to compare variations both within and
among the five communities (using, among other methods, factor analysis). Regarding between-culture differences, they found the Spanish-
American group and the English-speaking communities at opposite extremes, with the Indians somewhere in the middle (pp. 352–353). The
Spanish-Americans were oriented toward the present, toward "being" as
opposed to "doing," and toward a view that subjugates man to nature.
The Texans and Mormons were quite similar to each other, although the
former were somewhat more individualistic, more inclined to emphasize
dominance over nature, and more geared to the present over the past
than were the Mormons. The Indian groups diverged somewhat—the
Zuni toward the polar position of the Spanish-Americans, the Navaho in
the direction of the English-speaking communities—but they were closer
to each other than either was to the other groups studied.

In his discussion of the political implications of this project, Guy J.
Pauker (1966, p. 220) wrote:

> The character, elaboration, and intensity of political process within the five
> groups does not seem determined by the amount of real or seeming freedom
> from external pressure, political or economic, but by internal factors.
> Navaho and Spanish-Americans are not strongly organized to defend their
> interests in a socio-political environment dominated by Anglos, whereas
> Zuni are. Texans, Navaho, and Spanish-Americans are not organized for
> community action, although this would seem highly desirable in view of the
> precarious character of their subsistence economic basis. Situational factors,
> external to the cultures of all the groups, do not appear to be major
> determinants of their political processes. . . .

Power, prestige, or authority were central values implicitly rather than
explicitly (pp. 220–221). Thus the Zuni and Navaho sought political
office only indirectly: "Candidates wait to be drafted and show reluct-
ance to assume positions of leadership." But for members of the other
communities, "political ambition is considered normal and acceptable,
with certain reservations in the case of the Texans." A similar division
occurred with respect to political decision-making (pp. 221–222).

"Navaho and Zuni prefer lengthy and patient confrontation of opinions, carrying on debate until consensus, preferably unanimous consent, is achieved." The Navaho, however, "enhance the role of the individual" whereas the Zuni subject themselves to the will of the community into which they have submerged their individuality. The Mormons and Spanish-Americans relied upon external authority—the Bishop and the church hierarchy in the former case, the *patrón* in the latter—to guide their decisions; but, in the absence of authority, the Mormons were able to act on their own whereas the Spanish-American community found itself "disoriented and paralyzed." The Texan homesteaders "will not accept any 'boss' but will appoint ad hoc committees for whatever decisions have to be made and then act, if at all, even more informally through such members of the community as happen to be available." Findings of this sort make it clear that a cross-national study of variations in value orientations, using the approach outlined here, would make a serious contribution to our knowledge of political culture and behavior.

Another project, cross-national as well as cross-cultural, sprang from the research interests in childrearing of Whiting and Child (1953), discussed above. As a first approximation they expanded the sample of their previous study from 75 to 111 societies, and performed more sophisticated types of analysis with the data (see, for example, Barry, Child & Bacon, 1959; Barry, Bacon & Child, 1967). Then, after an exhaustive search of the HRAF material and a series of conferences, they formulated a field manual for guiding original cross-cultural research on socialization (Whiting, Child, Lambert et al., 1966, pp. 2–3):

> The major focus of theory is on the child-training practices that are important in the development of individual and cultural differences in aggression, dependency, and the internalization of various mechanisms of behavior control. These general variables have been broken into components (habit and motivation systems) of theoretical relevance. . . .
>
> The design represents an integration around several different kinds of hypotheses: (a) those viewing child-training techniques as leading to individual differences in personality; (b) those relating child-training practices to cultural expressive systems; (c) those relating social structure to child-training practices; (d) those relating certain "universal" stimulus patterns to "universal" response modes.

The study was ultimately carried out during 1954–1955 in small communities of six cultures (see Whiting, 1963a): The Gursii community of Nyansongo in Kenya (LeVine & LeVine, 1966); members of the Rājpūt caste in Khalapur, India (Minturn & Hitchcock, 1966); the Mixtecans of Juxtlahuaca, Mexico (Romney & Romney, 1966); the New England community of "Orchard Town" (Fischer & Fischer,

1966); the Ilocos barrio of Tarong in the Philippines (Nydegger & Nydegger, 1966); and the Okinawan village of Taira (Maretzki & Maretzki, 1966).

The instruments used to study socialization in these six cultures included both direct observation and interviews with mothers and children (Whiting, 1963a, p. 4):

> Intraculturally, . . . 24 mothers in each society were studied as individuals in their relationship to one of their children, and each of the 24 children (ages 3 to 10) was observed and interviewed in a standard manner in the hope of detecting behavioral and personality differences. . . . The cross-cultural measures included material on child-training practices and also religious beliefs, theories of disease, recreational activities, and so on, collected by standard ethnographic techniques.

To take a simple example, one of the variables pertaining to dependence and independence was "achievement-oriented behavior." In a carefully controlled series of observational sessions, the field researcher rated the children on a seven-point scale ranging from very much to very little achievement-oriented behavior. Parents were asked (Whiting, Child, Lambert et al., 1966, p. 80):

> How satisfied do you feel about how well P [child] does things (specify)?
> (a) What do you do when he does something well?
> (b) Do you care more about his getting them done or doing them especially well?
> (c) What do you do if he is careless?
> (d) How about when he does poorly?

Children, in turn, were asked (p. 120):

> How do you feel about doing something better than anybody else your age? When you're not the best, do you ever practice so you can get better? When you are the worst, what do you do? How do you feel? Suppose you're in the middle. How do you feel?

Data on such topics became the basis for monographs on each of the six cultures, with their focus on intracultural variations; and they will ultimately provide the basis for an extensive intercultural study.

One important aspect of this broader intercultural study has already appeared (Minturn, Lambert et al., 1964). It factor analyzed data stemming from interviews conducted by the field teams with 133 mothers in the six cultures. Using both the responses to direct questions asked of the mothers and ratings based on a content analysis of the interview protocols, the investigators found a total of 28 items that they could scale for their factor analysis: general warmth of mother, for instance, or consistency of aggression rules, or frequency and intensity of physical punishment. The analysis revealed seven independent dimensions of behavior (in addition to three weaker ones which the authors did not discuss in any detail), altogether accounting for 38.4 per cent of the total variance in the data. And, in some cases, they were able to compare their findings with those from a cross-cultural study based upon HRAF data.

Their analysis of the antecedents of childrearing suggested that within-society variation was greater on all dimensions of behavior than the variation between societies. By way of a general finding, the authors wrote (pp. 290–291):

> . . . Most studies in this area have approached socializing practices as if the parents of the investigations were operating in terms of blueprints and curriculums that are guided largely by either cognitively-monitored theories about what is good and bad for the long range development of children, or, at the other extreme, molded by the parents' own unconscious motives and anxieties, which translate themselves into behavior and, in turn, mold the children's psyches without the parents' knowledge or control.
>
> It now appears that the pressures impinging upon the growing child are much more in the nature of by-products of the horde of apparently irrelevant considerations that impinge upon the parents. These considerations of household composition, size of family, work load, etc., determine the time and energy that mothers have available to care for children. They determine the range and content of mother-child relations and the context in which these relations must take place. . . .

The mothers of these six cultures lived in substantially different worlds. "Each must solve the problems of these worlds and pass on to her children, both the problems and their solutions." The messages transmitted, the authors concluded (p. 291), were "more a function of the problems than of a theory of child rearing."

The Cross-Cultural Study of Personality

"One of the great hopes and aims of cross-cultural personality study," wrote Bert Kaplan (1961a, p. 251), "has been the feeling that a better understanding of personality functioning itself might be achieved if cultural factors could be given more serious consideration." And, in turn, to the extent that personality is a determinant of political behavior, such an aim assumes great importance. This and preceding chapters have reported many approaches to and findings about the cross-national and cross-cultural study of personality. What remains is to put these and other studies into a somewhat broader, if also necessarily brief, framework (see Hsu, 1961; Kaplan, 1961b; Singer, 1961; Hill, 1962; Holtzman, 1965; LeVine, 1966b).

The Distribution of Personality Characteristics. One general approach seeks to determine which personality characteristics are universal among mankind and which are to be found only in certain cultures. "Ethnological evidence," noted Dorothy Eggan (1961, p. 552),

> indicates that there are pan-human qualities in man, among them ambivalence toward death and a capacity for emotional involvement with others, which are more invariant than variant. But cultural provision for different ways of adjustment to universal problems does alter many visible facets of personality, and quite probably weights many elements of it toward culturally valued norms.

The task of sorting out the universal from the culture-bound aspects of personality is one that behavioral scientists have approached with a variety of research techniques—content analysis of cultural artifacts (see, for example, McClelland, 1961), cross-cultural studies based on files of anthropological data (Whiting & Child, 1953), projective tests (Kluckhohn & Strodtbeck, 1961; see also Henry, 1961; Kaplan, 1961a; Lindzey, 1961), observation (Minturn, Lambert, et al., 1964), use of the semantic differential (Osgood, 1964), cross-national elite studies (Edinger, 1964; Wolfenstein, 1967), and use of standardized questionnaires on nationwide samples (Almond & Verba, 1963), as well as special samples with a limited focus (Doob, 1967).

A case in point is the study of dreams—something which, it turns out, almost all people throughout the world have. But what cross-cultural generalizations can be made about dreaming? First of all, in her summary of anthropological research on dreams, Dorothy Eggan (1961, p. 552) found "much affirmative evidence, both experimental and ethnographic," to support the idea that dreams are "both a projection of the personality and a reflection of culture." That is, people in all cultures transform the latent content of their psyches into dreams with content at once manifest and, in certain circumstances, subject to recall; and the cultural environment of the dreamer impinges upon the content of his dreams. Second, some latent themes appearing in dreams seem to be pancultural. Thus, for instance, in research resting upon McClelland's notion (1961; see Chapter 3 above) of a need for achievement, Robert A. LeVine (1966a) found substantiating evidence in the dreams of Hausa, Ibo, and Yoruba high school boys in Nigeria. Others, however, such as the appearance in dreams of supernaturals who give important powers, aid, ritual, and information, are culture-specific (see, for data, Murdock, 1967). Third, although the symbolism embodied in dreams varies from one culture to the next, it is present wherever men dream. Roy G. D'Andrade (1961, p. 327) has even pointed to some patterns of symbols recurring cross-culturally:

There are a number of small bits of evidence to support the thesis that symbolism in dreams is a universal phenomena [*sic*]. If true, this means that man either innately or due to experience establishes a set of identities or equivalences without cultural tuition, and without awareness, and that these equivalences are in constant use.

Thus the bear-hunting dream of the Attawapiskat Cree, reported by John J. Honigmann (1961), and the symbolism it contained, would have fit well into the notebook drafted by Sigmund Freud on the basis of his Viennese clientele and his wide reading in the classics. (A fourth point may be mentioned, although it is more appropriate to an earlier section of this chapter: the societal uses of dreams show some persistent cross-cultural uniformities.)

Dreams are but one aspect of personality that can be studied fruitfully on a cross-cultural basis. Irvin L. Child (1954) found cross-cultural uniformities in nine systems of behavior: oral, excretory, and sexual behavior; aggression, dependence, and achievement; and affection or affiliation, reproductive behavior, and fear. Robert R. Sears (1961) later argued strongly for aggression, dependency, and competition as candidates for transcultural motivation systems. More specifically, Leonard W. Doob (1966, pp. 13, 29) reported that the ability to have eidetic imagery—"images which are reported to appear in front of the eyes (whether or not the eyes are open), to persist after stimulation by an external stimulus for a period of time generally longer than an ordinary after-image, to be scannable, and to be colored positively rather than negatively (that is, the image from a red object is red, not green)"—is "one which transcends culture; it may be as universal as belching or having the negative after-image of black spots in front of one's eyes after staring at the sun." And, to cite one last example from a list that could be multiplied many times over, William N. Stephens (1962) found substantiation in data from about 100 cultures for his hypothesis about the universality of the Oedipus complex.

The variant and invariant aspects of personality across cultures has posed a challenge to psychiatrists, who are interested in therapy as well as analysis (Opler, 1959; Carstairs, 1961; Murphy & Leighton, 1965). Little need be said here on cross-cultural psychiatry except to note its orientation. According to Jane M. Murphy (1965, pp. 274–275),

a major task of a comparative approach to psychiatry is to develop a scheme whereby we can discover populations or subpopulations that are freer of some kinds of disorders than are other populations. If such low-symptom and high-symptom populations can be found, then the task is to begin winnowing down the associated factors of sociocultural environment to those which may be causal. . . .

One taxonomy (Savage, Leighton & Leighton, 1965) lists its major concerns as brain syndromes (including senility, metabolic disorders, and the like), mental deficiency, psychoses without demonstrable organic diseases (such as schizophrenia, paranoid states, and depression and manic states), psychophysiologic conditions, psychoneuroses (anxiety reactions, depressions), personality disorders, and sociopathic disorders.

Modal Distributions Within a Society. Usually of more interest to political scientists than a concern solely with individual personality characteristics is the effort to describe entire cultures or national groups in terms of the distribution of such personality traits within them. There are doubtless few serious scholars who would assert that personalities are uniform in any given culture or nation: Any collection of human beings contains a range of personality characteristics and types. To say that "the German" or "the Ibo tribesman" does this or that is usually patent nonsense—although, to be sure, it would probably be possible to find some Germans or some Ibo tribesmen behaving in precisely the manner ascribed to the groups of which they are members. Despite the fact of variation within a culture or national group, it is usually possible to find some aspects of the attributes for which we have satisfactory quantitative indicators: the central tendency of the population, expressed in terms of the modal category responding to the measuring instrument; the degree of variation around the mode; and the range of this variation.

Alex Inkeles and Daniel J. Levinson (1954, p. 983) termed the set of "relatively enduring personality characteristics and patterns that are modal among the adult members of the society" that society's modal personality structure. If the society comprises the population of a nation-state, then we may speak of national character (Duijker & Frijda, 1960; see also Cattell & Gorsuch, 1965). It should be stressed that both a society's modal personality structure and a nation-state's national character are hypothetical constructs. It may well be impossible to find any single individual whose own personality structure precisely parallels the mode for the group of which he is a member; yet it is quite likely that his personality will be structured more like the group's mode than like the mode for some other culture or national society of which he is not a member. It should also be noted that a complex industrial society may be multi- rather an unimodal, that is, personality patterns may cluster around two or even more dominant personality structures. Finally, that it is possible to discover a modal personality structure for a given culture should not disguise the fact of variation within the culture around the mode. Any indicator of what is modal should also include an estimate both of the range and the degree of variation around it.

Like any other aggregate indicator (as discussed in Chapter 2), the modal personality structure concept makes possible a wide variety of comparisons across nation-states or cultures. And it is precisely this fact that makes much of the psychologically oriented research of recent years exciting to political scientists interested in the comparative approach. Most simply, a cross-national sample survey asking people questions about their hopes, fears, and other items that provide an insight into their personality yields indicators of this sort (see, for example, Cantril, 1965). And so do content analyses of elite and other publications that use the General Inquirer, with its basis in social-psychological theory (Stone, Dunphy, Smith & Ogilvie, 1966). As Bert Kaplan (1956–1962) has shown, it is possible to compare Rorschach and Thematic Apperception Test (TAT) studies across cultures. The development of cross-cultural psychiatry may enable us to use schizophrenia indices as we now use other "event statistics," such as the outbreak of anomic violence (Rummel, 1963). And, in principle at least, it would be possible to factor analyze on a comparative basis, survey data (Puchala, 1968), semantic differential scores (Osgood, 1964), and projective test scores (Kluckhohn & Strodtbeck, 1961; Comrey, Meschieri, Misiti & Nencini, 1965), and then to compare the various cultures' or nations' loading scores on the major factors. In each case, however, the success of such efforts rests upon the degree to which the research instruments are valid cross-culturally or cross-nationally —and this is a particularly thorny issue in the case of projective tests— and the samples used are truly representative of the cultures' or nation-states' population. But, methodological issues notwithstanding, we can expect to see the inclusion of more psychological scales in the cross-national research of the coming years.

REFERENCES

Almond, Gabriel A., and Sidney Verba. *The Civic Culture: Political Attitudes and Democracy in Five Nations*. Princeton, N.J.: Princeton University Press, 1963.

Anderson, Harold H., and Gladys L. Anderson. "Cultural Reactions to Conflicts: A Study of Adolescent Children in Seven Countries." In Gilbert (1956) pp. 27–32.

Anderson, H. H., G. L. Anderson, I. H. Cohen, and F. D. Nutt. "Image of the Teacher by Adolescent Children in Four Countries: Germany, England, Mexico, United States," *The Journal of Social Psychology*. 50:1 (August 1959), 47–55.

Banks, Arthur S., and Robert B. Textor. *A Cross-Polity Survey*. Cambridge, Mass.: M.I.T. Press, 1963.

Barry, Herbert, III, Margaret K. Bacon, and Irvin L. Child. "Definitions, Ratings, and Bibliographic Sources for Child-Training Practices of 110 Cultures." In Ford (1967), pp. 293–331.

Barry, Herbert, III, Irvin L. Child, and Margaret K. Bacon. "Relation of Child Training to Subsistence Economy," *American Anthropologist*. 61:1 (February 1959), 51–63. Reprinted in Ford (1967), pp. 246–258.

Cantril, Hadley. *The Pattern of Human Concerns*. New Brunswick, N.J.: Rutgers University Press, 1965.

Carlston, Kenneth S. *Social Theory and African Tribal Organization: The Development of Socio-Legal Theory*. Urbana: University of Illinois Press, 1968.

Carstairs, G. Morris. "Cross-Cultural Psychiatric Interviewing." In Kaplan (1961b), pp. 533–548.

Carter, Roy E., Jr. "Some Problems and Distinctions in Cross-Cultural Research," *The American Behavioral Scientist*. 9:7 (March 1966), 23–24.

Cattell, Raymond B., and Richard L. Gorsuch. "The Definition and Measurement of National Morale and Morality," *Journal of Social Psychology*. 67:1 (October 1965), 77–96.

Child, Irvin L. "Socialization." In Lindzey (1954), pp. 655–692.

Cohen, Ronald. "Power, Authority and Personal Success in Islam and Bornu." In Swartz, Turner & Tuden (1966b), pp. 129–139.

Comrey, Andrew L., Luigi Meschieri, Rafaello Misiti, and Rodolfo Nencini. "A Comparison of Personality Factor Structure in American and Italian Subjects," *Journal of Personality and Social Psychology*. 1:3 (March 1965), 257–262.

Count, Earl W., and Gordon T. Bowles, editors. *Fact and Theory in Social Science*. Syracuse, N.Y.: Syracuse University Press, 1964.

D'Andrade, Roy G. "Anthropological Studies of Dreams." In Hsu (1961), pp. 296–332.

Doob, Leonard W. "Eidetic Imagery: A Cross-Cultural Will-o'-the-Wisp?" *Journal of Psychology*. 63:1 (May 1966), 13–34.

Doob, Leonard W. "Scales for Assaying Psychological Modernization in Africa," *The Public Opinion Quarterly*. 31:3 (Fall 1967), 414–421.

Duijker, H. C. J., and N. H. Frijda. *National Character and National Stereotypes: A Trend Report Prepared for the International Union of Scientific Psychology*. Amsterdam: North-Holland Publishing Company, 1960.

Easton, David. "Political Anthropology." In Siegel (1959), pp. 210–262.

Edinger, Lewis J. "Political Science and Political Biography: Reflections on the Study of Leadership," *The Journal of Politics*. 26:2 (May 1964), 423–439; and 26:3 (August 1964), 648–676.

Eggan, Dorothy. "Dream Analysis." In Kaplan (1961b), pp. 551–577.

Evans-Pritchard, E. E. *The Nuer: A Description of the Modes of Livelihood and Political Institutions of a Nilotic People*. Oxford: Clarendon Press, 1940a.

Evans-Pritchard, E. E. "The Nuer of the Southern Sudan" [1940b]. In Fortes & Evans-Pritchard (1940a), pp. 272–296.

Farrell, R. Barry, editor. *Approaches to Comparative and International Politics*. Evanston, Ill.: Northwestern University Press, 1966.

Fischer, John L., and Ann Fischer. *New Englanders of Orchard Town, U.S.A*. New York: John Wiley & Sons, Inc., 1966. Appears also in Whiting (1963b), pp. 869–1010.

Ford, Clellan S., editor. *Cross-Cultural Approaches: Readings in Comparative Research*. New Haven, Conn.: HRAF Press, 1967.

Ford, Clellan S. "On the Analysis of Behavior for Cross-Cultural Comparisons," *Behavior Science Notes*. 1:2 (1966), 79–97. Reprinted in Ford (1967), pp. 3–21.

Fortes, M., and E. E. Evans-Pritchard, editors. *African Political Systems*. London, New York, Toronto: Published for the International African Institute by the Oxford University Press, 1940a.

Fortes, M., and E. E. Evans-Pritchard. "Introduction" [1940b]. In Fortes & Evans-Pritchard (1940a), pp. 1–23.

Friedrich, Carl J., assisted by Morton Horwitz. "Some Thoughts on the Relation of Political Theory to Anthropology," *The American Political Science Review*. 62:2 (June 1968), 536–545.

Friedrich, Carl J. "The Uses of Anthropological Materials in Political Theory." In Count & Bowles (1964), pp. 127–139.

Gilbert, G. M., editor. *Psychological Approaches to Intergroup and International Understanding: A Symposium of the Third Interamerican Congress of Psychology*. Austin: The University of Texas, Hogg Foundation for Mental Hygiene, 1956.

Gillespie, James M., and Gordon W. Allport. *Youth's Outlook on the Future: A Cross-National Study*. Garden City, N.Y.: Doubleday & Company, Inc., 1955, by permission of Random House, Inc., publisher.

Gluckman, Max. *Politics, Law and Ritual in Tribal Society*. Chicago: Aldine Publishing Company, 1965.

Greenstein, Fred I. *Children and Politics*. New Haven and London: Yale University Press, 1965.

Greenstein, Fred I., editor. "Personality and Politics: Theoretical and Methodological Issues," *The Journal of Social Issues*. 24:3 (July 1968), 1–158.

Henry, William E. "Projective Tests in Cross-Cultural Research." In Kaplan (1961b), pp. 587–596.

Hess, Robert D., and Judith V. Torney. *The Development of Political Attitudes in Children*. Chicago: Aldine Publishing Company, 1967.

Hill, Reuben. "Cross-National Family Research: Attempts and Prospects," *International Social Science Journal*. 14:3 (1962), 425–451.

Holtzman, W. H. "Cross-Cultural Research on Personality Development," *Human Development*. 8:2–3 (1965), 65–86.

Honigmann, John J. "The Interpretation of Dreams in Anthropological Field Work: A Case Study." In Kaplan (1961b), pp. 579–585.

Hsu, Francis L. K., editor. *Psychological Anthropology: Approaches to Culture and Personality*. Homewood, Ill.: The Dorsey Press, Inc., 1961.

Human Relations Area Files. *A Laboratory for the Study of Man: Human Relations Area Files Report, 1949–1959.* New Haven, Conn.: Human Relations Area Files, n.d.

Inkeles, Alex, and Daniel J. Levinson. "National Character: The Study of the Modal Personality and Sociocultural Systems." In Lindzey (1954), pp. 977–1020.

Kaplan, Bert. "Cross-Cultural Use of Projective Techniques" [1961a]. In Hsu (1961), pp. 235–254.

Kaplan, Bert, editor. *Primary Records in Culture and Personality*. 4 vols.; Madison: University of Wisconsin Press, 1956–1962.

Kaplan, Bert, editor. *Studying Personality Cross-Culturally*. Evanston, Ill., and Elmsford, N.Y.: Row, Peterson and Company, 1961b.

Kluckhohn, Florence Rockwood, and Fred L. Strodtbeck, with the assistance of John M. Roberts, A. Kimball Romney, Clyde Kluckhohn, and Harry A. Scarr. *Variations in Value Orientations*. Evanston, Ill., and Elmsford, N.Y.: Row, Peterson and Company, 1961.

Lambert, Wallace E., and Otto Klineberg. *Children's Views of Foreign Peoples: A Cross-National Study*. New York: © Meredith Corporation, reprinted by permission of Appleton-Century-Crofts, 1967.

Lentz, Theo. F. "Japan vs. USA: A Comparative Public Opinion Study," *Journal of Peace Research*. 2:3 (1965), 288–294.

LeVine, Robert A., with the assistance of Eugene Strangman and Leonard Unterberger. *Dreams and Deeds: Achievement Motivation in Nigeria*. Chicago: The University of Chicago Press, 1966a.

LeVine, Robert A. "Toward a Psychology of Populations: The Cross-Cultural Study of Personality," *Human Development*. 9:1–2 (1966b.), 30–46.

LeVine, Robert A., and Barbara B. LeVine. *Nyansongo: A Gusii Community in Kenya*. New York: John Wiley & Sons, Inc., 1966. Appears also in Whiting (1963b), pp. 15–202.

Lindzey, Gardner, editor. *Handbook of Social Psychology*. 2 vols.; Cambridge, Mass.: Addison-Wesley Publishing Company, Inc., 1954.

Lindzey, Gardner. *Projective Techniques and Cross-Cultural Research*. New York: Appleton-Century-Crofts, Inc., 1961.

Llewellyn, K. N., and E. Adamson Hoebel. *The Cheyenne Way: Conflict and Case Law in Primitive Jurisprudence*. Norman: University of Oklahoma Press, 1941.

Maclay, Howard, and Edward E. Ware. "Cross-Cultural Use of the Semantic Differential," *Behavioral Science*. 6:3 (July 1961), 185–190.

Mair, Lucy. *Primitive Government*. Baltimore, Md.: Penguin Books, 1962.

Maretzki, Thomas W., and Hatsumi Maretzki. *Taira: An Okinawan Village*. New York: John Wiley & Sons, Inc., 1966. Appears also in Whiting (1963b), pp. 363–539.

Masters, Roger D. "World Politics as a Primitive Political System," *World Politics*. 16:4 (July 1964), 595–619.

McClelland, David C. *The Achieving Society*. Princeton, N.J.: D. Van Nostrand Company, Inc., 1961.

Merritt, Richard L., and Donald J. Puchala, editors. *Western European Perspectives on International Affairs: Public Opinion Studies and Evaluations*. New York: Frederick A. Praeger, Publishers, 1968.

Minturn, Leigh, and John T. Hitchcock. *The Rājpūts of Khalapur, India*. New York: John Wiley & Sons, Inc., 1966. Appears also in Whiting (1963b), pp. 203–361.

Minturn, Leigh, William W. Lambert et al. *Mothers of Six Cultures: Antecedents of Child Rearing.* New York: John Wiley & Sons, Inc., 1964.

Moore, Frank W., editor. *Readings in Cross-Cultural Methodology.* New Haven, Conn.: HRAF Press, 1961.

Murdock, George Peter. "Cross-Cultural Sampling," *Ethnology.* 5:1 (January 1966), 97–114.

Murdock, George Peter. "The Cross-Cultural Survey," *American Sociological Review.* 5:3 (June 1940), 361–370. Reprinted in Moore (1961), pp. 45–54.

Murdock, George Peter. *Ethnographic Atlas.* Pittsburgh, Penna.: University of Pittsburgh Press, 1967.

Murdock, George Peter. *Social Structure.* New York: The Macmillan Co., 1949.

Murdock, George Peter. "World Ethnographic Sample," *American Anthropologist.* 59:4 (August 1957), 664–687. Reprinted in Moore (1961), pp. 193–216.

Murdock, George P., Clellan S. Ford, Alfred E. Hudson, Raymond Kennedy, Leo W. Simmons, and John W. M. Whiting. *Outline of Cultural Materials.* 4th rev. ed., 2d printing; New Haven, Conn.: Human Relations Area Files, 1965.

Murphy, Jane M. "Social Science Concepts and Cross-cultural Methods for Psychiatric Research." In Murphy & Leighton (1965), pp. 251–284.

Murphy, Jane M., and Alexander Leighton, editors. *Approaches to Cross-Cultural Psychiatry.* Ithaca, N.Y.: Cornell University Press, 1965.

Naroll, Raoul. *Data Quality Control—A New Research Technique: Prolegomena to a Cross-Cultural Study of Culture Stress.* New York: The Free Press of Glencoe, 1962.

Naroll, Raoul. "Scientific Comparative Politics and International Relations." In Farrell (1966), pp. 329–337.

Nieuwenhuijze, C. A. O. van. *Cross-Cultural Studies.* The Hague: Mouton & Co., 1963.

Nydegger, William F., and Corinne Nydegger. *Tarong: An Ilocos Barrio in the Philippines.* New York: John Wiley & Sons, Inc., 1966. Appears also in Whiting (1963b), pp. 693–867.

Opler, Marvin K., editor. *Culture and Mental Health: Cross-Cultural Studies.* New York: The Macmillan Company, 1959.

Osgood, Charles E. "On the Strategy of Cross-National Research into Subjective Culture," *Social Science Information.* 6:1 (February 1967), 5–37.

Osgood, Charles E. "Semantic Differential Technique in the Comparative Study of Cultures," *American Anthropologist.* 66:3 (June 1964), 171–200.

Osgood, Charles E., George J. Suci, and Percy H. Tannenbaum. *The Measurement of Meaning.* Urbana: University of Illinois Press, 1957.

Park, George K. "Kinga Priests: The Politics of Pestilence." In Swartz, Turner & Tuden (1966b), pp. 229–237.

Pauker, Guy J. "Political Structure." In Vogt & Albert (1966), pp. 191–226.

Puchala, Donald J. "Factor Analysis in International Survey Research." In Merritt & Puchala (1968), pp. 142–172.

Pye, Lucian W., and Sidney Verba, editors. *Political Culture and Political Development.* Princeton, N.J.: Princeton University Press, 1965.

Rokkan, Stein. "An Experiment in Cross-National Research Cooperation: The Organization for Comparative Social Research," *International Social Science Bulletin.* 7:4 (1955), 645–652.

Romney, Kimball, and Romaine Romney. *The Mixtecans of Juxtlahuaca, Mexico.* New York: John Wiley & Sons, Inc., 1966. Appears also in Whiting (1963b), pp. 541–691.

Rummel, Rudolph J. "Dimensions of Conflict Behavior Within and Between Nations." In *General Systems: Yearbook of the Society for General Systems Research,* vol. viii, 1963, editors Ludwig von Bertalanffy and Anatol Rapoport. Ann Arbor, Mich.: Society for General Systems Research, 1964, pp. 1–50.

Savage, Charles, Alexander H. Leighton, and Dorothea C. Leighton. "The Problem of Cross-cultural Identification of Psychiatric Disorders." In Murphy & Leighton (1965), pp. 21–63.

Sawyer, Jack, and Robert A. LeVine. "Cultural Dimensions: A Factor Analysis of the World Ethnographic Sample," *American Anthropologist.* 68:3 (June 1966), 708–731.

Sears, Robert R. "Transcultural Variables and Conceptual Equivalence." In Kaplan (1961b), pp. 445–455.

Seeman, Melvin. "Alienation, Membership, and Political Knowledge: A Comparative Study," *The Public Opinion Quarterly.* 30:3 (Fall 1966), 353–367.

Siegel, Bernard J., editor. *Biennial Review of Anthropology, 1959.* Stanford, Calif.: Stanford University Press, 1959.

Singer, Milton. "A Survey of Culture and Personality Theory and Research." In Kaplan (1961b), pp. 9–90.

Stephens, William N. *The Oedipus Complex: Cross-Cultural Evidence.* New York: Free Press of Glencoe, 1962.

Stone, Philip J., Dexter C. Dunphy, Marshall S. Smith, Daniel M. Ogilvie with Associates. *The General Inquirer: A Computer Approach to Content Analysis.* Cambridge, Mass.: M.I.T. Press, 1966.

Swanson, Guy E. *The Birth of the Gods: The Origin of Primitive Beliefs.* Ann Arbor: The University of Michigan Press, 1960.

Swartz, Marc J. and Victor W. Turner and Arthur Tuden. "Introduction" [1966a]. In Swartz, Turner & Tuden (1966b), pp. 1–41.

Swartz, Marc J., Victor W. Turner, and Arthur Tuden, editors. *Political Anthropology.* Chicago: Aldine Publishing Company, 1966b.

Textor, Robert B. *A Cross-Cultural Summary.* New Haven, Conn.: HRAF Press, 1968.

Udy, Stanley H., Jr. *Organization of Work: A Comparative Analysis of Production among Nonindustrial Peoples.* New Haven, Conn.: HRAF Press, 1959.

Vogt, Evon Z., and Ethel M. Albert, editors. *People of Rimrock: A Study of Values in Five Cultures.* Cambridge, Mass.: Harvard University Press, 1966.

Whiting, Beatrice B. "Introduction" [1963a]. In Whiting (1963b), pp. 1–13.

Whiting, Beatrice B. *Six Cultures: Studies of Child Rearing.* New York: John Wiley & Sons, Inc., 1963b.

Whiting, John W. M. "The Cross-Cultural Method." In Lindzey (1954), pp. 523–531. Reprinted in Moore (1961), pp. 283–291.

Whiting, John W. M., and Irvin L. Child. *Child Training and Personality: A Cross-National Study.* New Haven: Yale University Press, 1953.

Whiting, John W. M., Irvin L. Child, William W. Lambert, Ann M. Fischer, John L. Fischer, Corinne Nydegger, William Nydegger, Hatsumi Maretzki, Thomas Maretzki, Leigh Minturn, A. Kimball Romney, and Romaine Romney. *Field Guide for a Study of Socialization.* New York: John Wiley & Sons, Inc., 1966.

Wipper, Audrey. "A Comparative Study of Nascent Unionism in French West Africa and the Philippines," *Economic Development and Cultural Change.* 13:1, pt. I (October 1964), 20–55.

Wolfenstein, E. Victor. *The Revolutionary Personality: Lenin, Trotsky, Gandhi.* Princeton, N.J.: Princeton University Press, 1967.

7

THE FUTURE OF
SYSTEMATIC COMPARATIVE RESEARCH

The study of political phenomena has seen tremendous growth in recent decades. Whereas the number of colleges and universities in the United States slightly more than doubled from 1910 to 1965 (from 951 to 2,173), the number of such institutions with separate departments of political science increased fourfold by the most conservative estimate (Merritt, 1966; U.S. Bureau of the Census, 1967, p. 136). Since 1910, membership in the American Political Science Association grew by a factor of fifteen, the circulation of the *American Political Science Review* by a factor of eleven, and the number of doctorates in political science from about 10 per annum to well over 300 yearly. Of the 550 periodicals for which dates of initial publication are listed by a standard directory (Graves, 1966, pp. 586, 710–716, 843–858) under the rubrics Defense, International Relations, and Political Science, only 89 (16 per cent) existed before 1940 and as many as 154 (28 per cent) sprang up in the half decade between 1961 and 1965. A glance at the dates of major systematic studies in comparative politics discussed in earlier pages of this book will also reveal that the productive curve is rising steadily and rather sharply.

The growth of political studies—indicative, by the way, of the entire academic profession (see Machlup, 1962)—has brought with it several other developments that will affect future scholarship. Not the least important of these has been a changed orientation toward research. Scholars are far more willing now than in former times to engage in cooperative research, and the number of research institutes has mushroomed in recent years. Then, too, the development of highspeed electronic computers has greatly facilitated research for those who both know how to maximize their use and have research problems that can benefit from their use. With these remarkable gains, however, have come problems of organization, data retrieval, and training. It is with such problems that those interested in systematic research in comparative politics will have to contend in the immediate and long-range future.

Cooperative Research: Myth or Reality?

Perhaps no shibboleth has been dearer to the hearts of social scientists than the crying need for cooperative research, yes, even interdisciplinary research. Over forty years ago the eminent American social historian, J. Franklin Jameson (cited in Ogg, 1928, p. 17n), cast a longing glance at the physical sciences:

> Research in the physical sciences is perhaps more certain to be directed toward useful ends than research in humanistic fields, because the former is most commonly carried on in organized laboratories, where consultation is almost inevitable and a consensus of opinion as to what is worth while is easily formed, and has its effect on the investigator, whereas in most humanistic subjects the researcher can work in comparative isolation.

More recently, in his stimulating book *The Future of Political Science* (1963, pp. 233–234), Harold D. Lasswell envisioned centers for advanced political science, where physical and biological scientists, specialists in history, prehistory, social anthropology, economics, and linguistics, communication engineers, sociologists and, above all, political scientists "recruited from the several fields within the profession" could come together on a more or less permanent basis "to consolidate and improve the advances that have been made in integrating frames of reference among scholars and scientists and between them and the responsible decision-makers of government and other social institutions."

There is much to be said for cooperative research. Cooperative research—and let it be clear at the outset that what is meant are successful efforts in this direction—enables a more satisfactory division of labor among participants in a project than would be possible were there but one scholar trying to deal with all aspects of the topic. Sometimes it does not require two—a political scientist and an economist, possibly joined by a sociologist and a social psychologist—to dance the particular tango of a research project on, let us say, American aid to developing countries; but such cooperation is often more satisfactory in terms of results as well as more economical in terms of research time and funds. An ever more important factor favoring cooperative research is the cost of acquiring and maintaining the plant and equipment necessary for many forms of political analysis. This problem is especially acute for the growing number of political scientists who are using punchcard equipment and large computers in their research. Cooperative research may also produce intellectual stimulation and cross-fertilization that is often a welcome relief to the individual scholar who may have spent too long communicating solely to his typewriter or computer console. Then, too, participation in cooperative projects gives the fledgling researcher a chance to soar the heights of knowledge with his older and more experienced colleagues. At the very least he may learn something of the discipline required to carry out joint or individual research projects.

In no area is the need for cooperation more apparent than in the systematic study of comparative politics. If the scholar's concern is with a pair or even a small group of culturally and geographically contiguous states, then perhaps many years of study and travel will equip him to make sound judgments and valid generalizations for his limited area of concern. But increasingly scholars are interested in a broader range of countries. Time and again this volume has stressed the pitfalls awaiting those who would generalize too quickly from their own experience to the behavior of peoples with whom they are not intimately familiar. And yet we cannot expect any scholar to vest himself with intimate knowledge of a hundred or more polities. This turns out to be the case even if he is concentrating only upon a narrow aspect of their political life. In short, the very nature of his research task forces him to rely upon the knowledge, judgments, and insights of those more expert in some areas than himself. And this is particularly the case if he is seeking quantitative indicators relevant to the politics of these areas.

To date, political science has not made the transition, forecast about a generation ago by the Research Committee of the American Political Science Association (1945) as well-nigh inevitable, "from atomistic effort to collective, organized, cooperative or administered activity." The force of argument and the sincerity of the advocates of cooperative and interdisciplinary research notwithstanding, and in spite of some of the spectacular results that have emerged from such joint projects, what may be termed a vestigial element of anarchy has prevented the social scientist from subjecting his own research interests entirely to those of a research group. Perhaps rightly so. The scholar who escapes from his freedom too wholeheartedly subjects himself to the (possibly fatal) disease of "projectitis" (Dodds, 1954, pp. 91–92)—the pursuit of research with limited and immediate objectives at the cost of basic research and broad reading that would contribute to his long-term intellectual growth. The other problems of cooperative and particularly interdisciplinary research are well known—problems of communication (which are not limited merely to practitioners of different arts), of paperwork and administration, and of interpersonal relationships (see Bennis, 1956; Luszki, 1958).

Cooperative research in political affairs is nonetheless gaining headway, if often slowly and painfully. From 1933 to 1937, 3 per cent of the articles and 16 per cent of the items in the book review section in the *American Political Science Review* were the result of joint effort; by the period 1963 to 1967 these percentages had risen to 18 and 19 per cent, respectively (see Merritt, 1966, p. 388). In some of the newer American quarterlies geared toward empirical political research, the percentage of multiple-authored articles is still higher: 25 per cent of the main articles in the *Public Opinion Quarterly* from 1963 to 1967 had joint authorship (as opposed to 9 per cent in the six years from 1937 to 1942); and roughly a third of the main articles appearing in *Behavioral Science* since its inception were written cooperatively.

Somewhat more remarkable than this growth in joint authorship as an indicator of cooperative research, however, is the development of formal organizations to facilitate such research on political topics. Since 1913, when only four university research bureaus and institutes in all of the United States and Canada concentrated upon politically relevant studies, the number of such organizations has doubled approximately every eight years. By 1965, the last year for which comprehensive data are available, their number had grown to 406 (Palmer & Kruzas, 1965, pp. 193–211, 411–429, 431–478). Of these, for which founding dates are given, 102 focus on "regional and area studies." And, in turn, of these, more than three-quarters sprang up since 1950, and more than a quarter in the years between 1961 and 1965 alone.

The Organization of Political Research

In the course of these years since 1913, four different organizational approaches to political research have emerged. One of these, by far the most prevalent in the American political science profession, can be called the *all-purpose research institute*. It is dedicated to the anarchic principle of the sovereign scholar and, paradoxically enough, to the principle of equity in scholarship. At its center stands the individual scholar with his specific research interests. Although collaborative or cooperative research may be a result, it is often the by-product of the institute's allocation of funds rather than any sort of precondition (see Gee, 1934).

In its most primitive form the all-purpose research institute may exist as no more than a departmental committee, charged with the responsibilities to review research projects proposed by individual members of the department and to make necessary arrangements for the allocation of teaching and research time. With the passage of the years the committee, by now distinguished by the use of its own letterhead, may set up an office with typists, mimeograph machines, and other equipment and comforts. Not only do such accoutrements provide the scholar with a home, but they also enable him to point to existing research facilities as a cost-cutting attraction for research grants. At a later stage the faculty committee may transform itself into a research bureau empowered to seek out and facilitate the flow of research funds to individuals in the department. It may even draw upon the credit that particularly prominent members of the department have built up for themselves in the academic world to secure financing for projects undertaken by staff members of less experience or fame. To the extent that the board of directors of the research bureau is successful in securing grants that are not earmarked for specific individuals or specific projects, it gains a measure of control over the general allocation of research funds among its members. The research bureau may eventually reach the stage of organizational sophistication where it terminates its brokerage function altogether and acts only to disburse its funds to worthy applicants. It may even hire a permanent research staff or solicit applications from scholars at other universities.

The variant forms of the all-purpose research institute are numerous. One of the more prominent of these is the research organization with special fields of interest. Another is the multidisciplinary institute. Prior to the end of World War II, such institutes were most often marriages of convenience—sometimes merely collective security agencies designed to divert research funds normally destined for the more highly organized physical and natural sciences—rather than genuine attempts to merge diverse disciplines in a common research effort. The notable exception in the 1920s and 1930s was the Social Science Research Committee at the University of Chicago. Under the tutelage of Charles E. Merriam, as Harold D. Lasswell (1963, p. 158) has pointed out, an entire generation of American political scientists learned to mind their "p's and q's— the emphases on psychology and quantity." Still a third variant turns toward public service, acting as a consultant for state and local governmental agencies. And, of course, some all-purpose research institutes seek to fill all these roles—supporting monographs, providing a multidisciplinary framework for research, serving the public interest—and perhaps several others.

More recently, emphasis has turned to the interdisciplinary as opposed to the multidisciplinary or specialist character of political research. This has been accompanied by a trend toward the creation of a second type of institutional framework, specifically organized to encourage scholars from different disciplines to pool their knowledge and techniques in the common pursuit of solutions to research problems.

Truly *interdisciplinary research institutes* may be an outgrowth of the all-purpose research centers or—and it would seem that this is the more frequent origin—arise from the realization by specialists in different fields of study that they have many interests in common. The student of political organizations, for example, may notice that the problems and principles that intrigue him are closely related to aspects of industrial firms, streetcorner gangs, and, somewhat more generally, physical organisms (such as the Portuguese man-of-war), the human nervous system, and the human brain. The creation of a formal research center to house experts in such diverse topics may bring to fruition research on important ideas that are not easily pigeonholed into one or another of the separate academic disciplines.

Such interdisciplinary research centers have flourished in the years since the close of World War II. The Institute for Social Research at the University of Michigan, for instance, contains two separate institutes of this sort: the Survey Research Center, which applies sample survey methods to such psychological, sociological, economic, and political problems as leadership and organizational behavior, organizational change, economic behavior, public communication and influence, student development, mental health, as well as, of course, political behavior (see Campbell, Converse, Miller & Stokes, 1966); and the Research Center for Group Dynamics, which concerns itself with the practice as well as the theory of group behavior. Another such center, also at the University of Michigan, is the Mental Health Research Institute. Although an integral part of the psychiatry department and under the direction of a psychiatrist, James G. Miller, its full-time staff includes biochemists, psychologists, historians, mathematicians, social psychologists, industrial engineers, physicists, neurophysiologists, chemists, psychobiologists, mathematical biologists, and political scientists. The interests of the Institute are clearly in the field of mental health. The field is broad enough, however, to include a number of subjects that political scientists consider important in their own work, such as general systems analysis, mathematical models, deterrence and arms control, and conflict resolution.

Along with the rise of organizations infusing ideas and methods from other disciplines into political research came the development of more refined ancillary services—specialized libraries, bibliographies, and collections of data—to aid the political researcher in his work. The convenience of having a collection of relevant books and documents in a central location has led many a political science department to found its own library, either within or apart from the main university libraries. In many instances it is necessary to have up-to-date collections of IBM punchcards or other types of research material and equipment that the budgets or policies of university libraries do not cover. Such departmental research libraries may also serve as training grounds to familiarize both undergraduate and graduate students with the techniques of modern empirical research (Merritt & Lane, 1965). Similarly, a number of efforts are under way to provide political researchers with the bibliographic information they need. A more recent development is the creation of political data banks that not only serve as a new type of library but also as research institutes.

The idea underlying the *institute for basic research and data* is certainly not new. As any father of a small child knows, man's urge to collect anything small enough to be moved emerges almost simultaneously with his curiosity about his environment. With the invention of alphabets and tools for writing came the beginnings of libraries to store the accumulated knowledge about the past and ideas about the present and future. The political data bank concentrates upon the acquisition of information about man's political environment, perspectives, and behavior. This entails not the amassing of a general or eclectic collection of books and other documents, but the systematic collection of specific bits of information that are then put into a form rendering them immediately useful for analysis. Such is the function of the Human Relations Area Files, which has gathered and organized data on all aspects of human behavior and social life in primitive cultures throughout the world, as well as such historical cultures as imperial Rome and such modern cultures as twentieth-century Japan and Connecticut. Also important for students of cross-national behavior is the World Data Analysis Program (formerly the Yale Political Data Program), which concentrates on quantitative data useful for international and comparative research.

A key problem for basic data and research centers is making data accessible to scholars at other institutions. The Human Relations Area Files has sought to solve this problem by placing printed or microfilmed information at a number of universities. The Yale World Data Analysis Program, as well as such larger data banks as the Inter-University Consortium for Political Research, make available at nominal cost whatever data they have in their files. This represents a significant shift from the era when a scholar's collection of data and ideas was held to be at least as inviolable as his wife and daughters. This is not to say that all duplication of effort in political research has been eliminated, or even that we shall realize this particular vision of utopia in the foreseeable future. By fostering a communal attitude toward research data, however, and by expanding the links of communication both within the political science profession and between it and other disciplines, we may be reducing the probability of wasteful duplication.

An equally prominent trend is the emergence of men and women who direct their energies solely toward political research instead of trying to fulfill the traditional multifunctional role of the academic scholar. In some cases the normal academic situation imposes restrictions upon research—faculty and staff meetings, undergraduate courses, the need to counsel students and to fill out their recommendation forms, and, sometimes, the latent or active hostility of the university's administration to departures from the job of providing a liberal arts education to a body of undergraduate students—that, although stimulating to some scholars, may prove burdensome to others. Possibly more frequent is the case where scholars of like interest at different institutions want to spend more time working together in their field of specialization, even if this means terminating their university affiliation. In either event the result may be a decision to found a research institute outside the academic environs.

Although the *independent research institute* is a fairly new idea in the social sciences, extramural research has an honorable history. In an earlier age scholarship was often the profession of gentlemen who were not forced to rely upon institutional support to finance their work. Indeed, some of the finest scientific and humanistic research stemmed from such gentlemen-scholars. More recently we have seen the proliferation of independent research institutes in the natural and physical sciences, composed of men who were scientific entrepreneurs or who sought government contracts to sustain their operations. The development of non-academic research institutes (other than government operated agencies) in the field of political science is still newer.

In their early stages such independent centers for political research often resemble the "Invisible College" of seventeenth-century England, that band of scientists and artisans which met frequently to discuss joint interests and which eventually, in 1662, formed the Royal Society of London. Of modern invisible colleges in the sciences, Derek de Solla Price (1961, p. 99n) has written:

> Starting originally as a reaction to the communication difficulty brought about by the flood of literature, and flourishing mightily under the teamwork conditions induced by World War II, their whole *raison d'être* was to substitute personal contact for formal communication among those who were really getting on with the job, making serious advances in their fields. In many of these fields, it is now hardly worth while embarking upon serious work unless you happen to be within the group, accepted and invited to the annual and informal conferences, commuting between the two Cambridges,

and vacationing in one of the residential conference and work centers that are part of the international chain.

In the Center for Advanced Study in the Behavioral Sciences at Stanford, California, and in the numerous conferences on such topics as arms control and general systems analysis that tend to be self-regenerative, the political scientist may recognize his own profession's invisible colleges.

The Center for Advanced Study in the Behavioral Sciences is a particularly interesting development in empirical research. Each year the Center invites approximately fifty political scientists and other scholars, from both the United States and abroad, to sojourn in the rolling foothills of California, away from their academic chores, working on research projects of their own choice or merely deepening their knowledge of their own and other disciplines. The Center does not organize an extensive program to occupy the Fellows' time, nor does it seek to exert supervisory controls over their activities during the year. In accepting their invitations, however, the Fellows tacitly agree to spend at least some of their time working on systematic research or theory-building cutting across traditional academic or disciplinary boundaries. The Center carefully nurtures a suitable collegial atmosphere, often by inviting a number of scholars from different disciplines who are working on the same or related projects to be Fellows during the same year. By now, although only a dozen and a half sets of scholars have "graduated" from the Thinktank, as it has come affectionately to be called, the fellowship is regarded as a badge of distinction for political scientists interested in empirical and cross-disciplinary research.

Far more formal and project-oriented than the invisible colleges or the Center are the independent research institutes organized to conduct research on a contract basis. Perhaps the best known of these is the RAND Corporation, founded in 1946 in Santa Monica, California, to work on broad military problems for the United States Air Force (see Smith, 1966). Similarly, the Department of Defense, in the mid-1950s, conceived the Institute for Defense Analyses, a nonprofit corporation comprising a number of universities brought together as a means by which experts could be enlisted in the service of America's national defense policy. As is the case with the RAND Corporation, the IDA is supported by such private organizations as the Ford Foundation as well as by federal agencies. In a like manner the Hudson Institute, located in Croton-on-Hudson near New York City, will secure government and private contracts to study problems of national security and international order. The Center for the Study of Democratic Institutions at Santa Barbara, California, has a broader scope of interest—the free society. In contrast to the usual research situation, in which a group of scholars searches for funds to pursue their research interests, the Center arose out of the desire of a foundation to put its funds to good use. An off-spring of the Fund for the Republic, founded in 1952 with a grant from the Ford Foundation, it is a part of the Fund's continuing effort to clarify and publicize the basic issues of civil liberties and civil rights.

Clearly the independent research institute, no less than the all-purpose research institute, the interdisciplinary research institute, and the institute for basic research and data, has established itself as a permanent feature in the landscape of organizations devoted to empirical research of a political nature. To date, however, unclassified cross-national research has remained almost exclusively in the hands of academic centers. It nonetheless seems reasonable to expect that, as the demand for cross-national studies grows, more nonacademic centers will emerge to undertake them.

A particular advantage that a well-funded research institute has frequently enjoyed over the solitary scholar is its access to modern equipment for processing and analyzing data. This gap, however, is closing. Universities are increasingly recognizing the immense value of electronic computing facilities to researchers and are taking pains to make them available to the social scientist as well as to his colleagues in the physical sciences. But, then, how useful to the political scientist is the computer anyway?

The Computer and Political Research

The political scientist's decision to use or not to use a computer in his research is a simple one indeed. If his data are amenable to computer analysis, then it is the most rational way to proceed. He would be foolish not to make the best use of his own research time and resources.

Such a decision does, of course, imply subsequent tasks—tasks that, depending upon the political scientist's level of mathematical acumen and technological sophistication, will be less or more painful to resolve. One of these is to select or to write computer programs that will process the data efficiently and produce meaningful results. Another is the almost purely technological problem of preparing and processing the data. These tasks should not be belittled. Not only are they time consuming, they also can be extremely complicated and may necessitate considerable intellectual effort. They nonetheless entail problems that can be resolved —if not by the researcher himself, then through assistance from his university's computer center; if not immediately, then probably in the not too distant future. In short, once the political scientist commits himself to computer analysis, the next steps are clear.

More crucial than the decision to utilize computers in research or the many subsequent decisions required to implement a research design is the antecedent decision to think in mathematical terms. At one level this suggests the need to seek out and use quantitative data. These may be percentages of people responding in a particular way to the pollsters' questions, figures on the distribution of space in newspaper editorials, or indicators of gross national product or the number of working days lost due to strikes. Or they may be qualitative data that we can categorize along nominal, ordinal, or interval scales—in effect assigning numbers to them, numbers that are then subject to mathematical modes of analysis. At another level such an antecedent decision involves the use of statistical techniques to describe events and processes in terms of central tendencies, variances, and other attributes; to generalize about the characteristics of an entire population through sampling procedures; and to show relationships between variables through correlative tests. And at still another level it may entail the use of mathematical models to show the interaction of a complex set of variables. Until the political scientist is willing to take the plunge into mathematical modes of thinking, the question of whether he can or should use computers is superfluous. And, as this volume has demonstrated, increasing numbers of political scientists have seemed willing to take this step.

The political scientist's uses for the computer are various. For one thing, the development of computer technology has vastly *expanded the potential data base* for politically relevant research. It has done this in three ways: First, methods currently being devised for the storage and retrieval of information make data more readily accessible than at any previous time in our century. By no means are comprehensive data retrieval systems operational, but it is in this area that we may expect to see the most rapid advances in the next few years. Second, the use of computers has enlarged the capacity of the analyst to handle the data available to him. Instead of trying to organize in his mind interrelationships among three or four variables, or using a desk calculator to manipulate perhaps a dozen variables, he can now deal with several hundred variables and their interaction. It is also possible, as we shall see later, to store whole banks of survey data in the machine's memory and, under certain conditions, to treat all the smaller surveys as a single survey comprising hundreds of thousands of responses to individual questions. Third, the development of computer routines for content analysis has enhanced markedly the speed and accuracy with which this type of data can be produced. Indeed, as the earlier discussion of the

General Inquirer and similar routines suggested, computers have made feasible for the first time large-scale content analyses that scholars would never have dreamed of undertaking with techniques using hand coding.

However important the use of digital computers for broadening the data base for political research has been, to date it has been the role of computers in *data processing,* and particularly statistical analysis, that has been of most use to political scientists. Computers are frequently used simply as glorified desk calculators. The rapidity with which they perform the statistical tasks of summarizing data, generalizing them, and providing measures of relationships makes them tempting objects of exploitation for any researcher.

There is no need to eschew the use of the computer as a work-horse. It is, to be sure, often an inefficient use of such a powerful tool. It may nonetheless be efficient in the sense that it frees the researcher for his more important analytical chores, while at the same time giving him a wealth of processed data to work with. A table program that correlates all variables in an analysis with each other, for instance, may produce some significant findings that would never have occurred to the researcher to investigate. Moreover, there is much to be said for using the computer to perform even the most trivial of calculating operations. In the first place, it reduces the likelihood of error. Unlike the computer, the researcher may well tire of running regression coefficients after the first dozen or two, and begin to misread his data or mispunch the buttons on his desk calculator. Similar errors in his programming or preparation of data will in all likelihood cause the computer to reject the program and give him a diagnosis of what went wrong at what stage. Second, it permits the researcher to expand his analytical tools. The man with a desk calculator and little time to spend will often settle for one measure of significance, one that he thinks will be the most powerful for his own set of data. By way of contrast, if he processes his data using table programs available at most academic computing centers, he can select subroutines for the program that will produce as many as eight measures of the strength and significance of association—and at the cost of only a few seconds of machine time. Finally, it may reduce the researcher's initial anxieties about computers. When he becomes familiar with the computer as a research assistant, he may be willing not only to use it more often but also to initiate more sophisticated research projects.

Increasingly, computers are being used to process information through statistical techniques that would be prohibitively time consuming if done by hand on desk calculators. One of these techniques, to which this volume has made repeated reference (see, in particular, Chapter 2), is factor analysis. Among other things, it seeks to reduce an unwieldy mass of data to a few underlying dimensions (factors) that describe or otherwise account for variation in the data. Another useful statistical model is that for the analysis of transaction flows, which stems from the joint interests of I. Richard Savage and Karl Deutsch (1960) in large-scale political integration. It seeks to answer the questions "What is integration?" and "How can we measure it?" in terms of transaction flows of all types—labor migration, for instance, or international trade and attention patterns. A key aspect of integration is the emergence of high levels of transactions that are continuing, autonomous, and reciprocal— all attributes suggesting that the populations concerned approve of the transactions and find them mutually beneficial. But, then, given the fact that the number of transactions among any group of countries shifts from year to year, what constitutes "high levels" of such transactions? The model postulates that a special kind of interaction or partnership among countries occurs when the actual level of their transactions is significantly higher than that which would result from a purely random distribution of transactions.

Since to date transaction flow analysis has been used more to look at processes by which countries integrate themselves into larger political units than to examine cross-nationally levels of internal integration in a set of countries, a useful example to demonstrate the model may stem from the area of international trade. The model looks first of all at the propensity of each of a set of countries to accept imports from all other countries and in turn to have its own exports accepted by those other countries. These propensities are expressed as ratios of the total trade of the group of countries being considered (adjusted to take into account the fact that the model excludes a country's exports to itself). Next, the procedure constructs a matrix ("null model") showing the distribution of imports and exports among the countries that would result from a purely random distribution of trade based solely upon the propensities of the countries to import and export. A comparison of the actual distribution of trade over a given time with the expected distribution of the null model produces an index of a country's *relative acceptance* (RA) of trade from any other country. Relative acceptance scores, which tell not only the extent but the direction of divergence from expected trade patterns, can give us an idea of whether any pair or group of states is increasing or decreasing its mutual trade flow beyond what we might expect, given normal shifts in the quantity of trade transactions. A special relationship in a statistical sense is thus used to measure integration in a political sense.

Hayward R. Alker, Jr., and Donald J. Puchala (1968) used transaction flow analysis to examine trade patterns in prewar and postwar Europe, looking particularly at trade within and between the Common Market bloc (the "Six" of the EEC) and the Free Trade Association bloc (the "Seven" of EFTA). Besides finding major changes in the structure of Western European trade patterns from the prewar to the postwar years, the authors also found that "the period of all-Western European partnership is over." After the unity artificially imposed through Marshall Plan assistance came increasing divergence between EEC and EFTA countries. This does not mean, however, that the Six are enjoying closer economic ties. Indeed, using their relative acceptance figures, Alker and Puchala argue that economic integration among the Six did not move forward from the 1950s to the 1960s. They interpret these findings to mean that "unless further structural change intensifies the EEC partnership, movement toward *further* political unity in the area is unlikely."

What to my mind is the most exciting use of computers for political research is in the area of *gaming and simulation.* Broadly speaking, both entail the construction of an operating model of a dynamic system. The model must be sufficiently detailed that it functions in its most important respects (that is, those most relevant for the researcher's interests) just like the system modeled. If this is the case, then similar changes in either the environments or the structures of the model and the real system will produce similar outcomes. And if the model is sufficiently representational, then it is possible, as Martin Shubik (1964b, p. 71) has pointed out, to infer "properties concerning the behavior of the actual system" by "studying the operation of the model." Other purposes of simulation and gaming may include training personnel, laboratory sessions for students of political science, and theory-building. As heuristic devices, they force the researcher to make explicit some of his assumptions and to relate them to hypotheses about behavior; or, by observing the behavior of participants in a simulated environment, he can learn what to look for and what questions to ask in analyses of comparable real-world environments.

Despite some similarities, simulation and gaming differ in important respects. *Simulation,* according to Shubik, takes as given the behavior of the components (organism) of the model and adjusts the inputs (stimuli) to see what the outcomes (responses) will be. Note, however, that this need not mean a total disregard for the process by which the organism moves from stimulus to response. As we shall see later, scholars are currently trying to gain insight into these intervening stages by simulating series of interim outcomes. *Gaming,* by way of contrast, may or may not alter the stimuli, but focuses primarily upon the operation of the organism; any concern with outcomes is usually only incidental to this task. Thus, it studies real people playing roles in simulated or experimental environments (which may but need not include computerized inputs) whereas simulation does not need the actual presence of individuals.

The earliest use of simulation and gaming to study social processes (we may ignore uses in the physical sciences, such as simulating the flight of a Gemini spacecraft or engine testing in a wind tunnel) were in the field of military science. For example, a study conducted at the Systems Research Center of the RAND Corporation in the early 1950s, concerned with improving the effectiveness of air defense, simulated the environments of an air defense direction center in an effort to find out something about the response of its crews to enemy attacks (Chapman, Kennedy, Newell & Biel, 1959). The most extensive gaming exercise of direct interest to political scientists is the Inter-Nation Simulation carried out by Harold Guetzkow and his colleagues at Northwestern University (1963). Although it combines the use of live experimenters with that of computers, the emphasis is strictly on the human element.

Other researchers simulating social processes have turned directly to electronic computers. One research team succinctly outlined the procedures involved in such undertakings (Pool, Abelson & Popkin, 1965, p. 3):

> In a computer simulation the entities studied (and also their attributes) are represented by symbols in computer registers. These symbols are changed step by step to represent expected changes in real-world entities as known variables act upon them. The transformation rules that specify which symbols are to change, when, and how, are contained in a set of computer instructions called "the program." Thus, simulation is a way of making a computer act out a history of expectable processes that could occur in a complex real-world system.

In recent years several branches of the social sciences have begun to utilize computerized techniques of simulation: Norman H. Jennings and Justin H. Dickens (1958) sought to simulate operations in a bus terminal during peak hours; Allen Newell, J. C. Shaw, and Herbert A. Simon (1958) worked on human problem-solving; Carl I. Hovland (1960) and his associates at Yale University undertook other studies of thinking processes; Silvan S. Tomkins and Samuel Messick (1962) reported several attempts to simulate human personalities; and James S. Coleman (1962) examined such social phenomena as cliques and reference groups. In still another extensive study, Edward P. Holland and Robert W. Gillespie (1963) attempted to determine the effects of development planning and balance-of-payments policies on an underdeveloped economy, using data from India. And Rudolf Wildenmann, Werner Kaltefleiter, and Uwe Schleth (1965) simulated the differential effects of various electoral systems on the outcome of the 1961 Bundestag election in West Germany.

Several other simulations deserve special mention because of their immense potential for the cross-national study of politics. The first major use of computer simulation in political science was the Simulmatics project, carried out by Ithiel de Sola Pool, Robert P. Abelson, and Samuel Popkin (1965), which attempted to predict outcomes in the 1960 American presidential election. Its data base comprised 50 (and in some instances 65) nationwide sample surveys of the American population conducted between 1952 and 1958 (and in some instances 1960). By treating all these individual surveys, selected for the comparability of the questions asked in them, as a single national survey with more than 100,000 respondents, it was possible to break down the population surveyed into a large number of "voter types" based on seven socioeconomic variables: region, city size, socioeconomic status, sex, religion, ethnicity, and political identification. The total possible number of voter types was then reduced to 480 meaningful categories (such as Eastern, metropolitan, lower-income, white, Catholic, female Democrats or Southern, rural, upper-income, white, Protestant, male independents), each with a sufficiently large number of respondents to enable statistical treatment. The authors then isolated 52 issue clusters of questions contained in the surveys: Anti-McCarthyism, Favor Committing Troops Abroad, Pro-Labor, Soft Policy to Red China, and so forth. By delineating the distribution of attitudes on each issue cluster within each voter type, as well as the distribution of voter types among 32 states outside the South, and by making shrewd (and in retrospect accurate) guesses as to what the major issues of the 1960 campaign would be, the authors were able to predict the most likely state-by-state reactions and voting shifts in response to campaign positions that the candidates could conceivably have taken on each of these major issues.

Perhaps the most interesting aspect of the Simulmatics project is the fact that it was conducted during the midst of a hotly contested campaign, which means that its results could be used by the sponsors of the study—the Democratic National Committee—in planning their campaign strategy. The authors, for instance, advised the Kennedy strategists as early as August 1960 to meet head on the religious issue (Kennedy's Catholicism) and to play down foreign policy issues (on which Vice-President Nixon seemed to be particularly strong in the view of poll respondents). The extent to which the Simulmatics project directly influenced candidate Kennedy's ultimate actions, we can at best only

SYSTEMATIC APPROACHES TO COMPARATIVE POLITICS

guess. In their own evaluation of their impact, Pool, Abelson, and Popkin write (p. 21):

> In a Presidential campaign there are only a limited number of policy alternatives, and there are myriad voices arguing for each of them. Our own contribution, if any, was to bolster by evidence one set of alternatives. With one exception they were the alternatives that the candidate ended up choosing.

They conclude by noting that "certainly no one can say how much pause it might have given John F. Kennedy if the research results had co-incided with the views of the equally shrewd advisors on the opposite side of the issue" (p. 22).

Another point raised by this simulation is its usefulness vis-à-vis other types of data (particularly survey data) in predicting election outcomes. A product-moment correlation between the position of the 32 non-Southern states ranked according to the simulated estimate of how well Kennedy would fare in each of them (using only data from surveys conducted between 1952 and 1958) and the actual vote for Senator Kennedy in November was 0.82; that contrasts with a 0.53 correlation between the actual vote and straw-polls conducted in October 1958. "The simulation, in short," according to the authors (p. 57), "portrayed trends that actually took place between the time the data were collected and election day two years later." To be sure, polls taken closer to the election were more accurate than those of 1958; they also reflected judgments made during the heat of the campaign about the salience of specific issues. The point to be noted here, however, is slightly different (p. 58):

> A simulation is not as good as a poll if the problem is to learn how voters have already made up their minds. The way to learn that fact is to ask it. But the simulation did take old data collected before the voters had made up their minds and acted out how they would make up their minds before they did so.

Close guesses in 1958 about the candidates who would face one another two years later and some of the major issues that would shape the campaign (or even about alternative sets of candidates and issues) would have enabled simulations that could have had profound effects upon the electoral process itself.

The goal of the Simulmatics project was not to ascertain the decision-making processes of individuals but rather to predict the final voting patterns. What intervened between the voter's predispositions of 1958 and his ballot in November 1960—that is, the process of attitude formation and change—was not the project's focus of attention. Moreover, it should be noted that the individuals making up the voter types were treated in a plebiscitary, "one man, one vote" fashion; there was no effort to assess the relative importance of the individuals in the decision-making process.

In subsequent research the participants in the Simulmatics project concentrated more on process than on prognostic simulation. One of the more interesting of these studies is the simulation of a fluoridation campaign by Abelson and Alex Bernstein (1963). They included three types of information in their computer program: (1) social background data about the inhabitants of a small Connecticut town, derived from actual sample surveys and including demographic variables, predispositions, exposure to communication media, frequency and nature of face-to-face contacts, level of participation in local politics, interest in the issue of fluoridation, and so forth; (2) a set of rules, based on experimentally established principles of attitude formation and change, specifying the conditions under which any individual would have his attitudes reinforced, modified, or changed; and (3) predetermined amounts and types of information emanating from communication media (data which, in a real situation could be found through content analysis). "Following exposure to the assertions in the channels for a simulated week, the individuals in the computer population are allowed to hold 'conversations' with each other" (p. 95).

> The simulation is designed so that each person's exposure to arguments and conversation rate depends upon his level of interest in the issue, which in turn depends upon previous exposure to arguments and information, and the outcomes of prior conversations. The system is such that it is possible for 'nothing much to happen' or, on the other hand, for interest gradually to build up until certain segments of the population become quite active and involved (though other segments may remain relatively dormant) (p. 96).

Cycles of exposure to communication media and "conversations" are repeated weekly during the whole of the campaign period (which in the case of this project was about ten weeks), at which time it would be possible either to simulate the voting turnout or to state the level of interest, activity, and attitude of each of the individuals. The ulimate outcomes, however, are of considerably less importance for the researchers than the social process of attitude formation and change as indicated by interim outcomes reached after each iteration of the cycles.

Even more recently Abelson and J. Douglas Carroll (1965) simulated the belief system of a "well-known right-winger." Using the published remarks of the individual as a basis not only for the content but also for the structure of the computer's "memory," their program then enables the computer to evaluate statements according to their credibility, and, if they prove not to be credible given the individual's belief system, to enable the computer to "rationalize" away the statements. In addition to being able to produce "responses of a resistive character," the system can itself be changed through the interaction of statements put into it and its responses (p. 28):

> In the course of its machinations, the system undergoes four types of changes: 1) the creation of new instances to include in its vertical memory structure; 2) the gradual development of a "style" of rationalization for particular contents; 3) the storage of new beliefs found credible and not later denied or rationalized; 4) gradual evaluative changes.

In a similar type of model, Pool and Allan Kessler (1965) simulated the processing of information by decision-makers in a crisis situation, concentrating upon messages between Kaiser Wilhelm II and Tsar Nicholas during the week in which World War I broke out.

> More specifically it is designed to represent the ways in which psychological mechanisms enter into their processing of the information they receive. It is designed to simulate the process whereby two different decision-makers acquire in their own minds quite different pictures of the world in which they are interacting. A flow of messages representing the real world comes to the decision-makers. They selectively attend to different messages in this flow leaving each decision-maker with a quite different image of the world from that of the other (p. 32).

The techniques of computer simulation such as Abelson, Pool, and others are developing hold great promise for the future simulation of national decision-making systems and other social processes of key importance for the cross-national study of political perspectives and behavior. What will be needed, however, are comparable banks of survey and other data from many countries, as well as cross-national validation of some of the assumptions that social psychologists make about the ways in which people perceive things and behave.

What has been accomplished to date using computers for political research—broadening the data base, data processing and statistical analysis, and simulation—makes it clear that we are on the threshold of even greater advances. But if this development, along with the others discussed in this chapter, promises brilliance for the future of political science, it also points to glaring gaps in the organizational framework for political research.

Systematic Political Research: Future Needs

The sheer *quantitative growth of the profession* will bring with it myriad problems. If present trends continue (and it seems likely that they will), by the middle of the 1980s there will be some 3,000 American universities and colleges, as many as 2,000 university research bureaus and institutes devoted at least in part to the study of politics, 35,000 members of the American Political Science Association, 700 new Ph.D.'s annually in political science, international relations, and public administration, as well as approximately 60 major American quarterlies (containing between 1,500 and 2,500 articles per year) devoted primarily or exclusively to the scholarly study of political science and international relations. (These figures assume that the trends now under way do not reach their natural limits before this time; that such trends cannot continue indefinitely has been made clear by Derek de Solla Price [1961, p. 113]: "To go beyond the bounds of absurdity, another couple of centuries of 'normal' growth of science would give us dozens of scientists per man, woman, child, and dog of the world population.")

This quantitative growth, although highly desirable in many respects, will also intensify some problems that are already very much with us. One of these is the problem to which political scientists from Plato to Lasswell have devoted so much of their attention—that of clarifying the goals of political science. The proliferation of research institutes and journals together with the rapid growth of the number of scholars hardly seem calculated to produce a unified approach to the discipline and its purposes; we can only hope that, in the absence of a consensus, the continuing debate will prove to be more fruitful than debilitating. One point nonetheless seems clear now: The profession will become much more cross-national in its orientation, as parochial concerns with institutions, perceptions, and behavior in single countries (even the United States) give way to a desire to establish generally valid principles of politics.

A second issue is one of guidance for our research. In one sense, of course, the value of any piece of competent research depends upon the extent to which it fulfills the goals that the scholar sets for himself. But in another sense there are certain societal criteria of value, often determined by people who base decisions upon their own perception of societal or professional goals. This is particularly true—and will become increasingly true in the future—in the case of the scholar dependent upon foundation or government support for his research projects. In the Social Science Research Council and the American Political Science Association, especially since the early 1950s, political scientists have found mentors with vision, organizations willing to support, promote, and even initiate empirical research on man's political behavior. More recently the federal government has begun to play a major role in financing political research, particularly that of a basic character. . Sponsorship

SYSTEMATIC APPROACHES TO COMPARATIVE POLITICS

and financing of cross-national research are even more problematic, and will require a growing degree of international cooperation, possibly coordinated through UNESCO and the International Social Science Council, with its headquarters currently in Paris (see Deutsch 1966a, b).

Among other perennial problems exacerbated by quantitative growth is the need for improved training facilities for graduate students, for better means to educate the larger public in political affairs, for organizational developments, both in the universities and in the various sources of financing, to accommodate the changing nature and emphases of political research. Above all there is a growing need for competent political scientists—teachers and researchers—since the demand for full-time teachers of political science is outstripping the annual production of doctorates in the field. There is, moreover, a subtler aspect to the manpower shortage in the political science profession. Of the natural and physical sciences, Derek de Solla Price (1961, pp. 117–118) has written:

> If the cumulative expansion of science rapidly outpaces all efforts we can make to feed it with manpower, it means that more and more things will arise naturally in the life of science and require attention that cannot be given. There will be too many discoveries chasing too few workers. At the highest level we must come to a situation at which there are too many breakthroughs per square head.

It does not take much foresight to see that political science, too, is fast approaching this point.

Recent *developments in computer-based research* underline an increasingly desperate need to take action now. At the individual level these developments imply certain tasks for the researcher if he wants to take advantage of computer technology. He must learn to think in terms of data processing when he is in the planning stages of any project. To facilitate the preparation, processing, and analysis of his data, he must plan his statistical analysis before setting out to gather data—at least to as great an extent as possible. In organizing the financial aspects of his project, he will have to learn to plan for machine time, programming, statistical consultation, and similar contingencies. And, of course, it will be imperative that he, himself, become familiar with higher levels of mathematics, statistics, and computer programming—at least familiar enough to communicate with technicians who can help him.

Future progress also rests upon the creation of an organizational framework that can effectively accomplish three tasks. For those political scientists already in the profession and who are interested in this type of research, it is necessary to provide means for them to retool. In the first instance this implies personal initiative, but it also implies a need for funds both for individual study grants and for sponsoring training conferences, as well as for appropriate training tools such as textbooks on data processing and analysis. Fortunately there are some bright spots in the gloom of current efforts to fulfill this training function. The brightest of these—a training program that may well serve as a model for more massive efforts—is that conducted for the Inter-University Consortium for Political Research (ICPR) by the Survey Research Center of the University of Michigan.

Second, training in quantitative approaches and computer technology must be provided for graduate and undergraduate students who want to enter the political science profession. This in turn may mean extensive curriculum changes, summer training facilities, and in all likelihood considerable financial assistance, at least at the outset. In time, as some of the scholars and students who are now being trained in these techniques move about in the academic environment, this set of problems will be eased considerably.

Third, and implicit in the first two points as well, is the need for an organizational framework to facilitate and promote empirical research in political behavior. National and even international coordination is possible provided that the scholars who are creating and running individual training programs and the foundations providing financial support are agreed upon what is needed and how best to implement their plans. In the Council of Social Science Data Archives (CSSDA), set up in September 1965 by representatives of more than a dozen universities in the United States, and now containing several times that number of members, there is just now beginning to be a semblance of such organization among data archives and users; its technical subcommittee has been meeting since late 1964 to discuss such problems as data format, storage and retrieval, and program sharing. A European Federation of Social Science Data Archives is seeking to perform the same function. Given the quantitative and qualitative level of contacts among members of the two organizations, international coordination seems quite feasible.

In his review of some recent uses of computers in social science research, Harold D. Lasswell (1965, p. 3) wrote:

> In the frame of reference of a society that accepts and in no small measure approximates the goals of human dignity, the cultural norm of disclosure must be reiterated and applied to every innovation that affects the advancement of knowledge. . . .
>
> The sanguine predictions that have been made by responsible persons have begun to be realized as the computer revolution rolls along. The potentialities of the human brain are augmented as *more factors* are *more speedily* interrelated with one another. By enlarging the span and accelerating the process of combination every intellectual task is affected. . . . Scientific speculation, too, is enormously influenced by the possibility of proceeding at

once to the study of complex interconnections that were only recently beyond the scope of disciplined inquiry.

To harness this massive potential to fruitful political research, however, is a task that will require concentrated effort, both intellectual and organizational, on the part of political scientists.

The phenomenal growth of political research has brought still a third set of problems to the fore—those of *documentation*. The need for more efficient systems of data retrieval is becoming increasingly apparent. Although we cannot agree with it entirely, there is a ring of truth in Robert Oppenheimer's remark (cited by Price, 1961, p. 121), "We need new knowledge like we need a hole in the head." If we could organize and comprehend fully the information we already have, we could make great strides forward in our political research. We must know what that information is, however, before we can organize it. And, given the growing number of relevant publications, research centers collecting quantitative data of one sort or another, and commercial firms as well as academic organizations sampling public opinion, the tasks of knowing what we already know and knowing how to locate it are becoming more difficult all the time.

We need not give up hope at this stage. Man apparently has a unique capacity to invent solutions just before he is inundated by the problems he is seeking to solve. In the case of data retrieval, the best prospect seems to lie in the area of electronic information systems, an area currently being explored by numerous private and governmental agencies. In recent years, political scientists, notably those at some of the institutes for basic research, have begun to direct their attention to such retrieval systems. But the road is long. The realization of that utopia in which every political scientist, through electronic equipment, has fingertip control over the precise information that he needs in his research is yet to come.

Two other needs, not quite so dramatic perhaps, are nonetheless of increasing importance, particularly in the area of cross-national studies. The first of these is for competent syntheses of research in progress. With an increase in the number of invisible colleges and separate research institutes, the load on the communications system within the discipline of political science has become well-nigh intolerable. The scholar who immerses himself in the study of legislative behavior, for example, often does not have time to keep abreast of developments in the area of general systems analysis. And yet, knowledge of the latter subject will aid him immensely in the pursuit of his specialty. The second need is for carefully organized replicate studies of past empirical research, both of the country for which the original study was done as well as for other countries. In any empirical science a check on research results serves a useful purpose. At best such checks can add depth to our knowledge about the subject analyzed; at worst they may expose shoddy craftsmanship. Unfortunately, syntheses and replicate studies are often of low prestige value for their authors. Professional recognition and advancement seem to accrue to chiefs rather than to braves; research funds seem to go to the innovator rather than to the syntheziser or the replicator.

The clear need for syntheses and replicate studies and the profession's clear preference for original research and theory building pose a dilemma for which there seems no solution at the present time. Unlike our problems of data retrieval, which appear to be essentially technical in nature, this dilemma hinges on our attitudes toward the proper role of the political scientist. Man may well be endowed with a capacity to prevent in the nick of time his technical inundation, but this genius does not always cover problems stemming from differing attitudes.

The need for an adequate abstracting journal for political scientists is also becoming increasingly pressing. In the late 1960s there were well over 30 scholarly journals in the United States devoted exclusively or primarily to serious research in political science and international relations. An average of 315 articles appeared in the ten most general of these publications during each of the five years from 1958 to 1962— one article for each day of the year excluding Sundays (Merritt, 1966). The political scientist with specialized interests, however, must read or at least scan more than just these ten or even three dozen journals, and the student of cross-national political behavior must also take into account the plethora of general and specialized journals published abroad. There are probably 2,000 journals in the world today that touch directly upon aspects of the political process. If present trends continue, these figures will have doubled by the mid-1980s.

The modern political scientist, however conscientious he may be, simply does not have the time to keep on top of this information explosion. True, he gets some assistance in the form of bibliographies that some journals and research institutes publish. But tracking down titles listed in bibliographies is often not the best use of research time; even if the journal in which a particular title appears is available, it may turn out that the title is misleading as far as the content of the article itself is concerned. True, there are some annotated bibliographies and abstracting journals available to the political scientist. Among the most notable of these are the *International Political Science Abstracts* and the bibliographic sections of such journals as the *American Behavioral Scientist*. Such publications are far from comprehensive—even the former searches only 124 journals—and, moreover, often include over-lapping citations.

With respect to abstracting journals, the field of political science comprises a vast underdeveloped area. Derek de Solla Price (1961, p. 98) has noted that the first abstracting journal in the natural and physical sciences came in 1930, when the world's scientists were publishing about 300 journals. In the years since then the growth of abstracting journals has kept pace with the growth of scientific journals at the steady ratio of about 1 to 300. In 1950 there were about 90,000 scientific journals and close to 300 abstracting journals. The field of political science, judging by these standards, should have at least 6 abstracting journals. In fact we do not have a single comprehensive abstracting journal, although the *International Political Science Abstracts* is certainly a start in the right direction. In considering the possibility of such a journal, we might do well to look to our sister discipline, sociology. Today, a decade and a half after its birth, *Sociological Abstracts* annually catalogues and cross-references about 5,000 abstracts of articles from close to 500 journals.

The future of empirical political research does not rest upon past developments alone. We have reached the stage—actually we have been in its midst for seven or eight years now, and it will probably continue for that length of time again before burying us in the growth mass of information—where we must make some decisions that will be crucial in determining the character of this future. Data retrieval systems, syntheses and replicate studies, abstracting journals—in short, the whole range of documentation needs—rank high in the list of developments necessary to prevent a further deterioration of channels for the flow of information within the political science profession.

The quantitative growth of the profession, the new requirements of computer technology, and documentation needs currently constitute barriers to the expansion of systematic approaches to comparative politics. And yet, as this volume has tried to show, significant progress is being made—in terms of theory, methods for gathering data, and techniques for analysis. Moreover, the potential for further growth is great. To reduce the effects of these barriers to growth and to encourage these needed developments are two of the major tasks facing the contemporary student of cross-national institutions, perspectives, and behavior.

REFERENCES

Abelson, Robert P., and Alex Bernstein. "A Computer Simulation Model of Community Referendum Controversies," *The Public Opinion Quarterly*. 27:1 (Spring 1963), 93–122.

Abelson, Robert P., and J. Douglas Carroll. "Computer Simulation of Individual Belief Systems," *The American Behavioral Scientist*. 8:9 (May 1965), 24–30. (Sage Publications, Inc., Beverly Hills, Calif.)

Alker, Hayward R., Jr., and Donald J. Puchala. "Trends in Economic Partnership: The North Atlantic Area, 1928–1963." In Singer (1968), pp. 287–316.

Bennis, Warren G. "Some Barriers to Teamwork in Social Research," *Social Problems*. 3:4 (April 1956), 223–235.

Campbell, Angus, Philip E. Converse, Warren E. Miller, and Donald E. Stokes. *Elections and the Political Order*. New York: John Wiley & Sons, Inc., 1966.

Chapman, Robert L., John L. Kennedy, Allen Newell, and William C. Biel. "The Systems Research Laboratory's Air Defense Experiments," *Management Science*. 5:3 (April 1959), 250–269. Reprinted in part in Guetzkow (1962), pp. 172–188.

Charlesworth, James C., editor. *A Design for Political Science; Scope, Objectives, and Methods*. Philadelphia: The American Academy of Political and Social Science, December, 1966.

Coleman, James S. "Analysis of Social Structures and Simulation of Social Processes with Electronic Computers." In Guetzkow (1962), pp. 61–69.

Deutsch, Karl W. "Recent Trends in Research Methods in Political Science" [1966a]. In Charlesworth (1966), pp. 149–178.

Deutsch, Karl W. "Social Resources for the Growth of Science: Some Issues for Research and Policy." In *Public Policy*, Volume XV, editors John D. Montgomery and Arthur Smithies. Cambridge, Mass.: Harvard University Press, 1966b, pp. 179–198.

Dodds, Harold W. Address at Princeton University, 20 September 1953. Reprinted in part as "The Dangers of Project Research," *Social Problems*. 1:3 (January 1954), 90–93.

Gee, Wilson. *Social Science Research Organization in American Universities and Colleges*. New York: Appleton-Century Company, 1934.

Graves, Eileen C., editor. *Ulrich's International Periodicals Index*. 2 vols.; New York and London: R. R. Bowker Company, 1966.

Guetzkow, Harold, editor. *Simulation in Social Science: Readings*. Englewood Cliffs, N.J.: Prentice-Hall, Inc., 1962.

Guetzkow, Harold, Chadwick F. Alger, Richard A. Brody, Robert C. Noel, and Richard C. Snyder. *Simulation in International Relations: Developments for Research and Teaching*. Englewood Cliffs, N.J.: Prentice-Hall, Inc., 1963.

Holland, Edward P., with Robert W. Gillespie. *Experiments on a Simulated Underdeveloped Economy: Development Plans and Balance-of-Payments Policies*. Cambridge, Mass.: M.I.T. Press, 1963.

Hovland, Carl I. "Computer Simulation of Thinking," *American Psychologist*. 15:11 (November 1960), 687–693. Reprinted in Guetzkow (1962), pp. 16–28.

Jennings, Norman H., and Justin H. Dickens. "Computer Simulation of Peak Hour Operations in a Bus Terminal," *Management Science*. 5:1 (October 1958), 106–120. Reprinted in part in Guetzkow (1962), pp. 151–165.

Lasswell, Harold D. *The Future of Political Science*. New York: Atherton Press, 1963.

Lasswell, Harold D. "The Shape of the Future," *The American Behavioral Scientist.* 8:9 (May 1965), 3. (Sage Publications, Inc., Beverly Hills, Calif.)

Luszki, Margaret B. *Interdisciplinary Team Research: Methods and Problems.* New York: New York University Press, 1958.

Machlup, Fritz. *The Production and Distribution of Knowledge in the United States.* Princeton, N.J.: Princeton University Press, 1962.

Merritt, Richard L. "The Organization and Promotion of Political Research in the United States." In Merritt & Rokkan (1966), pp. 383–409.

Merritt, Richard L., and Robert E. Lane. "The Training Functions of a Data Library," *Social Sciences Information.* 4:3 (September 1965), 118–126.

Merritt, Richard L., and Stein Rokkan, editors. *Comparing Nations: The Use of Quantitative Data in Cross-National Research.* New Haven and London: Yale University Press, 1966.

Newell, Allen, J. C. Shaw, and Herbert A. Simon. "Elements of a Theory of Human Problem Solving," *Psychological Review.* 65:3 (May 1958), 151–166.

Ogg, Frederic Austin. *Research in the Humanistic and Social Sciences.* New York: Century, 1928.

Palmer, Archie M., and Anthony T. Kruzas, editors. *Research Centers Directory.* 2d ed.; Detroit, Mich.: Gale Research Company, 1965.

Pool, Ithiel de Sola, Robert P. Abelson, and Samuel Popkin. *Candidates, Issues & Strategies: A Computer Simulation of the 1960 and 1964 Presidential Elections.* Cambridge, Mass.: M.I.T. Press, 1965.

Pool, Ithiel de Sola, and Allan Kessler. "The Kaiser, the Tsar, and the Computer: Information Processing in a Crisis," *The American Behavioral Scientist.* 8:9 (May 1965), 31–38. (Sage Publications, Inc., Beverly Hills, Calif.)

Price, Derek de Solla. *Science Since Babylon.* New Haven and London: Yale University Press, 1961.

Research Committee, American Political Science Association. "Report of the Research Committee of the American Political Science Association on Opinions as to the State of Research in the Profession, together with Suggestions for its Strengthening," *The American Political Science Review.* 39:1 (February 1945), 148–166.

Savage, I. Richard, and Karl W. Deutsch. "A Statistical Model of the Gross Analysis of Transaction Flows," *Econometrica.* 28:3 (July 1960), 551–572.

Scheuch, Erwin K., and Rudolf Wildenmann, editors. *Zur Soziologie der Wahl.* Köln and Opladen: Westdeutscher Verlag, 1965.

Shubik, Martin, editor. *Game Theory and Related Approaches to Social Behavior: Selections.* New York: John Wiley & Sons, 1964a.

Shubik, Martin. "Game Theory and the Study of Social Behavior: An Introductory Exposition" [1964b]. In Shubik (1964a), 3–77.

Singer, J. David, editor. *Quantitative International Politics: Insights and Evidence.* New York: The Free Press, 1968.

Smith, Bruce L. R. *The RAND Corporation: Case Study of a Nonprofit Advisory Corporation.* Cambridge, Mass.: Harvard University Press, 1966.

Tomkins, Silvan S., and Samuel Messick, editors. *Computer Simulation of Personality: Frontier of Psychological Theory.* New York: John Wiley & Sons, Inc., 1962.

United States Bureau of the Census. *Statistical Abstract of the United States: 1967.* 88th ed.; Washington, D.C.: United States Government Printing Office, 1967.

Wildenmann, Rudolf, Werner Kaltefleiter, and Uwe Schleth. "Auswirkungen von Wahlsystemen auf das Parteien- und Regierungssystem der Bundesrepublik." In Scheuch and Wildenmann (1965), pp. 74–112.

Index

INDEX

Abelson, Robert P., 141, 143, 178, 189, 241–245, 252, 253
Abrams, Mark, 129, 135
Abrams, Philip, 142, 151, 184
Abu-Lughod, Ibrahim, 95, 99
Achievement motivation, 15, 30, 53–56, 78–80, 96–97, 216
Adamec, Cenek, 158, 184
Adelman, Irma, 59, 60
Adorno, T. W., 130–131, 135
Aggregate data, 17–18; summation vs. syntality, 24; as indicators, 25–27; types, 27–36; error in, 36–44; validity as indicators, 44–45; univariate analysis (rank-order profiles), 45–49; bivariate analysis, 49–51; multivariate analysis, 51–59
Albert, Ethel M., 225, 226
Alford, Robert R., 181–182, 184
Alger, Chadwick F., 241, 252
Alker, Hayward R., Jr., ix, 9, 14–15, 22, 23, 30, 36, 41–42, 45–58, 60, 239–240, 252
Allport, Gordon W., 194–196, 223
Almond, Gabriel A., 29, 60, 106, 121, 135, 143, 151–152, 154, 164–167, 174, 184, 218, 222
American community, symbols of, 74, 76, 80
American Political Science Association, Research Committee, 229, 253
Anderson, Dale, 184
Anderson, Gladys L., 196–197, 222
Anderson, Harold H., 196–197, 222
Anderson, Nels, 160, 176, 184, 189
Angell, Robert C., 77–78, 80, 85, 95, 99
Ansbacher, H. L., 155–156, 184
Anthropology, political, 20, 200–217; case studies, 203–206; cross-cultural secondary analyses, 206–212; cross-cultural research, 212
Arms Control and Atlantic Community (Yale Project), 80–83, 95, 117–118, 123, 175. *See also* European unity
Aron, Raymond, 106–107, 121, 135
Aronson, Elliot, 64, 99
Association Française de Science Politique, 184, 186
Atkinson, John W., 78–79, 99, 131, 135
Aubert, Vilhelm, 161–162, 184

Axelrod, Morris, 147, 184

Backstrom, Charles H., 140, 184
Bacon, Margaret K., 215, 222
Bales, Robert F., 70, 103
Banks, Arthur S., 34–35, 58–59, 60, 61, 211–212, 222
Barber, James D., 20, 22, 122, 125, 135
Barioux, Max, 158, 191
Barry, Herbert, III, 215, 222
Barthes, Roland, 152, 184
Bauer, Mary Lou, 114, 136
Bauer, Raymond A., 37, 38, 44, 60, 61, 171, 187
Beck, Carl, 134, 135
Becker, Sam L., 145, 184
Bell, Wendell, 114, 129, 135, 138
Bemis, Samuel Flagg, ix
Benda, Harry J., 121–122, 135
Bendix, Reinhard, 188
Bennis, Warren G., 229, 252
Berelson, Bernard, 64, 88, 99
Bernaut, Elsa, 84, 101
Bernd, Joseph L., viii, 99, 101, 135, 138
Bernstein, Alex, 244, 252
Berry, Brian J. L., 57–58, 60
Biderman, Albert D., 37, 38–39, 44, 60
Biel, William C., 241, 252
Bindman, Aaron M., 147, 154–155, 184
Blalock, Hubert M., Jr., 14, 22, 88, 99
Blood, Robert O., Jr., 149, 150, 184
Bloomberg, Warner, Jr., 114, 136
Bogart, Leo, 140, 184
Bonjean, Charles M., 114, 135
Bosses, political, 133
Bottomore, T. B., 104, 107, 110–111, 135
Bower, Robert T., 152, 186
Bowles, Edmund A., viii–ix
Bowles, Gordon T., 222, 223
Breul, H., 24, 61
Brewer, Thomas L., 68, 69, 70, 77, 82–83, 95, 101
Brody, Richard A., 241, 252
Brouwer, Marten, 151, 160, 162, 175–176, 178, 184, 185
Brown, Roger, 97, 99
Bruck, H. W., 125, 139
Bryson, Lyman, 99, 100

Buchanan, William, 8, 22, 29, 60, 122, 139, 151, 158–160, 185
Budd, Richard W., 64, 99
Bush, Henry C., 95, 99

Cahalan, Don, 146, 185
Campbell, Angus, 12, 22, 177–178, 185, 186, 232, 252
Campbell, Donald T., 12, 16–17, 23
Cannell, Charles F., 144, 146, 185, 187
Cantril, Hadley, 29, 60, 151, 158–160, 167–168, 182, 185, 221, 222
Carlston, Kenneth S., 200, 202, 204–205, 222
Carroll, J. Douglas, 244–245, 252
Carstairs, G. Morris, 219, 222
Carter, Roy E., Jr., 146, 185, 202, 222
Cattell, Raymond B., 24, 56, 57, 60, 61, 220, 222
Census data, 28; and sample surveys, 142
Center for Advanced Study in the Behavioral Sciences, 234–235
Chapman, Robert L., 241, 252
Charlesworth, James C., 252
Child, Irvin L., 207–209, 215–216, 218, 219, 222, 226
Childrearing studies, 207–209, 215–217
Children: youth's outlook, 194–196; reaction to conflict, 196–197; views of foreign peoples, 197–198; socialization, 207–209, 215–217
Churchill, Winston S., 131–132
Civic culture, 151–152, 164–167
Clark, Russell A., 78–79, 101
Clifford-Vaughan, Michalina, 116, 135
Cnudde, Charles F., 172–173, 188
Coale, Ansley J., 37, 61
Cobb, William J., 146, 147, 187
Coddington, Alan, 95, 99
Cohen, I. H., 196–197, 222
Cohen, Jacob, 87–88, 99
Cohen, Ronald, 203, 222
Coleman, James S., 241, 252
Coleman, James Smoot, 60
Collins, Orvis F., 133, 139
Colombotos, John, 147, 186
Columbianum (Genoa), 64–65, 99
Communications: content analysis as research tool, 64–65; inferences about consequences, 89–90; sources, 90–91; motivation for, 90–97; communicator as representative, 92–97; among elites, 124–125; flow, simulations, 244–245
Comparative politics, as field of inquiry, vii–viii, 3–4; traditional approaches, 4–5; recent approaches (micro- and macro-politics, middle-range), 5–7; behavioral mood, 6–7; systematic approaches, 7–10
Computer research, 236, 247–249; expanding data base, 237–238; data processing, 238–240; simulation, 240–245
Comrey, Andrew L., 221, 222

Concept analysis, 76–77
Conflict: civil violence, 27, 32–34, 39–40, 51–52; foreign and domestic, 30–31, 42–43, 57–58; stability, 31–32, 50; and integration, 70; resolution in tribal society, 204–205
Content analysis, 18–19, 64–98; as aggregate data, 29–30; role in study of communications, 64–65; procedures for, 65–83; qualitative, 83–85; coding reliability, 85–88; inferences from, 88–97; future prospects, 97–98; and elite perspectives, 127, 130
Converse, Philip E., 12, 22, 177–178, 183, 185, 186, 232, 252
Cooperative research, 228–230, 245–247. See also Research institutes
Count, Earl W., 222, 223
Crane, Wilder W., 128, 137
Crespi, Leo P., 142, 146, 147, 155, 158, 185, 186
Cross-Cultural Summary, 211–212
Cross-Polity Survey, 34–35, 58–59, 211
Crossley, Archibald M., 158, 186
Crossley, Helen M., 146, 188
Crotty, William J., 10, 22
Culture, political. See Children; Civic culture; Human concerns; Personality, modal distributions; Anthropology, political; Semantic differential; Time budgets; UNESCO Tensions Project; Values, distribution of; Voting behavior
Cutright, Phillips, 53, 61

Dahl, Robert A., 6, 22, 107, 109, 117, 124–125, 135, 202
D'Andrade, Roy G., 218–219, 222
D'Antonio, William V., 114, 135–136
Danzger, M. Herbert, 114, 136
Data, 7–8; interplay with theory, 10; measurement and indicators, 11–13; pitfalls in use, 13–16; unobtrusive, 16–19; intrusive, 19–21; archives, 172, 182–183, 232–234, 248–249; expanding data base through computers, 237–238; computer processing, 238–240
Davis, Morris, 180–181, 186
De Gaulle, Charles, 178
Deming, W. Edwards, 141, 186
Dennis, Wayne, 65, 99
Dentler, Robert A., 61, 62
Deutsch, Karl W., ix, 12, 22, 23, 26–27, 30, 36, 38, 41–42, 45–53, 58, 60, 61, 72–73, 89–90, 99, 117–118, 125, 127, 136, 137, 239, 247, 252, 253
Development, economic, 45, 46–47, 50–51, 57, 59, 96–97
Development, political, 26–27, 35–36, 50, 59; social mobilization, 26–27; stability, 31–32, 50. See also Modernization in the Middle East
Dexter, Lewis A., 128, 136

125–126, 137
Kendall, Patricia L., 172, 187
Kennedy, John Fitzgerald, 109; family, 124; 1960 election, 242–244
Kennedy, John L., 241, 252
Kennedy, Raymond, 206–207, 225
Kessler, Allen, 245, 253
Kish, Leslie, 141, 187
Klapper, Joseph T., 89, 100
Kline, F. Gerald, 146, 185
Klineberg, Otto, 197–198, 224
Kluckhohn, Clyde, 213–215, 218, 221, 224
Kluckhohn, Florence Rockwood, 213–215, 218, 221, 224
Kolabinska, Marie, 110, 137
König, René, 187, 190
Krippendorff, Klaus, 64, 85–86, 100
Kruzas, Anthony T., 230, 253

Lamb, Robert K., 124, 137
Lambert, Wallace E., 197–198, 224
Lambert, William W., 215–217, 218, 225, 226
Landsberger, Henry A., 154, 187
Lane, Robert E., ix, 125, 131, 137, 140, 187, 233, 253
Langeschmidt, Waldo, 188
LaPalombara, Joseph, 6, 22
Lasswell, Harold D., ix, 3, 20, 22, 23, 30, 36, 41–42, 45–53, 58, 60, 62, 63, 64–65, 73–76, 77, 80, 89–90, 93–95, 96, 100, 101, 102, 104–106, 107, 108–109, 110, 121, 125, 133, 137, 138, 139, 228, 231, 246, 248–249, 253
Lazarsfeld, Paul F., 9, 14, 23, 25, 45, 62, 124, 137
Leighton, Alexander, 219, 220, 225, 226
Leighton, Dorothea C., 220, 226
Leites, Nathan, 64, 83–84, 101, 103, 127, 137
Lenin, V. I., 131–132
Lentz, Theo. F., 194, 224
Lerner, Daniel, 30, 62, 64, 73–76, 80, 89–90, 91–92, 93–95, 101, 102, 110, 115, 120, 121, 127, 128, 137, 138, 139, 142, 146, 154, 172–174, 188
LeVine, Barbara B., 215–216, 224
LeVine, Robert A., 207, 211, 215–216, 217, 218, 224, 226
Levine, Sol, 148, 188
Levinson, Daniel J., 130–131, 135, 220, 224
Lewis, Ralph, 146, 188
Lichtheim, George, 39
Lindblom, Charles E., 125, 135
Lindzey, Gardner, 218, 222, 224, 226
Linz, Juan J., 29, 62, 108, 138, 156, 188
Lipset, Seymour Martin, 34, 62, 179–180, 188
Llewellyn, K. N., 203, 224
Lochner, Louis P., 80, 84, 101
Lodge, Milton, 77, 101
Lowe, Francis E., 144, 188
Lowell, E. L., 78–79, 101

Luszki, Margaret B., 229, 253

McCarthy, Philip J., 140, 141, 143, 189, 190
McClelland, David C., 15, 30, 53–56, 62, 78–80, 96–97, 101, 218, 224
McCormick, Thomas C., 144, 188
McCrone, Donald J., 172–173, 188
McDonagh, Edward C., 147, 188
McGranahan, Donald V., 64, 101
Machlup, Fritz, 227, 253
MacIver, R. M., 99
McKechnie, J. Thomas, 134, 135
Maclay, Howard, 198–200, 224
MacLean, Malcolm, Jr., 89, 101
MacRae, Duncan, Jr., 29, 62, 141, 143, 189
Macridis, Roy C., 4, 6, 23, 117–118, 127, 136
Macropolitics, 5–7
Magid, Frank N., 147, 188
Mahl, George F., 74, 83, 91–92, 101
Mair, Lucy, 206, 224
Malenbaum, Wilfried, 44
Maletzke, Gerhard, 138
Mann, Floyd, 145, 188
Maretzki, Hatsumi, 215–216, 224, 226
Maretzki, Thomas W., 215–216, 224, 226
Markham, James W., 95, 101
Marks, Eli S., 141, 143, 188, 189
Martin, Norman H., 133, 139
Masters, Roger D., 203–204, 224
Matthews, Donald R., 116, 122, 138, 147, 184
Mauss, Marcel, 203
Meadow, Arnold, 149–150, 191
Measurement, and indicators, 11–13
Meehan, Eugene J., 7, 8, 23
Meldrum, James A., 29, 62
Merriam, Charles E., 231
Merrill, John C., 94, 101
Merritt, Anna J., ix, 162, 188
Merritt, Richard L., viii–ix, 12, 22, 23, 24, 29, 38, 61, 62, 63, 70, 74, 76, 80–81, 89–90, 94–95, 96, 99, 101, 117–118, 124, 125–126, 127, 136, 138, 144–145, 151–152, 162–164, 174–175, 176, 184, 186, 188, 191, 224, 227, 230, 233, 250, 253
Merton, Robert K., 6, 23
Meschieri, Luigi, 221, 222
Messick, Samuel, 241, 253
Metzner, Helen, 145, 188
Micropolitics, 5–7
Miguel, Amando de, 108, 138, 156, 188
Miller, S. M., 179–180, 186, 188
Miller, Warren E., 12, 22, 177–178, 185, 186, 232, 252
Mills, C. Wright, 72, 100, 107, 109, 124–125, 138
Minturn, Leigh, 215–217, 218, 224, 225, 226
Mintz, Alexander, 68, 101
Misiti, Rafaello, 221, 222
Mitchell, Robert Edward, 89, 101, 142, 149, 151, 189

Rokkan, Stein, viii, ix, 22, 23, 24, 40, 61, 62, 63, 138, 141, 160–162, 177, 184, 185, 186, 188, 190, 194, 225, 253
Rommetveit, Ragnar, 156–157, 190
Romney, A. Kimball, 213–216, 218, 221, 224, 225, 226
Romney, Romaine, 215–216, 225, 226
Roos, Leslie L., Jr., 143, 178, 190
Roos, Noralou P., 143, 178, 190
Rosenau, James N., 94, 102, 122, 124, 129, 139
Rosenberg, Morris, 25, 62, 140, 190
Rosenblum, A. Leon, 147, 188
Rosenthal, Howard, 143, 178, 190
Rosow, Irving, 187
Rothwell, C. Easton, 110, 121, 137
Ruge, Mari Holmboe, 95, 100
Rummel, Rudolph J., 30–31, 39, 41, 42–43, 56, 58, 62, 63, 221, 226
Russett, Bruce M., 22, 23, 30, 36, 41–42, 45–56, 58, 60, 63
Ruttenberg, Charles, 27, 32–34, 39, 42, 51–52, 61

Saavedra, Antonio, 154, 187
Sampling, for content analysis, 66–69; "prestige papers," 93–95; elites, 115; public opinion (random, stratified, quota, cluster), 141–144, (functional equivalence), 150–152; limited surveys, 192–200
Sanford, R. Nevitt, 130–131, 135
Sapin, Burton, 125, 139
Saporta, Sol, 70, 102
Savage, Charles, 220, 226
Savage, I. Richard, 239, 253
Sawyer, Jack, 207, 211, 226
Scarr, Harry A., 213–215, 218, 221, 224
Scheuch, Erwin K., ix, 14, 23, 24, 63, 141, 142, 166, 170–171, 190, 191, 253
Schleth, Uwe, 242, 253
Schneider, Annerose, 170–171, 191
Schramm, Wilbur, 95, 102
Schröter, Gerhard, 171, 190
Schubert, Glendon, 178, 190
Schueller, George K., 120, 138, 139
Schutz, William C., 86, 102
Schwartz, Richard D., 12, 16–17, 23
Scott, William A., 87–88, 102
Searing, Donald D., 123, 136, 139
Sears, David O., 140, 187
Sears, Robert R., 219, 226
Sechrest, Lee, 12, 16–17, 23
Seeman, Melvin, 194, 226
Seligman, Lester G., 116, 139
Semantic differential, 80, 131, 152–153, 198–200, 218, 221
Sereno, Renzo, 105, 106, 116, 139
Shaw, J. C., 241, 253
Sheatsley, Paul B., 141, 190
Shubik, Martin, 240–241, 253
Sibley, Elbridge, 44
Siegel, Bernard J., 222, 226

Sills, David L., 172, 190
Simmons, Leo W., 206–207, 225
Simon, Herbert A., 9, 14, 23, 241, 253
Simulation, 240–245
Simulmatics Project, 141, 143, 242–245
Singer, J. David, 8, 23, 77, 102, 139, 252, 253
Singer, Marshall R., 116, 123, 129, 139
Singer, Milton, 217, 226
Sjoberg, Gideon, 154, 190
Small, Melvin, 101, 102
Smelser, Neil J., 106, 138
Smith, Bruce L. R., 235, 253
Smith, Charles P., 85, 99, 102
Smith, Dilman M. K., 142, 187
Smith, Marshall S., 69, 76–77, 85, 98, 100, 101, 103, 127, 139, 221, 226
Smith, Paul A., 61, 62
Snyder, Richard C., 125, 139, 241, 252
Solomon, Herbert, 22, 23
Soviet and American elite values project, 77–78, 80, 95
Space analysis, 71–72
Statistics, use of, 6; measures of distribution, 45–49, 148; measures of correlation, 49–51, 148, 210–212; multivariate analysis, 51–59, 148; factor analysis, 54–59, 82–83, 148, 175, 211, 213–215, 238–239; contingency analysis, 81–82; use of computers for, 238–240
Steinkemp, Stanley, 146, 187
Stember, Charles Herbert, 146, 147, 187
Stephan, Frederick F., 37, 61, 140, 141, 143, 189, 190
Stephens, William N., 219, 226
Stern, Eric, 158, 190, 191
Stoetzel, Jean, 177, 186
Stokes, Donald E., 12, 22, 177–178, 185, 186, 232, 252
Stone, Philip J., 64, 69, 70, 76–77, 85, 96, 100, 101, 103, 127, 139, 221, 226
Stouffer, Samuel A., 141, 143, 189
Strangman, Eugene, 218, 224
Strodtbeck, Fred L., 213–215, 218, 221, 224, 225, 226
Strunk, Mildred, 182, 185
Stycos, J. Mayone, 146, 190
Suchman, Edward A., 144, 145, 190
Suci, George J., 80, 102, 131, 138, 198–200, 225
Sudman, Seymour, 146, 191
Sullivan, Robert L., 154, 191
Sunshine, Morris H., 114, 136
Survey research, 21, 140–183; as aggregate data, 29; readership studies, 89–90; assumptions and procedures, 140–148; functional equivalence, 149–157; original analyses, 157–171; secondary analyses, 171–176; replications, 176–178, 249–250; comparisons of national surveys, 178–183; limited samples, 192–200
Swanson, Guy E., 207, 210–211, 226
Swartz, Marc J., 201–203, 222, 225, 226

Symbol analysis, 72–76
Syntax, simplification of, for content analysis, 70–71
Szalai, Alexander, 170–171, 191

Takeshita, Yuzuru John, 149, 150, 184
Tamulonis, Valerie, 146, 185
Tannenbaum, Percy H., 80, 102, 131, 138, 198–200, 225
Tanter, Raymond, 30–31, 42–43, 58, 63
Taylor, Charles Lewis, 24, 63
Teune, Henry, 6, 23, 156, 189
Textor, Robert B., 34–35, 58–59, 60, 207, 211–212, 222, 226
Thayer, Paul W., 144, 191
Thematic analysis, 77–80. *See also* Anthropology, political; Personality
Thompson, Victor A., 124, 139
Thorp, Robert K., 64, 99
Time, 158, 191
Time budgets, 170–171
Tomkins, Silvan S., 241, 253
Torney, Judith V., 198, 223
Transaction flow analysis, 239–240
Translation: in content analysis, 69–70; of questionnaires, 152–153; in semantic differential, 198–200
Truman, David B., 141, 143, 189
Tuden, Arthur, 201–203, 222, 225, 226
Turner, Victor W., 201–203, 222, 225, 226

Udy, Stanley H., Jr., 207, 210–211, 226
UNESCO Tensions Project, 151, 158–160, 176
United Nations voting patterns, 56–57
United States, Bureau of the Census, 227, 253
United States, Department of State, Office of Intelligence Research, 162, 191
United States Information Agency (USIA) surveys, 29, 36, 144–145, 151–153, 162–164, 174–175, 176
Units for content analysis, 71–80; space, 71–72; symbols, 72–76; concepts, 76–77; themes, 77–80
Unterberger, Leonard, 218, 224
Usui, Mikoto, 45, 63

Valen, Henry, 177, 185, 191
Validity of indicators, 13; aggregate data, 44–45; of symbols in content analysis, 73–76; in elite surveys, 128–129; of limited sample surveys, 192–194
Values, distribution of, 3, 48–49; and land reform, 76; in Soviet and American elite publications, 77–78, 80, 95; elites and,

104–113; orientations, 213–215
Van Riper, Paul P., 133, 139
Verba, Sidney, 20, 23, 29, 60, 141, 143, 151–152, 154, 164–167, 180–181, 184, 186, 190, 207, 218, 222, 225
Verner, Helen W., 146, 185
Vincent, Jack E., 56, 63
Vogt, Evon Z., 225, 226
Voting behavior, 177–178; in United Nations, 56–57; and social class, 181–182; simulations, 242–244

Wahlke, John C., 122, 128, 137, 139
Wallace, David, 147, 158, 191
Wallace, David L., 73, 90, 101
Walton, John, 117, 139
Ware, Edward E., 198–200, 224
Warner, W. Lloyd, 133, 139
Wayne, Ivor, 64, 101, 103
Webb, Eugene J., 12, 16–17, 23
Welsh, William A., 10, 22, 119, 137
West Indian elites, 115, 118, 129
White, James R., 151, 158–160, 185
White, Ralph K., 164, 191
Whiting, Beatrice B., 215–216, 223, 224, 225, 226
Whiting, John W. M., 202, 206–209, 215–216, 218, 222, 225, 226
Wildavsky, Aaron, 20, 23
Wildenmann, Rudolf, 190, 242, 253
Wilkinson, Rupert, 122, 139
Wilks, S. S., 141, 143, 189
Williams, Thomas Rhys, 141, 191
Wilson, Elmo C., 158, 191
Wilson, Woodrow, 73–74, 131, 132–133
Wipper, Audrey, 194, 226
Wispé, Lauren G., 144, 191
Wolfenstein, E. Victor, 131–132, 139, 218, 226
Wolfenstein, Martha, 64, 103
Wolfinger, Raymond E., 114, 139
Woodward, Julian L., 158, 191
Wuelker, Gabriele, 158, 191
Wylie, Laurence, 150, 191

Yale Political Data Program (now, Yale World Data Analysis Program), 36, 41–42, 45–55, 58, 233
Ylvisaker, Hedwig, 158, 191

Zaninovich, M. George, 68–69, 70, 101
Zapf, Wolfgang, 111, 139
Zelan, Joseph, 110, 139
Zerega, Virginia Van S., 151, 158–160, 185
Zetterberg, Hans L., 179–180, 188
Zinnes, Dina A., 68–69, 70, 101
Zurcher, Louis A., Jr., 149–150, 191

Printed in U.S.A.